MIDNIGHT AT THE CROSSROADS

HAS BELLY DANCE SOLD ITS SOUL?

ALIA THABIT

DANCE ART PRESS

Copyright © 2017 by Alia Thabit

All rights reserved.

No part of this book may be reproduced in any form or by any electronic or mechanical means, including information storage and retrieval systems, without written permission from the author, except for the use of brief quotations in a book review.

Contact the author at midnight@aliathabit.com

Publisher: Dance Art Press

Editor: Lizabet Nix, *Wordcredible!*

Illustrations: Alia Thabit

Cover Design: Benjamin Carlson

Hardcover ISBN 978-0-9971888-0-6

Softcover ISBN 978-0-9971888-2-0

E-Book ISBN 978-0-9971888-1-3

First Edition. Second printing.

Printed in the USA

CONTENTS

Important Note about Names   ix
Introduction   xi

PART I
THE FEELING IN THE MOMENT
1. What is Belly Dance?   3
2. Music Made Visible   19
3. The "Mysterious" East   31
4. Culture Clash   39

PART II
SAME BUT DIFFERENT
5. Tick-tock Technique   57
6. The Flaming Jekyll-Hyde of Belly Dance   69
7. Through the Door   83
8. SEX   99

PART III
BRING THE JOY
9. Improvisation—the Belly Dance Bête Noire   123
10. Mind   127
11. Body: The Lock   137
12. Body: The Key   149
13. Soul   169
14. Midnight at the Crossroads   189

PART IV
HOW-TO
15. Practice: the door to healing, soul, and joy   203

Acknowledgments   217
About the Author   221

This book is dedicated to the dance and to all who love her

"The world is full of magic things patiently waiting for our senses to grow sharper." —WB Yeats

Important Note about Names

This book uses the terms *Eastern* and *Oriental* in their vintage sense, to encompass the lands of the dance, primarily North Africa, the Near East, and the Mediterranean basin; I also use Eastern and Oriental dance as synonyms for belly dance.

Why Oriental? Orient means East. In much of the world (including the Near and Middle East), Oriental dance is the accepted term. Early versions of American nightclub-style dance were called *danse orientale*, or Oriental dance. It is still often known as Vintage Orientale. The term Oriental, however, has racist connotations for people of Asian descent. *Asian* is the accepted term for people. But one may refer to *things* as Oriental, for example, carpets, isms—and dance. Since Oriental dance is a preferred term in the Middle East and much of the world, and because dance is a thing, not a person, I use Oriental here.

Why not use the Arabic term *raqs sharqi*? *Sharq* means east; *raqs* means dance. *Raqs Sharqi*, means Dance of the East—which distinguishes it from the dances of the West—but it is often seen as the modern stage dance, and I plan to discuss more than the stage version of the dance. Moreover, some of the dance's home countries are not Arabic-speaking (for example, Greece and Turkey).

For all these reasons, I will use Eastern, Oriental, and belly dance as catch-all terms for the nonce.

Western will generally be understood to encompass North America, Europe, and any other place that has adopted Western dance values (particularly ballet)—for example, Russia and Eastern Europe.

INTRODUCTION

Belly dance... A magical phrase, it conjures images of sultry harem girls, exotic perfume, tinkling finger cymbals, and undulating hips. People are so drawn to this imagery one rarely finds mention of the dance that doesn't evoke it. Yet this trope is only one facet of the jewel that is belly dance.

People see and use the dance in many ways. It is a movement vocabulary, a way to express sensuality, a venue for perfectionism, a sexy treat for the male gaze, a pretty bauble, an elastic medium adaptable to anyone's preconceptions and values. It is a fun way to get exercise, a dress-up opportunity, a bonding experience. It is entertainment, even art. But as we delve deeply into the dance, we find much more than this. Why do millions of people love this beautiful, joyous dance? What secret does belly dance carry, deep in its wild heart?

This book makes the case for the dance not only as an ancient, beautiful art, but also as a soul and spirit-healing venue for joy, a mind-body practice that equals (and in some ways, may surpass), yoga, tai-chi, sitting meditation, etc., in its effectiveness and power.

Really?

Yes.

Sparkly little belly dance has immense power. People are drawn to it because they sense this, though they may not know how to access it. When they come to a class, they are usually taught a sterilized version--stylized, choreographed, counted, body-control to recorded music. This is not the dance they were looking for. But it's all they can find, all that's available, so okay.

It is not okay with me. I am here to shine a light on the magic and mystery of our dance. There is a more to this dance than meets the eye, and those less-visible elements are its most vital and rewarding--for dancers, their guests, and the world.

This book is NOT an academic research project. The few citations mostly come from conversation with beta readers as the book grew and from memorable revelations as I have grown as a dancer and come to understand its—and my—culture of origin.

This book IS a love letter to the dance that has nourished me for forty-five years. It is a manifesto, the conclusions to which I have come over decades of devotion to this dance. It is for those who want something deep and real. It is given as a beacon of light welcoming dancers home to the soul of their beloved dance.

We are drawn to this dance because we feel something from it, something deep and soulful. It is real. It is there. The dance waits for you, a hidden seed, trembling with life, ready to blossom in your heart and soul. It is filled with joy--beautiful, loving, and free--and so are you.

I invite you to step into joy.
Let's dance.

PART I
THE FEELING IN THE MOMENT

"Dance is music made visible." —Morocco (and George Balanchine, and Martha Graham)

1
WHAT IS BELLY DANCE?

BACK IN THE 70S, I WORKED AS A FIGURE MODEL FOR ART CLASSES, mostly at the long-gone Brooklyn Museum art school and at Pratt Institute. This was how I financed my dance education. There was a professor at Pratt whom I liked a lot, and I often worked for his classes. In addition to still poses, each semester we ran through a sequence of sessions for his Illustration class as his students learned to draw objects in motion. For the capstone of the series, I brought my dance gear to class, put on belly dance music, and danced in full costume while the class frantically sketched. It was a lot of fun.

One day, during this class, a dark-haired student burst into the room. He took in the scene—the madly sketching students, the glittery dancer, the white-haired, bearded professor—and demanded, "Who is playing this music?"

"I am," I said.

"This is John Berberian!" he exclaimed.

Uh-oh. I wondered if he were going to yell at me for dancing to this music. Instead, it turned out the kid was Armenian (as is John Berberian). He told me Berberian was about to perform at an Armenian Church supper. He eagerly invited me to the supper, because anyone who loved John Berberian was family. So I went. With my Mom, who had introduced me to John's music.

∽

The church was packed, and food was everywhere. My Mom and I were both shy, but the kid from school saw us, thanked us for coming, and found us seats. Everyone made us welcome, even though we didn't know anyone. My Mom and I sat in a happy daze with the swirl of activity all around us. Soon it was time for the concert. Or so we thought.

When Berberian's band took the stage, *everyone* jumped up to dance. Young, old, male, female—the floor was packed with ecstatic people of every age and size boogieing down in every way, shape, and form. As I watched, it slowly dawned on me—all these people were belly dancing!

Everyone loves to belly dance

Now, I am Levantine on my father's side (Lebanon, Syria, Palestine), but no one in my family danced. I had already taken belly dance classes for a while, primarily with renowned dancer and choreographer Ibrahim Farrah. I could dance—but I had never seen belly dance "in the wild." These folks danced solo, in groups, as couples—and all the things I had learned in class were their natural expression of the music: hip drops, shimmies, undulations —the works. It was belly dance in its natural habitat. It was a revelation. I didn't dance that night; I watched. But I learned a lot, and I never forgot.

You would think the answer to "What is belly dance?" would be obvious— you see the people dancing, the hip drops, shimmies, and undulations—and there it is.

You would be wrong about that.

The definition of belly dance is surprisingly contentious.

Belly dance is a made-up term.

It was the most salacious possible English translation of the French term *"danse du ventre"* (dance of the stomach). The original danse du ventre was a specialty dance of the Algerian Ouled Naïl (pronounced *weled nile*), in which a dancer manipulated a metal belt up and down her abdomen with her stomach muscles. Was that what we think of as belly dance? Did it become that because of the name? Who knows?

What *is* belly dance as we have come to know it?

Belly dance, in its home countries, is literally the dance without a name—or with many names. Other folk dances of the region, such as debke or tahtib, have specific names. Not this one. Our dance is so ubiquitous that in Arabic it is often simply called *raqs*, which means dance, or *raqs baladi*, dance of my country. Dr. Mo Geddawi, *drmogeddawi.com*, suggests Egyptian dance as the proper term, since, in his experience, other Arab-speaking countries referred to the dance as *raqs al Masri* (dance of Egypt). In Lebanon, it is often called *raqs al farrah*, the dance of happiness, as it is a staple of any celebration. In Egypt, it is often called *raqs sharqi*, Dance of the East, to differentiate it from dances of the West.

Leila Farid, *leilainegypt.com*, an American dancer who lived and worked in Cairo for over a decade, says that in Egypt, "*Raqs Sharqi* seems to encompass everything but Western dance. It is a mishmash of everything Eastern plus some of the performer's stuff she wants to put in—most people assume you will mix in some folk dance from your native village." It is the home-style dance of millions of women and men, young and old, in Cairo, Egypt, and many millions more in other places around the globe. It is a dance that elicits passionate attachment—and controversy.

For folks of the culture who dance in their homes (this is the vast majority of folks), belly dance is a fun, playful endeavor, and it is improvised. Dr. Najwa Adra, a Lebanese anthropologist and field researcher who studies dance, describes this in her article, "Belly Dance: an Urban Folk Genre." She opens her description of the dance with, "Traditional belly dance is an improvised genre, led by music that may also be improvised." She goes on to describe the isolations, shimmies, modest footwork etc. You can read Dr. Adra's article on her website, *NajwaAdra.net*.

One of Adra's most interesting observations is that the dance's function is primarily that of play. It is done for fun. It is stress release, a playful, enjoyable pastime. In the East, most of the millions of people who belly dance are not professional performers. The dance is a social dance, something fun to do with family and friends. The stage versions of the dance are largely more dramatic versions of the home dance. And many home dancers are as skilled (sometimes more so) than professional dancers.

In the West, the question "What is Belly Dance?" has become rather complex. There are almost as many opinions as there are dancers. Is it a folk dance, a stage dance, or what? What we know as "belly dance" is already inclusive of many fusion elements. Modern belly dance has adopted elements of ballet (and a lot of Western values). We have added Sa'idi stick dance and Turkish Romani dance among many others. There are Egyptian, Lebanese, Turkish, Greek and assorted regional variations, and they come in stage styles and social styles.

There are various forms of "Tribal" dance, from ATS® to fusion (none of which, Leila notes, would be recognized as raqs sharqi in Egypt but play alongside it in the West), a host of ethnic and other fusions, and all the theatrical approaches. Many bear little connection to the dance beyond a nod to the movement vocabulary. What do we do with this mishmash? What do we call it?

I am loath to kick anyone off the belly dance bus. Yes, I have concerns about some things, and will explore them as we go along. But as we come to value the Eastern soul of the dance, misconceptions fall away. There are classic qualities of our dance that underlie everything, and these are where we want to put our focus. The rest is window dressing.

To me, the vital elements of this dance are

- The foundation movement vocabulary, hip drops, shimmies, undulations, etc.
- Micromovement, the modulation of a movement's size, shape, direction, speed, and force to better fit the dancer's mood and the music
- Improvisation to improvised (preferably live, preferably Eastern) music or *loose* choreography/structured improvisation that can be changed or modified to each situation
- Expression of the dancer's physical and emotional feeling in the moment, including playfulness and fun
- Embodiment of the principles and values of Oriental music (more on this shortly)
- The Eastern music with which this dance has evolved. You can have all of the above with other music, but the music and dance go together, and they make special magic together.

The more of these principles we include in the mix, the closer we get to the soul of the dance.

The most important thing is the feeling

Ask any dancer of the culture and they will tell you. This is the emotional feeling from the music *and* the physical feeling of the movements, which are deeply pleasurable. They are tailor-made for the enjoyment and nurturance of the body. There is a lot to be said for this dance, for its capacity to heal—both daily stress and old, deep damage. Try this: Close your eyes. Slow down. Breathe. Notice how the dance *feels*, what you feel emotionally *and* what your body feels—the physical sensations of the movements themselves.

Traditionally, Oriental dance is a dance of improvisation, of on-the-fly musical interpretation, of subtle emotional timbres, somatic experience, and intuitive interaction between dancer and musician—and that musician plays improvised music, created in the moment as an expression of his feeling. For the musicians, dancers and guests, the goal is *tarab*, musical ecstasy. Every performance becomes a never-before seen, never-to-be repeated art happening, uniting performers and guests in a state of joy.

Oriental music and dance bring joy. Bringing joy is our calling as dancers. It is part of our dance's cultural heritage. And yet we see less and less joy as musicians retire, venues close, and culture clashes erode our connections to the heart and soul of our dance. Most people only see the outside of this dance—the sexy movement vocabulary, the pretty girl, the sparkly costume. The inner qualities—healing, joy, connection to the Divine—these treasures are hidden behind a secret doorway. Few know that they exist—fewer know how to find them.

This book is a map.

Let's unpack the riches of this treasure chest and return ourselves to this ecstatic state. Before we go there, here's a brief overview of my own path.

Who am I to say all this?

I am a white gal from Brooklyn, New York. What qualifies me to write this book and make these assertions?

For one thing, I'm a half-Arab white gal (more about this in a bit). I originally embraced this dance as a cultural activity. I've been at it for forty-five years, and the cultural aspect has been a driving force throughout. I began my dance journey in New York City back in the early 1970s.

Back then, there were three main teachers of Oriental dance in New York —Ibrahim "Bobby" Farrah, Serena Wilson, and Morocco (aka Carolina Varga Dinicu, *casbahdance.org*). I only met Serena once, late in her life. Morocco I've known since 1994. She is brilliant, generous, and adorable. She is also the only one of the three who is still around. However, I did not experience Rocky or Serena's teaching at the time. My foundation training came from Bobby Farrah, world-famous dancer and choreographer—and from his protégés and principal dancers, among them the incomparable Elena Lentini. Looking back, I am stunned at my good fortune.

Elena Lentini, a brilliant, fierce light of this dance, is an artist to her core. She is a treasured friend and mentor. From Elena I learned artistry, intensity, and emotional expression. I am who I am as a dancer because of her. She is my beacon, and has been for decades.

Bobby was a brilliant teacher. His methods were effective and quite farsighted. From Bobby, I learned structure—the moves, how to adapt and combine them, how to interpret and fit them to the music, and how to use a stage.

There were few resources back in the early 70s—no Internet, email, or message boards, no videos or DVDs, no online shopping or music downloading. We played vinyl records, and there were damn few of them. The main music sources were the import room at Tower Records (a pig in a poke, often), or the wonderful Rashid Music Store in Brooklyn, *rashid.com*, where Ray Rashid would suggest *and play* records to help you decide.

In 1977, I moved to Vermont, where there were even fewer resources (plus I soon had a couple of children to raise). Up through the early 90s, I danced pretty much in a vacuum. Over time, my situation evolved, and I was able to get back into dance.

At this time, I was shifting over from the Vintage Orientale musical repertoire to Egyptian music, as it had more dramatic shifts and changes. Since I was an improvisational dancer with only recorded music, this provided the energy I craved. But the complex, extended orchestral music made famous by revered artists like Farid el Atrash and Oum Kalthoum, evaded me. I didn't understand it. I couldn't dance to it. I didn't even like it.

Through weeklong workshops with Beata and Horacio Cifuentes, I began to understand this music. But the greatest learning was attendance at Simon Shaheen's Arabic Music Retreat, *arabicmusicretreat.com*. Through the Retreat, my knowledge and understanding of our music expanded beyond my wildest dreams. I learned to play the frame drum and the nay (a reed flute), and performed both with small ensembles and the Retreat Orchestra. I came to a much deeper understanding of how movement and music connect, and the potential these have for creating a shared state of joy.

From there I began to travel, embarking in 2004 on a five-week dance study tour including Egypt, Jordan, Lebanon, and Palestine, the centerpiece of which was attending Raqia Hassan's *Ahlan wa Sahlan* festival in Cairo. I met Leila Farid then. It was also in 2004 that I met Tamalyn Dallal and began to study with Dunya McPherson.

Over the years, I have traveled, studied, danced, and talked with many, many dancers. In 2006 and 2009, I mounted my Sofa Surfing Tours of Fame, meeting and conversing with dancers and musicians all over the USA. With Tamalyn Dallal, I visited Mercado Persa in Brazil, *mercadopersa.com.br*, and drove all over the American south. I returned to Egypt three more times with Leila Farid's Camp Negum, including during the Revolution in January 2011.

I have visited multiple continents and countries. I have talked, danced, and laughed with untold numbers of dancers from all over the world. I have taken countless workshops with brilliant dancers and musicians, many, many of the culture and others striving to embody it. These experiences and understanding permeate and drive this book. Yes, I have been around the block a few times. I have listened, learned, and connected the dots. This book contains my conclusions after forty-five years of fascination with our dance. The writing itself inspired many of them.

I invite you to read, think, and talk about these ideas with your dance friends. Weigh the material. Try some of the strategies. Come to your own conclusions. We'll start by taking a look at some of the differences between Eastern and Western mindsets, and how they underpin many misconceptions about the dance.

The difference between East and West

In the West, we have the Platonic Ideal.

There is a perfect form to which we aspire. This is a cultural aesthetic. We see it in our classical music and dance, particularly ballet. In ballet, every dance step or move has an ideal execution. Nothing else will do. In our classical music, each note has an ideal vibration. Nothing else will do. It must be exactly the same every time. It is what we in the West have come to expect of our classical arts. We strive for this idealized vision of how it is supposed to be. This involves extensive skill and can result in great beauty.

There is also an Asian aesthetic that is similar in its embrace of idealized execution, but different in its mindful, meditative approach. I mention this because Oriental dance is popular in Asia (remember that Eastern, for the purposes of this book, only refers to the homelands of our dance. Asia is not among the dance's homelands). In this model, there is again a perfect form to which the dancer aspires; however, the execution is like tea ceremony, calligraphy, or martial arts katas. The goal is to most effortlessly and beautifully express this sequence, in this case to music. This also involves extensive skill and can result in great beauty.

The cultural aesthetic for Oriental dance, however, is quite different. You "just feel it." Musicians play what they feel in the moment, and dancers make an improvised spontaneous expression. There may be a song, but it is a vehicle for expression rather than a set piece. Dancers allow the music in through their ears and out through their bodies, while connecting with both the musicians and guests in the shared moment. This also involves extensive skill and can result in great beauty.

None of these approaches is better or worse than any other. They are each different and unique to their cultures. Their cultural ethos shapes and gives meaning to the activity. When we learn tea ceremony, we strive to attain a Japanese aesthetic. When we learn ballet, we must rise to ballet's standard of excellence. It is the same for Oriental dance.

There is an Eastern standard of mastery to which we may aspire. However, in Oriental dance, we often apply the standards of our own culture rather than those of the East. Why is that? Often our own culture is simply the most familiar. But most of us never even heard of any Eastern standards. Well, let's change that right now.

~

What is the Eastern standard of mastery?

In the Eastern model, the focus is on fluid expression in the moment rather than idealized unchanging perfection. Eastern musicians embellish and adapt the structure, melody, rhythm—even the tones of the notes to suit their feeling. Improvisation is the rule. Eastern musicians pride themselves on never making a song the same way twice. The musician's goal is *tarab*, a state of musical ecstasy—a state shared with the audience (whom I shall call guests, a term I learned from Leila Farid).

A dancer performing to this improvised wealth of emotional expression dances what she feels. She lets the music come in through her ears and out through her body. Oriental dance is a sensual dance of joy; it takes pleasure in the sensations of the body from the music and from the movement itself. The music melts and shifts from performance to performance—as does the dance.

Just as musicians tweak even the timbre of the notes to suit their feeling in the moment, dancers command micro-movement (infinite variation in speed, size, texture, shape, and force of each move), to better express the music and their feeling from it. Each performance becomes a unique event, a synthesis of dancer and musicians.

Further, in a performance setting, these artists are in close contact with their guests. In the West, we often have what is called the Fourth Wall between the performers and the audience. What happens on stage is separate —there is no interaction between the performers and the audience.

In the East, there is no fourth wall. The performers share joy with the guests—in the case of the dancer, her joy in the music, her physical and emotional response to it, and her connection to the people. The dancer brings joy to the audience through her transmission of the music in a physical form. A shared ocean of delight unites the performers and guests as one. And every dance, every song, every show, is Different Every Time.

Different every time

Same Every Time vs. Different Every Time

Think about this for a moment.

Both involve technical skill. Both can result in incredible beauty—but the philosophy and intention in execution of the skills are wildly different. Few people understand this; if it is news to you, you are in good company. Keep reading—there is more.

So, what happens when East meets West?

Culture Clash! Western dance values applaud:

- Choreography
- Stylization
- Physical control
- Dancer as vehicle for choreographer
- External appearance, technique, precision, spectacle
- Dancer dominates the audience with her power

All of these are fine things. This system has worked for a long time, and it has a lot going for it. Plus, it is familiar and comfortable for most of us.

So, what's the problem?

Oriental dance comes from a different culture. It has its own, different, set of values and principles. What about them? Let's take a look. Eastern dance values applaud:

- Improvisation
- Micromovement & "Same but Different"
- Relaxation
- Dancer as free agent, expressing what she feels from the music
- Internal feeling, shared emotion, musical ecstasy, joy
- Dancer expresses playfulness and sexual confidence—in Arabic, *dala3* (more on this later)

Total opposite, right?

But what happens when Westerners come into Oriental dance? We bring our values with us. Even those of us who are not trained dancers have been shaped by our culture. Back in the 60s and 70s, there was a great appreciation and energy for improvisation; however, our current climate is far more structured, anxious, controlled, and Photoshopped. Oriental dance has become one more venue for stylized, choreographed perfectionism. Bye-bye improvisation, micromovement, relaxation, agency, and joy.

This clash of values and mindsets has multiple repercussions. Oriental dance suffers from a bad reputation. It is not viewed as "serious" (for many of the reasons that make it exceptional). In some circles, it is not even viewed as an art, but as "mere" entertainment. Many factors contribute to this marginalization of Oriental dance...

- Misperceptions of purpose and meaning (it's *fun*)
- Lack of traditional music comprehension
- Arab = terrorist (aka racism and xenophobia)

- September 11th and the death of ethnic dance
- Invisibility of micromovement
- Rise of recorded music
- Teacher ability levels
- Student comfort levels
- Those costumes
- Fear of women's sexuality
- Fear of improvisation

Because of this bad reputation, there is a desire to "elevate" the dance. This often translates to "make it more attractive to Westerners." In hewing to Western cultural tastes and an uneducated marketplace, we have too often sacrificed the dance's Eastern qualities. But the soul of our dance is improvisation, feeling, and joy—these are its treasures. They are its uniqueness, what makes our dance special. Yet now we applaud technique, choreography, stylization, and spectacle.

What gives?
In the mythology of the blues, there is the story of a musician who sells his soul to the devil in exchange for technical expertise. The deal goes down at midnight, always at a crossroads. The musician walks away with brilliance, but upon his death, the Devil gets his soul.

Have we sold our dance's soul?

Let's look more closely at this image.

Selling one's soul and magical midnight crossroads are common themes in the British Isles and parts of Europe.

But the old-world cultures and traditions that birthed the blues are African. A very different spirit attends the blues crossroads. The Keeper of the Crossroads, a revered deity, bestows wisdom, guidance, and skill, forever enriching the seeker's soul. It is He whom the blues artist meets at midnight. Surprise, right? We'll come back to this later on.

Belly dance has its own old-world cultures and traditions. Its path also leads to soul-enrichment. It has always been there for those who look. But we didn't know, or didn't care. We took that Western road. We threw our soul away without a backward glance.

Where is the feeling, the improvisation, the joy? Gone. Instead we have pretty girls in pretty costumes, doing stylized moves to recorded music in faux-Eastern drag. At the same time, our Western world demonizes Islam and women, particularly women of color and those of the original cultures. The focus is on choreographed, stylized, perfection, right down to facial expressions. The same, every time.

We threw out the baby—now all we have is the rather tepid bathwater.

Well, so what? Why not evolve? Who cares about soul, the feeling, or spirit connection? It's just a dance. We're artists. We can do whatever we want!

Okay. Sure. Fine. Go ahead.

But there's one little problem...

It's not *just* a dance. It's a superpower. There's magic and mystery hidden inside the dance. Belly dance is a lot bigger on the inside than it is on the outside. It comes with a lot of gifts, and it opens doorways to hidden treasure:

Effortlessness

Empowerment

Confidence

Creativity

Trauma healing

Connection to the Divine

JOY.

All of these exist organically within the dance (and we will discuss them individually as we go along). But we will not find them through stylization or rigid copying. They come from within, well up in response to the cultivation of intuitive movement. This treasure is inside each of us, waiting patiently for us to see, feel, and welcome it into our lives.

Another world is possible.

How do we get there? The first step is letting go of steps...

Technique is the servant of expression

As dancers, we have learned a lot of steps. We love our dance steps. We collect them. We polish them. We display them. We combine and recombine them, like Lego blocks or Pop Beads. We shop for more. We go to workshops, buy DVDs, and compare notes with our friends. We see how many steps we can cram into eight counts, and give ourselves extra credit for the hard ones, the ones we had to work at. Yes, we are justifiably proud of our moves.

Yet there's a big difference between learning steps and creating dance in the moment—just like the difference between learning language vocabulary and having a quick-witted conversation with native speakers, complete with jokes, allusions, and puns. Learning and using steps is the domain of the analytical mind. Steps are about thinking. To use one, we make a decision, have a debate, and select one from the many, over and over again. Intellectual decision-making may work when we construct choreography, but it's a disaster for improvisation.

In the moment, everything moves at warp speed. Decisions must be made on the fly. In the moment, we rely upon intuition. Musicians do not decide note-by-note what to play when they improvise; they just go. They trust their fingers to be there for them and play whatever reflects their feeling. As dancers, we must also *just go*. We leave our technique at the studio door and express what we feel in the moment. We trust our bodies. What comes out will be a glorious unity of intricate splendor: unique and ephemeral, each element individually shaped to mesh brilliantly with the whole.

We have few core moves in Oriental dance: circles, infinities, s-curves, lines, and accents, each segment of each one infinitely variable in size, speed, texture, height, direction, force, and weight. This variability is what we mean by micromovement. Each move can be infinitely customized to fit our feeling and the music. When people talk about famous dancers of the culture who only use four moves in their show, this is what they mean—the dancer may only use a few step families, yet the dynamic adaptation of each movement marries perfectly to the music, whatever it may be at the time. This is the heartbreaking thrill of intimate, tender art created spontaneously before one's eyes.

In the Eastern ethos, this is how music and the dance are meant to interact, complement each other, and become one. This ability to create dance in the moment is part of how we become masters of our art and develop our personal style—through discovering how our own bodies express the music.

But few of us have the chance to do this.

In dance class, most of us have been trained to copy. We are expected to exactly recreate the shape, size, and force of the teacher's chosen movements. If we are in a group dance, we all have to match. Some of the newer genres, such as the Tribal styles, employ limited and highly stylized movement vocabularies. Everyone learns these so they can be mixed and matched on the fly. Copying is a great way to learn something, but it is only one step on the road to mastery. As we shall see, stylization is foreign to Oriental dance. Yet many of us are only taught to copy, to stylize, and never progress.

Why do we dance this way? Yes, dancers (and teachers) import their Western aesthetics and hierarchies. But there is more.

- Students feel safer not having to think or act for themselves.
- Students want a product they can take home and show their friends.
- Group dances have become ever more ascendant. They allow the teacher to include entire classes in shows (because students feel safer in a group, being told what to do).
- Audiences love group dances.
- Recorded music has largely replaced live music. Few of us have an ensemble in our studio, ready to play at our beck and call (and when we do, we often expect them play the song just like the recording!).

Many of us came up in Western dance, where cultural biases and a competitive mindset reward technical perfection, memorization, and exact stylization. The move must be the same every time. There is also a status gulf between the dancer (to whom movement is assigned) and the choreographer (who makes the dance). The teacher's status as the creator of choreography supersedes that of the lowly dancer, who copies the higher-ranking teacher.

Yet the traditional nexus of Oriental dance is improvisation to live, improvised music. Learning choreography does not help us create dance in the moment. In fact, it makes this more difficult.

Why? Because: rote memorization and retrieval are relatively low-level cognitive activities. The intuitive synthesis of improvisation requires much higher-level processing. Additionally, copying choreographies discourages personal creativity, invention, and style. Yes, we need to learn technique, how to combine movements seamlessly. Yes, we copy to learn. But we also need to honor the dance's aesthetic and cultural values, including improvisation—responding in the moment to what we hear.

To learn this, we need to practice it.

Most of us think of practice as honing our technique, and we think of technique as the perfection of form—doing the moves "correctly." Oriental dance technique, however, consists of far more than its movement vocabulary and bodyline. Any of its aspects, including intuitive response to music, are skills that can be learned. But to learn anything new, one must practice it, in a deliberate, focused manner. We discover our own style, our own personality—how our body experiences and expresses the music. It is through practice of intuitive response that we go beyond imitation, find our true style, and, like Pinocchio, become real.

Why dance like someone else? You are you. You are special, unique, individual, precious. Nobody feels exactly what you feel. Nobody else's dance expresses your experience. Find your own voice. How do you do that? Let the music move you, physically and emotionally. Let those feelings infuse your body, from the expression on your face to the carriage of your arms, to the swing of your hip, to the turn of your foot. Radiate what you feel from the music, from sorrow to joy. Revel in the sensory experience of the dance. Let your body enjoy its connection to the music and share that connection. Dance what you feel. Literally.

Traditionally, the dancer shows any guests what she feels from the music. Traditionally, the music is live. Traditionally, musicians play what they feel. A dancer responds to what they play and communicates her feeling to her guests. The moves by themselves are empty. We can think of them in many ways, but they are vessels waiting to be filled. The dancer fills each vessel in the moment with physical and emotional feeling she gets from the music, the movement, the room, the whole package.

That double flip is awesome, and it took a long time to get it right, but it is a container for the feeling. A beautiful container, but empty—a bowl without food, a pot without a living plant, a box without a gift. We line these boxes up like Christmas morning—but when there is no gift inside all the pretty ribbons and wrapping, it's a sad day.

What gift is inside the wrapping?

Here's another way to look at it: Moves are like Lego blocks. We snap them together, interlocking units of Dance Construction. You can build a lot of things out of Legos, and some of them are pretty cool. But... you can't build drama out of Lego. You can't build pathos. You can't build laughter or tears, pleasure or pain, or any of the myriad emotions that we convey in dance. When the evening is over, a few people will remember that double flip. But everyone will remember that you made them cry. They will remember that you brought them joy. That's the true gift that you bring.

Wait, won't that bore an audience?

It seems hopeless to expect jaded Western guests to value feeling over the props and spectacle to which we have accustomed them. But maybe we haven't given them a chance to do so. Choreography can have feeling, or it can be empty. Improvisation can have feeling, or it can be empty. The dancer can respond joyously to the music or not—either way. What if we tried the way of feeling, of joy? It is riskier for the artist, yes, but the rewards are also greater.

Traditionally, the dancer's job is to bring joy through their interpretation of the music—and that means ALL of the music, not only the notes and rhythm. The music may be challenging. It may be scary to feel things. But allowing ourselves to feel and respond to the music is a giant step on the road to emotional and physical health, a worthwhile investment.

Famous dancers from Azza Sherif to Raqia Hassan to Tito Seif all agree: The most important thing is the feeling. I have personally heard each of these artists say this. Technique is the servant of expression. We acquire technique in the studio so that when we dance, our body has the strength and skill to support our expression—whatever we feel in the moment. As we practice intuitive response, we learn to trust our body to provide movement when we allow it to respond to the music.

∼

Let's take a moment to understand the music that underpins this dance. This music has a deep, rich history of its own. It has its own theory, which is quite different from that of Western music. We'll look at the traditional ensemble (the *takht*), the Arabic modal system (*maqam*), musical improvisation (*taqsim*), and how this all comes together with dance.

2
MUSIC MADE VISIBLE

CREATING MUSIC IN THE MOMENT

Traditionally, Oriental music is played by a *takht*, a small ensemble composed of classical instruments. These include the *qanun*, *oud*, violin, *nay* (reed flute), *riqq* (Arabic tambourine), *duff* (frame drum), sometimes a *tabla* (a vase-shaped drum, aka *darbuka, derbekke,* or *dumbek*), and a singer (with maybe two or three more in the chorus). For sound files of each of these instruments, please see *maqamworld.com*. Each instrument has a unique timbre; when played together, each stands out against the sonic whole.

Within the classical takht, the singer has the highest status. Singers don't have the safety of strings to pluck or holes to cover. They come to each pitch from deep training, and they let that go to improvise their response to the song. Next in line is the many-stringed qanun, one of the oldest instruments (its name means law). It is thought to most accurately correspond to the human voice—plus it is super hard to play. At the low end are the percussionists, who need not understand the maqam system, but only the rhythmic structures (the rhythms are called *iqa'*; plural *iqa'at*).

In Arabic music, there is no harmony (there are no chords, either). All the musicians play the same melody (*heterophony*) and rhythm (*heterorhythm*). This may seem simple; however, Eastern music has something extra, for each musician plays the song differently. When Eastern dancers speak of the dance, they talk about *Same but Different*. You may make the same move, or dance the same song, but you make it differently. It's the same for musicians.

Eastern musicians play what they feel in the moment, *and* they pride themselves on never making a song the same way twice. Each musician ornaments the musical line, playing sonic arabesques and curlicues around the established melody. Even a simple melody becomes a complex interaction of overlapping heterophonic interpretation, as each musician both ornaments as he pleases, and also listens and responds to the ornamentation of the others. Even in a simple song, i.e. verse, chorus, verse, there is a lot going on.

MAQAM

Another big difference between Eastern and Western music is the system of scales. Western scales are based mainly on two modes; major and minor. Eastern scales have many, many modes, called *maqamat* (the singular is *maqam*). Eastern scales are based on intervals—the spaces between the notes. You can start a maqam on any note, because the intervals are what drive the scale.

When musicians improvise, they journey from one maqam to another, often making daring leaps between deeply unlike maqamat, to the cheers of an educated audience who recognize the artistic mastery of this seeming discord.

Arabic music theory is venerable and complex. Entire suites (*wasla*), are built around one maqam—old-style shows had three *waslat* (suites), with each one mainly in a single maqam. Songs often begin with a short *taqsim* (instrumental improvisation), to set the maqam and allow the musicians to sink into the feeling of it. Musicians train rigorously—not to show off with ever-faster riffs, but to more freely express their feeling in the moment. Technique is considered the servant of expression, as it is for dancers.

MICROTONES

In addition to the ornamentation and modal scales, Eastern music simply has more notes. Think of a piano. The tones march up the keyboard in measured whole and half steps. The half step between A and B is called either A sharp (A#) or B flat (Bb). But Eastern music has notes *between* these notes. For example, A half sharp, a note between A and A sharp, or the B half flat, a note between B and Bb. These have their own notation indicators, too.

Those off-key sounds you may hear in Eastern music are not off-key; but since they don't exist in classical Western music, they may sound dissonant. NB: It was the search to represent these elusive Eastern microtones, or "blue" notes, on Western instruments that drove early African-American musicians to bend guitar notes with bottlenecks and knives (itself an African tradition), and create what we now know as the blues. Historians have found that "upward of 30 percent of the African slaves in the United States were Muslim, and an untold number of them spoke and wrote Arabic" (Curiel)*.

Though these notes are often called quarter tones, they are more accurately microtones. Why? Because Eastern musicians tweak the notes, pushing them sharper or flatter as the song or their feeling for the note indicates. So, we have individual ornamentation of the rhythm and melody, plus extra notes, *and on top of all this,* we have the musicians' modulation of those notes, the better to express their feeling in the moment. That is a lot of complexity.

archive.aramcoworld.com/issue/200604/muslim.roots.u.s.blues.htm

Putting it all together

These nuances give dancers abundant textures with which to interpret the music. When a traditional Eastern song is played without this decoration, the music is empty. When we have a half-dozen musicians adding texture, coloring the music with their ornaments, we have a rich palette of material upon which to dance.

Just as the musicians are free to play what they feel, dancers have equal artistic liberty. We have the freedom to pick and choose which lines to interpret, the melody or rhythm, which instrument and what aspect of it, with our bodies and our finger cymbals. How do we fully express these textures, timbres, and decorations? Welcome to *micromovement*...

MICROMOVEMENT

Just as the musicians use microtones to better express their mood, dancers use micromovement. We modulate each movement's size, shape, texture, direction, speed, and force to better fit our mood and the music, carving calligraphic lines through time and space. Just as calligraphy has thin and thick lines, our movement arcs have slower and faster segments, portions that are rich with tension and intensity coupled with sleek tracery. We cultivate a long, lazy line, dripping like thick, sweet, scented syrup. Some singers do this, too. Listen to Bobby Darin sing "Up the Lazy River." You'll hear it.

As with Arabic calligraphy, which fancifully tweaks letter shapes to better express the feeling and intention of the artist, we adapt moves to better fit the music and our feeling from the music.

Consider the textures and dynamics of the song *Ala eh Betloumy* (Links to this and other songs mentioned in this chapter are available at bellydancesoul.com/resources). As you listen, paint the music in the air with your hand. Vary speed and force to articulate the shifting quality of the sound. Close your eyes. Just feel it. Now let your body express the shapes of the sounds, from wide, sweeping strokes to elegant slender curves and cushioned accents.

Try it with the shapes of Arabic calligraphy. It's not about exact re-creation—it's about allowing the body's line to adapt to the shape, timing, and texture of the music. Radiate rich, exquisite lines into the hearts of your guests. Try this with the luxurious indulgence of Adaweya's *Bint al Sultaan*. Love the music with your body. Rub up against it like a cat. Feels good, doesn't it? That's the real deal.

Now let's step it up a bit further. Recorded music is great, but it is with live, improvised music that the dance finds its true home.

The music made visible

Live Music

When musicians play for a dancer, they watch the dancer as carefully as they listen to each other. They respond to the dancer's movement, literally playing what they see, the same as dancers dance what they hear. Master Egyptian tabla player Yousry Hefny maintains that his job is to watch the dancer's waist, and to *play whatever she does*. His job is to follow the dancer, not the other way around. The whole thing is a massive collaboration as everyone sparks off each other's interpretations.

TAQASIM, EMOTIONAL TIMBRES, AND IMPROVISATION

Eastern music (and belly dance) are profoundly elastic genres, expressing an array of emotional timbres. These timbres shift and change depending upon the nature of the composition. Music scholar and master musician Dr. George Dimitri Sawa, *georgedimitrisawa.com*, explains: "One and the same maqam can be sad or happy, depending upon the lyrics and the melodic movement. Both *Tel'ct Ya Mahla Norha* and *Zurumi Kalsana Marra* are in Ajam mode; however, the first is happy and the second is very sad" (links at *bellydancesoul.com/resources*).

With the musicians playing what they feel and the dancers dancing what they feel, that song is going to be played and danced differently every time, uniquely colored with today's feeling, this moment's feeling. This fluidity is most directly expressed in the *taqsim* (plural *taqasim*), a musician's solo improvisation.

A taqsim will begin on one note, then explore the maqam—first the lower *jins* (rhymes with hints), then the top jins. A jins (pl. *ajnas*) is a three to five-note building block of a maqam. Each maqam has two ajnas, the lower and the upper. The taqsim then winds from maqam to maqam, modulating through sometimes wild, heroic leaps. Where a musician goes depends entirely upon his feeling in the moment. Thus, the notes are a container for the feeling of the musician in the same way that movement is a container for the feeling of the dancer. Try it with a beautiful Farid al Atrash taqsim. Close your eyes; let the music move you.

Some movement elements that lend themselves to dancing on a taqsim are circles, infinities, undulations, shimmies and waves. The strong rhythm that underlies many taqasim is the Greek/Turkish rhythm, *chiftetelli*, an 8/4. It is so rich and compelling that many of us dance *only* on the rhythm, ignoring the melody instrument pouring its heart out—but that instrument provides much deeper, more dynamic material for interpretation. And there is much more to a taqsim than movement.

Dr. Sawa observes that, "embedded in any taqsim is the concept of *musical meaning*. And this is the hardest concept for non-Arab dancers." The taqsim most deeply expresses the musician's feeling in the moment. Unrestricted by melody or external structure, he is able to explore, allow his impressions to evolve, and his artistry to express itself. A dancer who accompanies this voyage of discovery opens herself to its fleeting shifts and wisps of emotional timbres and leaps of faith. *What* the dancer does is of far less importance than *the feeling, grace, and musicality with which she does it*. Her movement imbued at every moment with the essence of the musician's expression—the musical meaning—she expresses this for her guests. Leila Farid explains, "The dancer brings the audience to the music like a bridge."

∽

Sometimes the quality of the instrument's sound (even where it is played) is cited as a prescription for certain types of movement. Let's take a look at this. The two main melodic characterizations, *sahb* and *naqr*, apply to the timbre of the instrument's sound.

Sahb refers to smooth, flowing sounds, such as the voice, violin, and wind instruments. Naqr, the percussive sounds, includes all the drums—frame drums, *riqq* (Arabic tambourine), and *tabla* (aka darbuka, derbekke, or dumbeg). Naqr also characterizes the plucked instruments such as the qanun, oud, and buzuq (pictures and audio of these instruments are at *maqamworld.com*). Of course, each musician plays differently—some nays are more percussive, some ouds more flowing.

Sahb and naqr are often cited as injunctions upon the texture of the dancer's response—i.e., shimmy to the oud and the qanun, undulate to the violin, and lift the arms for the nay. I've repeated these recipes myself, and Leila points out that they can be a useful starting point for a taqsim, in which there is no "melody," per se. However, they do go against my early experience in the Five-Part Routine—and Dr. Sawa dismisses them completely.

Dr. Sawa explains that from the musician's perspective, the percussive quality of the qanun and other plucked instruments occurs because the sound dies away quickly; therefore, the musician has to keep plucking to *sustain* the sounds. He recommends that we dance more on each instrument's melodic elements rather than the percussive quality of the sustain.

I grew up in the days of the Five-Part Routine (1960s and 70s). Back then, we rarely shimmied to an oud or qanun taqsim—rather, we did floorwork. The floorwork of the time was a sensual, glorious roiling, with a few classic moves and a lot of long, languorous extensions. It was *wonderful*. Floorwork builds a *lot* of strength and flexibility and it adds a lot to one's practice. Sadly, it has fallen out of fashion for several reasons, among them the cost of costumes and the filth of restaurant floors. The other main reason is more interesting.

Because there is little to no floorwork in modern Egyptian style, Western dancers in search of authenticity thought that floorwork simply wasn't Egyptian, so they didn't do it. In reality, floorwork is illegal in Egypt, as the dance police deem it too sensual.

Nothing is made illegal unless a lot of people are doing it; one can safely assume there was plenty of floorwork prior to its criminalization (and one can only imagine the floorwork going down in Egypt; it must have been pretty hot). In any case, while it has continued in Turkish and Greek styles, Egyptian-influenced dancers (which is now most of us) dropped it. And while there has recently been a return to the floor, modern versions I have seen are more studied, contain modern and fusion movement, and exhibit far less sensual glory.

What's also interesting is that back in the Five-Part Routine days, everything was improvised. No one worried about which move to do with what music. We studied a *lot* (I went to class two or three times a week for two hours at a time), but we learned to dance what we felt and to infuse each step with our own flavor. As we will see, the brilliant polyglot blossoming of the American nightclub scene got short shrift later on for its lack of breeding; it pleases me to find that Dr. Sawa's advice supports its approach.

Okay, so far: Dancers use micromovement to express the microtonal, heterophonic nature of the music; they are free to follow whatever element of the music they like; the music is filled with improvised emotional timbres—feeling and representing them in concord with the music is more important than any specific steps; and the taqsim is the ultimate in musicians' expression.

Cool? Let's go on.

Improvising to taqsim

Dance makes the music visible. In a taqsim, when the musician plays, we dance. *When there is no music, we don't dance.* When the musician pauses (a pause is *qafla*; plural *qaflat*), we coast to a stop, gently fading the movement as the tone dies away, easing into motion as the notes recommence in the next phrase.

Within the music, we are free to choose what aspects of it we follow. We have the obvious elements of pitch, volume, frequency, and tempo. However, we also have more subtle elements—for example, the texture and the emotional feeling we get from the music. We may perceive feelings of happiness, sorrow, nostalgia, yearning, seeking, finding—even anger. Any feeling may appear in the music, depending upon the musician's intention and the dancer's perception, as a major feature or a mere wisp.

We let these feelings in through our ears and skin; we express them with our bodies. Far more important than any specific movement is the emotional quality with which that movement is expressed. This is why we say that the feeling is the most important thing. There are also physical sensations. Our open response to the music feels good to the body—we take pleasure in the sensation of our body's visceral response to the sounds. This, too, is part of the dance.

The dancer shows what she feels from the music—that emotional and physical feeling *is* her response to the music. The specific steps don't matter. The dancer's feeling and the timing of her physical response do. A dancer could stick with one move for an entire taqsim—for example, an undulation. Yet through the miracle of micromovement, all those dynamics—the timing, speed, size, and effort—shift and change according the music and the infinite shadings of the dancer's journey.

This understanding begins to coalesce as you listen to many taqasim—just listen. Dr. Sawa recommends listening extensively to a single musician's taqasim to get a feeling for how they phrase their improvisations. Rather than attempting to predict what the musician will do, relax into the music and let it move you. In the West, we are taught to be *on* the beat. In the East, dancers are often inside or behind the beat; they "sit inside the music," says Leila Farid.

Years ago, I heard on the radio about a study in which participants had to either predict or intuit where and when random points of light would appear. The study found that those intuiting the light were more accurate than those attempting to predict it. I could never find a citation for this, but I love that it happened. Allow yourself to relax and wait for the music. If you miss a note or a couple of accents, it's okay. Relax and have fun.

It is the dancer's honor and privilege to dance what she feels—this goes for naqr, sahb, anything. When you feel long, swooping curves, allow them to emerge. When you feel a shimmy, let it happen. I have seen video in which Fifi Abdou, an internationally revered Egyptian dancer, shimmies on a nay taqsim. If it's okay for Fifi, it's okay for us. It is a challenge to let go of "rules" and dance what we feel, but we are better dancers for it, and the dance is more rewarding this way, too—not only for the dancer, but also for the musicians and the guests.

Take your time. Feel the music—literally. Roll in it. Let it caress you and dance with you, like a curl of scent wafting through your dreams. Let yourself be a leaf in its wind, a twig on its stream, shaped by the sound. Now close your eyes and let a truly lovely *Taqsim Nay Kurd* into your heart. Ah!

There is joy in becoming one with the music. This joy is treasured in many cultures. It is especially revered in the cultures of this dance, where musicians and guests together seek the state of *Tarab*.

Joy

TARAB (طرب)

The goal of classical Eastern music (and art, and dance), is to enter into an exalted state. This state, *tarab* (rhymes with Arab), is often translated, insofar is it can be translated, as "ecstasy." Ecstasy is defined as a state of joy, but originally referred to a state of mystic self-transcendence (from the Greek *ekstasis* 'standing outside oneself'). There are many kinds of tarab; for our purposes, we will discuss musical tarab.

Tarab can be framed as a state of meditative entrainment, of being deeply in the present moment (the goal of Eastern arts in general). Expert dance artist Cassandra Shore, *jawaahir.org/cassandra,* defines musical tarab as "the hypersensitivity of consciousness that occurs between the performers and audience; one is not lost in the music, one is super aware and in sync with all the other artists, and the audience is in the same state, following, seeing, and hearing every nuance."

The joy of tarab is shared between the performers and the audience. Eastern audiences have an investment in the evening—they actively participate in the creation of this state. They encourage the musicians, call out, and engage with them, appreciating daring modulations, well-turned taqasim, etc. The best audience members are the *sammi'ah*, educated listeners. The job of the sammi'ah is to "cheer up" the musicians, to encourage them and appreciate their artistry.

Dr. Racy explains that Arabs embraced recording early on. In the early days of recording, musicians brought their sammi'ah with them to the recording studio, as engagement with the audience was such an integral part of the music-making process. For more, seek out *Tarab: Making Music in the Arab World,* by Dr. A.J. Racy.

You will often hear me say that Oriental dance has magical powers. The same is true for the music. With tarab as a goal, the music is consciously focused on ecstasy, embodiment, and soul connection.

Ecstasy and Dance

In classical usage, tarab does not include dancers or dance music, being primarily focused on specific genres meant for listening. However, the state of tarab exists for dancers as well. Many of us have felt it. We know it. We may not know how to name it, or how to reliably attain it, but we know it is there. This dance—and its music—connects us to the Divine.

As dancers, we create an opening in which all the participants in the moment feel that interconnection, a pervasive joy. This, too, is tarab. I find that with quality (preferably live), music and an experienced dancer, this state can be shared between musicians, dancer, and guests. Additionally, the canon of dance music has evolved to include songs originally intended for listening. The dance and the music evolved together, twining round each other in ecstatic union. It is a miraculous fusion, unique and marvelous.

To me, the dancer is one more musician, one whose instrument is seen rather than heard. Dr. Sawa agrees. From this perspective, we may include the dancer in the tarab equation.

NOTE: TARAB IS AN ALTERED STATE THAT INCLUDES THE PERFORMERS AND THE GUESTS. It is quite different from the modern trend of dancing on "tarab songs." Traditionally, these are songs made for listening and for generating feelings of tarab through the singer and the music. It's ironic, since dancers often precisely choreograph such pieces down to every wink and smile. Precision is not the purpose of these songs. Ecstasy is.

When our goal is musical ecstasy, our choices change. We may no longer feel satisfied with superficial music, recordings, stylized tricks, or stylized "emotion" built into busy, carbon-copy choreography. We listen more closely, more openly. We nurture our intuition. Ecstasy comes from expressing our feeling within the framework of the music, being in the moment, including an entire room in our joy. When ecstasy becomes our benchmark, we raise the bar—significantly.

I have experienced tarab as an audience member and as a dancer. It happens when dancing on quality music played by experienced musicians who understand this purpose. The feeling is that of being perfectly in tune with the moment, the music, and the guests. We are all one. Everything comes together and everyone shares this feeling of joy. When you experience this, you remember it.

I was fortunate to hear Dr. Racy lecture on tarab at the Arabic Music Retreat in Holyoke, MA. The minute he began to describe it, every person in the room leaned forward, intent upon his words. We all knew what he was talking about. He put into words what I had often felt but never been able to name. This is why we dance.

Whether we perform for others or dance for ourselves, we seek this sense of connection, of communion, of oneness, of joy. We look for it in our music and we look for it in our souls. This little folk dance has a deep magic. It need not be on stage to take us there. Dr. Racy says that genuine tarab persists, even in recordings. We hear it. We feel it. We dance it, wherever we may be—from the concert stage to the corner of our kitchen.

Tarab is but one of many elements of the dance that are hidden from first glance. We Western dancers struggle to learn, while Eastern dancers understand tarab intuitively from lifelong immersion in their culture. As we have seen, Eastern cultural mindsets and values are often quite different from those of the West. Let's take a deeper look.

Just what is life like for Eastern dancers?

30 | MIDNIGHT AT THE CROSSROADS

The Mysterious East?

3

THE "MYSTERIOUS" EAST

I TOOK UP BELLY DANCE WHEN I WAS SIXTEEN.

A woman down the block was giving lessons (Hi, Jeanne!) Being Lebanese/Palestinian/Syrian on my father's side, I thought it would be cultural—and sexy (did I mention I was sixteen?). My parents were fine with this.

My family was pretty bohemian—my mother, Frances, ran away from home in St. Louis to live in New York City. She became an actor with the Living Theater (her stage name was Fanny Mitchell). Ironically, it was she who interested me in Eastern music. On the Arab side, my father, Walter Thabit, was an advocate city planner who worked in East New York and Cooper Square. His mission was to empower redlined, impoverished neighborhoods to take charge of urban renewal.

A family friend, Fé Weinstein, was a belly dancer. I never saw her dance, but my mother said she had a great affect when she performed, like, "Aren't we all having a wonderful time?" That became what a belly dancer did.

It turned out to be an excellent model.

So, there I was in Brooklyn, NY, learning to shimmy and hip drop. Jeanne's classes lasted a few months; then she sent us to her teacher—Ibrahim "Bobby" Farrah. Luck can be your best friend. I stayed with Bobby for several years, attending two hours of classes two and three times a week.

One day, I proudly told my Uncle Eddie what I'd been doing. Eddie was my father's brother, and the nicest man on earth. He looked stricken. Then, very gently, he said, "You know, in the old country, dancers don't have the best reputation..." Well, I got all huffy and snarked him up one side and down the other: you'd think he'd be proud of me; I was doing something cultural, yadda yadda. He backed off and never said another word, and I went on my merry way. We lost Uncle Eddie far too early, but over the years, the rest of my family came around.

My father never cared if I danced; he came to see me perform several times and gave me some excellent advice. My Uncle Robert saw me dance Romani style to a Turkish band and wished I would dance "more Arabic." I asked him to point to someone who danced that way. He pointed out an excellent but (to me) empty dancer. My dad glanced at her and muttered, "No soul." So there you go.

My aunt Ethel asked me to perform at her 50th wedding anniversary (which made the party, especially getting her and her family up to dance). My aunt Gloria, at her 90th birthday party, insisted that I dance, and to make sure the kids would see and remember. I've had this same acceptance from many other diaspora folks who value dance. I understand now how lucky I have been. But way back in the 70s I had no idea that my horrified Uncle Eddie was 100% right. Dancers had (and have) a very bad reputation in the old country (it's not too great here, either).

Just how bad is it? Dancers are routinely seen as prostitutes, not to mention home-wrecking, dangerous, and thoroughly untouchable. You want one for your wedding, but you'd never allow your daughter to be one—or your son to marry one. There are a lot of reasons for this (thanks to patriarchy and misogyny rather than the dancers themselves).

I'll talk mostly about Egypt—scholars regard it as the likely birthplace of the dance, and it is the culture about which I know the most. Plus the dance is popular there—and divisive.

Culture

In the East, the family is the main unit of loyalty. Multiple generations often live under one roof and first cousin marriages are prized because they bring the family closer. Also, a wife usually goes to live in her husband's house; if he is a cousin, she is related to his male relatives. This way, if the family is conservative, she need not veil in front of them, which makes life easier for everyone. If a wife might have to veil in front of her husband's male kin, you can see why being uncovered on stage in front of random strangers is seen as shameful. Even to be *ibn al raqasa*—the son of a dancer—is a dire insult.

Since money for a house is hard to get, and because extended families are traditional, there may be several family groups living together. In addition, gender roles tend to be traditional, and women do most of the cooking, cleaning, childcare, etc.

Who is in the kitchen together? Women and children. What will they do to make the work lighter? Sing and dance. Yes, with each other, at home. Here you get the first inkling that this is not the dance of seduction. There is something far richer going on. Here's the thing: Belly dancing makes you happy. It does. Even a little dance to upbeat music can do it, and if you dance for twenty minutes or so, the positive effects can last for hours. We'll come back to this later. For now, let's go on.

Let's face it—for most women in the East, life is challenging. They work hard. They have few advantages. Sons are still the favored offspring, and if only one child is to get an education, guess who it's going to be? (Hint: not the girl.) On the other hand, I have often heard it said (particularly for Egypt) that, although women seem to have little freedom, they are in reality the boss of the house. The man is helpless in the face of pressure from the women—the mother, wife, daughters, etc.

Maybe this is true in the home—or some homes—but not in the larger society. The Damocles sword of Islamic law means the dependence enforced on most women is coupled with a man's right to beat his wife or to throw her out of the house at any moment, simply by saying, "I divorce you," three times. Should this occur, the woman is cast out into the world, without her precious children, hopelessly shamed. Where can she go? Back to her family? If they will even have her. Honor killings are sadly common. There is always insecurity, an uneasy balance that any woman must walk. She must watch herself and be careful.

The uneasy balance

Dance in the Culture

Despite all this, there is dance. It is an integral part of every celebration, every gathering, and everyday life. Dance strengthens the body and soul; it reminds us that we are beautiful and that we have agency. It gives us hope and opens up our dreams. No wonder conservative ideologies despise dance and music, twin stars of relief, pleasure, and joy. In the home, everyone dances—women, men, children, and old folks.

But, in the East, for a woman to have agency, to make her own decisions unfettered by the authority of a man, to earn her own money, have her own voice, and, in particular, show her body to men to whom she is not related, is the height of *haram*, forbidden.

The successful female dancer exemplifies every single thing that is taboo for a woman in the Eastern culture: She appears on stage and flaunts her body in front of men; she tells men what to do (her band, for example); she negotiates and participates in business; she is hard-headed and advocates for herself. This is why, historically, many dancers come from a class of performing families, like circus families, where the skills are handed down from parent to child and a separate culture forms aside from the main culture. Even in the case of folks from "straight" families who turn towards the arts, a culture of artists tends to form, so you and your friends share the same values.

Singing in public is considered bad enough for women, especially if men in the audience can see the singer's body. But dancing? In a two-piece costume? In front of men? That is beyond the pale.

Clearly, being a professional dancer in the East can be a choice of desperation. Maybe you are from a family that dances, and it is assumed you will go into the family profession. Maybe your family needs food, and you have no other way to make money (none that you can stomach, anyway). Maybe you have the privilege to make a choice. Whatever it is, there will be pushback.

As for male dancers, there is no shame in public dancing, particularly folklore, but dressing up in anything resembling a female dancer's *bedlah* (Arabic for suit or uniform, it refers to the typical two-piece bra and belt costume)? Oh, that you may not do. That is seen as gay. It's still illegal in Egypt to be gay, and you can go to jail. Nobody wants to go to Egyptian jail. No sir.

Like stripping in the West, belly dance is not considered a respectable occupation. Dancers must hide what they do or associate only with other artists who understand their alternative lifestyle. And, while dance was never a vaunted trade, the rise of Islamic conservatism means that conditions in the East have only worsened. Belly dancers are shamed in the same way that strippers are shamed in the West—cast as whores who dance to incite lust in men. Famous dancers have been offered huge sums of money to renounce dance and make the *hajj*—the pilgrimage to Mecca.

Ironically, we Western belly dancers often separate ourselves from strippers, saying, oh, we are not like *them*—what *we* do is family friendly! It's fine to present our performance as family friendly, but to disdain strippers is beyond hypocritical. Many Western belly dancers also have to hide what they do or risk losing jobs, children, and social respectability. All over the world, misogynist, right-wing, religious fundamentalism drives the demonization of women's agency, expression, and sexuality.

Every time we demean a stripper (or a sex worker, or any woman's sexuality), we support the oppression of women—and of belly dancers in the

East. We are all in this together. If we're going to do this dance, let's support the women from whom it comes. Let's be part of the solution.

Bad Reputation

Of course, many dancers and musicians, in addition to being artists, are also courtesans. For example, the women of the Algerian Ouled Naïl were famous courtesans. Mothers trained their daughters in dance and love, then sent them down to town to make their money. The girls danced, took lovers, and made boatloads of cash. Some stayed in the city and opened houses of their own, hosting new girls. Most came home draped with ropes of gold coins they had earned, chose husbands from their own people, and settled down to become what were regarded as exemplary wives.

The tribe had maintained this tradition for longer than anyone can remember. According to Lawrence Morgan in his lovely memoir, *Flute of Sand*, that they were also Islamic didn't bother them. Their tradition had always been, and no one questioned it. They didn't see any conflict, so there was no shame attached to this extended coming of age ritual. That's surprising, even for us "liberated" Westerners.

NB The Ouled Naïl probably didn't so much do what we think of as "belly dance." But they did have that *danse du ventre* (French for Dance of the Stomach), in which the dancer uses her stomach muscles to manipulate a metal belt up and down her midsection (it used to be a scarf, but they got fancier for the tourist trade). Morocco verified this during her time in Algeria—she and Aisha Ali, from whom I learned some of this intense stomach work, both did research with the Ouled Naïl back in the 1970s (yes, the same danse du ventre that inspired the term belly dance. Though it was not related to the dance we now know as belly dance, it has stuck determinedly since it was coined in the 1800s).

Arab dancers certainly have no patent on courtesanship—even in the West, art is rarely a wealth-making enterprise, especially for women. Dancers have always attracted wealthy "patrons." This hasn't helped our overall reputation. And in the East, the avid interest of Western men hasn't done the dancers—or the dance—any favors, either.

Let's look at what happened when the West came to the East.

Oriental dance is an abstract art. It is *not* about symbolic meaning; it *is* about the music and the dancer's feeling. Western art, however, is all about symbolic meaning. So, as Dr. Najwa Adra observes in her article, "Belly Dance, an Urban Folk Genre," *najwaadra.net*, when Westerners arrived, in particular, Western men, they took a look at the local entertainment, the sensual movement vocabulary, the *dala3* (playfulness and sexual confidence), of the dancers, and immediately decided that the dance was about sex.

"Nice dance," they said. "Can you take your clothes off?"

Historically, dancers' costumes were modest affairs—most performers wore their regular clothes (vest, long tunic, loose trousers, and a hip scarf or two, which somehow always goes with dance). But Western men had the money to get what they wanted. Costumes got skimpier. Nightclubs abounded, many following the new style set by Badia Masabni in her Casino Opera, who had a sharp eye for Western trends.

Note: According to Dr. Mo Geddawi, *drmogeddawi.com*, it was Badia who first coined the term Raqs Sharqi (dance of the east), to appeal to the upper classes she courted, as the dance's common name of raqs baladi (dance of the country), as "country" had an uneducated, low-rent tang. According to Morocco, Badia modeled her nightclub after a British music hall. The show went on—on time—every night, and included Western acts, such as ballroom dancers (one couple being Nadia Jamal's parents—and one of Badia's chorus sharqi dancers was the mother of famed costume designer Eman Zaki, *goldenlotus.com*, who accompanied her mother to work and teaches a marvelous workshop on this style).

In some less-savory nightclubs (*not* Badia's), dancers had to sit at customers' tables, encouraging them to drink. In Islamic culture, drink is *severely* frowned upon (and who got blamed for this practice? Hint: not the nightclub owners).

Egyptian films, ravenously consumed by the entire Arab world, at first showcased dancers as glamorous eye candy to drive box-office sales. Over time, however, this changed—dancers began to act in the films, only to be portrayed as home wreckers and harlots. An Egyptian woman I know struggled mightily with this dialectic. She knew she was a dancer, but she was certainly not a home-wrecking harlot. It took soul-searching and courage to reject this destructive stereotype and allow herself to dance. She became a highly regarded performer, teacher, and producer of quality events. She lived in America, which helped. But it took great courage to face down her cultural demons.

Of course, there was (and is) plenty of prostitution going down. Economics plays a huge part in this. Many (probably most) Egyptian women who dance publicly do it to make money (not art). In a society where it is incredibly difficult to get an education, where illiteracy is rampant, where boys are prized over girls, where jobs are difficult to find, and where the prospects for women are seriously curtailed, there aren't many options. Since the women may be in desperate straits, they face a lot of pressure from those who hire them—and we know where that goes.

This is why you never, ever, tell anyone you meet in the lands of this dance that you are a belly dancer—not the friendly passport guy at the airport, nor the taxi driver, nor your guide, nor even the desk clerk at your hotel. You will be quickly transformed into slut-stripper-harlot—with all the ickiness that entails.

But here's the point: It's tempting to look down upon the East for this viewpoint, but are we in the West any better?

Dance in the East is rarely a career path for those with connections and money. Consequently, dancers must often make a living on their backs, subject to the whims of those who employ them (this is why the shaming of sex workers, strippers, etc. undermines all women. There but for the grace of God... We'll talk more about this in the Sex chapter). And to be fair, not too long ago in the West (like, yesterday), dancers, actors, and performers of any stripe were largely regarded as dirty, louche people. Performers routinely slept with their benefactors. It was fine to see a show, but not a life you wanted for your kids.

Respect for belly dance has increased somewhat in the West (if not in the East), but we are nowhere near acceptance. Despite the fact that millions of people world-wide love this dance, despite the fact that you can now get a PhD for studying it, when you tell someone you are a belly dancer, you still get a dose of *nudge-nudge, wink-wink*. Some may be a hangover from the dance's bad rep in the old country, but much of it comes from the bad reputation carefully manufactured in the West, to sell the dance to Western audiences.

4
CULTURE CLASH

East comes West

The USA's first big exposure to the dances of the Near and Middle East came in 1893 at the World's Fair in Chicago. Oriental dance had already made it to the West, but this was the big time. There were Algerian, Syrian, Egyptian, and many other dancers. One of the impresarios who arranged for these dancers was the young Sol Bloom. Bloom needed a huge return to justify the enormous cost of importing an entire North African dance company, so he did a "smart" thing: He sold the show on sex.

The story goes that Bloom put the dancers in a tent, raised the admission price, and announced that only men were allowed to view them—the show was too crude for the eyes of ladies. He dubbed the dance with the French term *danse du ventre* (dance of the stomach), which he translated into the most salacious possible English: "belly dance." Remember, this was the Victorian age. Women wore corsets. Their hair was always put up. One glimpse of a woman's ankle was the stuff of erotic fantasy. Nobody even said arms or legs—just limbs.

And he calls it belly dance.

People were appalled. The dancers wore their hair loose, no corsets, bared forearms, and showed their ankles and feet. They were described as lewd, disgusting, and barely clothed. A few folks found some good, but mostly the shows were panned.

It was a roaring success. Welcome to America!

Dancers in the Egyptian Theater from the book The Dream City (1893). Bare arms and visible feet and ankles were scandalous at the time

Some of the Fair dancers (and locals who knew how to milk a good thing) later became staples on the vaudeville circuit or performed with circuses. According to the Library of Congress (LOC), Princess Ali had been a performer at the Fair and was a Barnum and Bailey circus performer when Thomas Edison filmed her in 1895. Though billed as Egyptian, her scarf work looks like what I've been taught as Algerian Ouled Naïl dance (Morocco also identifies her as Algerian).

Also in the LOC collection, American Mutoscope (founded by one of Edison's people), filmed Princess Rajah in 1904, dancing with a chair and doing enthusiastic shimmies and ghawazi-style footwork. Morocco identifies this Princess as American and adds that when the Eastern dance fad ended, Rajah became an opera singer.

In his Rare Glimpses DVD, Ibrahim Farrah mentions Fatima, filmed in 1896. Believed to be Fatima Djemmile, she may be the original Little Egypt—who became the notorious Little Egypt after performing at a party in New York City that was raided by the vice squad.

For links to all the above, see *bellydancesoul.com/resources* (fyi, any music you may hear in such old footage has been recently added).

Soon enough there were myriad Little Egypts, Cooch or Hoochie Coochie dancers, and, after the success of Maude Allen as Salome, countless Salomes flooding the circuit with their Dances of the Seven Veils. Modern dancers such as Ruth St. Denis developed their own interpretations of ethnic dances (St. Denis choreographed the Babylon sections of DW Griffith's epic, *Intolerance*).

The dance was here to stay. So, sadly, was its reputation as a lewd dance of seduction. That might have been the end of it, but for the influx of Near Eastern peoples immigrating to the US in the early 20th century. This is when my family arrived, entering the USA in the 1920s from what was then Syria (now Lebanon and Palestine), to "escape from the Turks."

*This early period in the West has been covered extensively by dancer-scholars Morocco, *casbahdance.org*, Dr. Laura Osweiler, *amaradances.com*, and by Donna Carlton in her excellent book "Looking for Little Egypt," *allaboutbellydance.com/egypt.html*.

The Golden Age of Greektown, USA

As the waves of Eastern immigrants surged into America, their collective longing for the arts and culture they left behind blossomed into a new form of music and dance. Greek entrepreneurs went into restaurants in a big way; consequently, a host of Greek nightclubs sprang up, catering to the tastes of their ethnic clientele. New York's 8th Avenue was a hotbed of such clubs, as was the Bay Area's North Shore.

Syrian, Greek, and Armenian musicians played together the folkloric and classical music of their homelands. Dancers were first imported (often from Turkey), then developed locally. The result was a miraculous organic fusion variously known as Turkish-Armenian style (many musicians came from Armenian families escaping the genocide in Turkey), American Nightclub style, Vintage Orientale, or more contentiously, American Cabaret Style, AmCab for short. Why contentious? Cabaret is not a dirty word in America, but in many other parts of the world (including Egypt), it connotes low sort of dive, and implies a low sort of dancer; therefore, we prefer the other names.

These clubs popularized the "Five-Part Routine." A great, durable dance vehicle, the Five-Part Routine starts out fast for the dancer's entrance, slows down to a bolero for veil work (largely an American innovation), speeds up again for table hopping, slows way down to a taqsim for floorwork, crescendos in a drum solo, then resolves into an upbeat finale, often in a 9/8 karşilama rhythm. Each part gets a different song. Back in the day, dancers played finger cymbals throughout their entire set—about half an hour. In the bigger nightclubs, there might be several dancers in an evening show; when the dancers were not dancing, they often played percussion on stage.

This Golden Age lasted from the 50s well into the 70s (when belly dance became a phenomenon, with classes springing up all over), up through the 80s and beyond. Live music was widely available in the nightclubs; at many Greek, Lebanese, and Armenian Church celebrations there was music and dancing galore. Recorded music for classes was less available (and much of it is now sadly out of print), but the music recorded then, by artists such as

George Abdo, John Berberian, and so on, is still cherished by dancers for its infectious joy.

This time alone is worth a few books. Many of the artists of the era are still alive, making music or dancing and teaching. Some of the print and online magazines have begun this collection process, but there is still so much to do.

The rise of "Tribal" style

Something else was going on in the belly dance world at this time. It started in California, and it got going back in the 60s and 70s.

Jamila Salimpour, a half-Sicilian circus artist, reportedly learned belly dance largely from Golden Age Egyptian films and Armenian neighbors in 1949. She later married an Iranian musician, who turned out to be, shall we say, non-supportive of her dance. He informed her (*after* the wedding), that if she ever danced in public again, he would break both her legs. Needless to say, that marriage didn't last—but it did produce Suhaila Salimpour, who has carried on the family legacy (as has Suhaila's daughter, Isabella), and it pushed Jamila into teaching and more to provide for her family. In the late 60s, Jamila developed the dance collective Bal-Anat. Ba'al and Anat are the Phoenician Sky Father and Earth Mother—but *bal* in this case was French for dance; thus, Bal-Anat, Dance of the Mother Goddess.

Did I mention California was kinda New Age at this time? San Francisco in the 60s and 70s was all laid back and groovy. The concept of "cultural appropriation" had not yet been born. It was a wide-open field; anything went. The economy was good, and you could live on next to nothing. There were lots of flower children, and the anti-war movement was strong. You could have a big group of people with enough time to develop something rich.

Bal-Anat had dancers and musicians. From her circus background, Jamila developed a winning format for presenting her amalgam of "ethnic" dance styles—which meant semi-authentic dance and music flashed up with what she called "hokum." Jamila wrote some articles about Bal-Anat for Habibi magazine—for one on its formation, see *bellydancesoul.com/resources*. Bal-Anat is often cited as the origin of Tribal Style; back then, it was just belly dance.

I met Jamila in the early 70s when Ibrahim Farrah sponsored her for a workshop at the Jerry LeRoy Studios (which later became Fazil's). She was an imposing presence in a gorgeous assuit dress, black hair, and thick black eyeliner. She also brought along her daughter, Suhaila (who must have been all of seven at the time), to demonstrate some of the more difficult moves, such as the drops (I still use her side drop). I also got Jamila's great one-page cymbal pattern sheet, which I am sure is still *somewhere* in my house.

Jamila's circus background gave her an understanding of showbiz and spectacle. She drew inspiration from paintings, pictures, variety acts—she had a creative mind and a mission. She crafted a scene that was perfect for the time and place in which she worked.

Bal-Anat was a large group. They often performed outdoors without amplification, so they had to be loud. A bunch of musicians played old school folkloric music with a lot of mizmar (doesn't get much louder than that) and big rhythm. The dancers clustered in a semicircle around the performance space, playing zils or drums and creating a critical mass. Small groups of three to five dancers would step forward and do a dance, maybe with pots on their heads or whatever—fairly simple steps but exotic costumes, and the mob of performers gave the whole thing a lot of oomph.

These groups were interspersed with solo dancers who did their more personal thing while the whole group provided a backdrop and cheering section. The dancers were mostly women, but several men danced with the company, some of whom, such as John Compton of Hahbi'Ru, went on to found their own dance companies and styles, as did many of the women—including Masha Archer.

Masha Archer (currently a jewelry and art-clothing designer at *masha.org*), was a trained artist. Her interests were eclectic, and her goal was beauty and artistry—according, of course, to her personal taste and style. She disliked dance in nightclubs and bars. Instead, she wanted to "elevate" the dance. She introduced group synchronized movement and Western music. She thought the costumes and floorwork degrading, so she dumped floorwork and covered legs with pantaloons and hair with turbans.

I totally get this. "Steal Like an Artist" and so on. Back in the 70s, no one thought about appropriation. You can't be arrested for laws passed *after* your actions. But Archer went further. She declared that the Eastern people, whose dance this was—and is—did not deserve it. Since they were ashamed of it, let them forfeit the dance. It belonged instead to Western women who valued it.

Now, it's true, the dance had (and has) a lousy reputation. Anyone who speaks to a random smattering of Eastern peoples could easily come to the conclusion that the dance is an unloved, embarrassing orphan. No one wants to own it. The Arabs and Greeks claimed the Turks made them do it and the Turks claimed to have learned it from the Arabs. Dancers were (and are) disdained by the larger society, generally seen as prostitutes.

That sort of disapproval is exhausting. And it is a complex situation, as

Eastern cultural norms prohibit women from performing—so dancers of the culture risk their safety and cultural respect. As much as we would love to have more dancers of the culture as teachers and performers, there is still this entrenched taboo against public performance. But that has never stopped anyone from dancing, particularly in the home—which millions of people do every day. Or having a dancer at weddings, celebrations, etc. (though that has declined, thanks to the current rise in hard-right religious fundamentalism).

No one had abandoned this dance. It was, and is, a living, breathing art, despite its checkered reputation. The disdain of dance is more of a patriarchal power play than anything that defines the Eastern ethos. Archer may have been unconcerned with this cultural background or may have not known of it (I began dancing in the early 70s, and there was little to no information out there). But she had her agenda, and that was that.

Archer's stance set a tone—and a precedent—in American belly dance for saying "Eff You," to the original cultures and all they hold dear, even though, back then, few people knew what that might be.

Cultural Heritage

Archer's student, Carolena Nericcio, founded Fat Chance Belly Dance. Fat Chance continued to use old-school mizmar and drum music, though the music was increasingly recorded, because, sadly, times have changed, and a good band is hard to find. Carolena developed a system of groups with shifting leaders and followers. The dancers use semi-structured improvisation with a cueing system and a limited, highly stylized movement vocabulary.

Nericcio's style became known (and trademarked), as American Tribal Style®. Its group aesthetic, flamboyant yet reserved costuming, and narrow scope have made it attractive to a lot of dancers. Tribal style sacrificed micromovement, the feeling in the moment, and dancer agency for a limited, stylized vocabulary, easy to learn and follow. It has worked well for them (though it does make for a challenging transition to the freedom and agency of Oriental dance).

Fast forward through Jill Parker's Ultra Gypsy—the reintroduction of soloing and the concept of Tribal Fusion—through Heather Stants' Urban Tribal, with its modern beat mixes and stop-motion fragmentation of the dance; and on to Rachel Brice's fame with the Belly Dance Super Stars, which spawned a tsunami of copies and a new style of urban, folk-funk tech music (which I like to call Clank and Crank).

As Masha Archer's stance rippled outward, dancers felt empowered to divest themselves of the Eastern roots of the dance, to mix and match however they pleased. Dancers now routinely fuse belly dance with hip hop, Bollywood, Flamenco, other ethnic dances, even burlesque (to much horror), all with varying degrees of success, depending upon the dancers' knowledge and artistry.

One of the fusions most interesting to me is theater. Brilliant artists such as Elena Lentini, *elenalentini.com*, have successfully brought Eastern values into Western forms and created marvelous work that is true to its Eastern roots. However, few dancers have her deep understanding of the dance or its cultural heritage.

Yes, there is a thriving trade in Egyptian dance festivals (and learning and honoring the roots is creeping into the Tribal community). Still, a lot of that interest is in mining music, steps, and choreography rather than delving into the conceptual framework of the dance and music (and some of the scholarship that does come down tends to be a tad self-righteous).

How do we find our way?

If we think of the dance as a movement vocabulary that can be mashed up with any other movement vocabulary, music, or costuming, then what difference does it make? The music, style, steps, whatever—these are the artist's prerogative. While it is artistically liberating, this classic Western point of view has a few drawbacks:

1. There is an uneasy line between "steal like an artist" and cultural appropriation. This line has gotten more and more uneasy as people of color/culture have begun to push back at the (largely white, often uninformed), Western sense of entitlement to their cultural treasures. Archer's stance, that the dance rightly belongs to the Western women who value it, to adapt as they please, is now understood to be classic appropriation.
2. The values and cultural identity of the dance have been displaced. Stylization and repetition have supplanted feeling, improvisation, and connection. Yes, Tribal style uses "improvisation," but it is a stylized, limited, rhythm-based movement vocabulary—the improvisation is in the *sequence* of the moves rather than their dynamics.
3. Dancers have been deprived of some remarkable gifts. The benefits of expression, improvisation, etc., are myriad. The next section explores these in detail.

These issues are ubiquitous—you can see them in any genre of belly dance (and many other arts). While wonderful dancers of all styles appreciate and promote the dance's cultural ethos, many Western belly dancers run as far away from the East as possible. Others become museum curators, presenting "accurate" reproductions of traditional dances rather than the glorious, anarchic living splendor that is live dance to live music.

We can do much better than this. And we will.

For now, let's get back to the East and see what was happening there.

The other Golden Age: cinema style

From the 30s and 40s through the 70s, Egyptian cinema was in its glory years. Hollywood had made a big impression on the East, particularly comedies and musicals. Egyptian cinema flourished, with big, splashy production numbers set in swank nightclubs, featuring famous musicians, composers, and dancers. These films showed men and women dressed in Western styles enjoying lush evenings of music and dance. Others were set *and filmed* out in country villages, bringing wonderful authenticity to the screen. Egyptian cinema was devoured throughout the East.

This was a fairly progressive time in Egypt. The style in films both mirrored and influenced the style in real life. It is eye-opening to see these films made such a short time ago, peopled with women in evening gowns and sundresses. You see this in film from Afghanistan from the 70s, too, and all over the East. Compare that with a walk down any street in Cairo today, with most women covering their heads, some even their faces and hands—or Kabul, swathed in burqas, any shred of women's personality hidden away.

Islamic conservatism has squeezed the East hard. And with "good" reason: there is a lot of money behind the effort to push women back into the home, hidden and powerless. And the East is not alone. As of 2017, Christian fundamentalism, its values alarmingly similar to its Islamic cousin, is rampant in the USA. This is important, and we'll get back to it shortly.

In any case, these films made their way to the West, thanks to pioneers like Rashid Music, *rashid.com*, the earliest purveyor of Arabic music and film in the USA. Dancers saw new and different styles, primarily Egyptian and Lebanese, depending upon the home country of the dancers turned film stars. Of course, these styles were already somewhat Westernized (thank you, Badia Masabni), as was the music to which the dancers performed. The top composers of the day listened to, and were influenced by, Western musical forms (Abdel Wahab even made his orchestra perform the music as written). But nobody understood that at the time, and besides, nobody cared—it was (and is) stunning music. Western dancers flocked to Egypt (and Turkey, and Lebanon) in the 80s and 90s to learn the dance in the places of its birth.

The dance they learned was different from the style of the Five-Part Routine. While Vintage Orientale favored simply-constructed folk songs with dance rhythms and multiple taqasim, the Egyptian orchestral music was far more complex—overtures from works composed for great singers such as Umm Kalthoum, or spectacular entrances composed for dance stars such as Nagwa Fouad, known for her tableaux and spectacles, and the first to commission big dance numbers from famous composers.

In addition, the Egyptian dance style was more melodic, nuanced, and subdued. Naturally, many dancers soon spurned the Five-Part Routine for what they thought of as the real thing—though the Five-Part Routine is a great contribution to the dance, rooted in earlier Egyptian and Turkish routines, and is what most Westerners (and many Easterners), think of when they think of belly dance.

The upshot of this is that suddenly there were styles, genres. You might dance Lebanese, Egyptian, or American Nightclub style. The nightclub scene changed. More Egyptian clubs sprang up, with Egyptian orchestras playing the music of the great composers (much of which was already old music by this time. Sadly, we have little excellent new music being composed for dance). But the ethnic audiences loved and supported the dance scene, and everything was going great.

Until September 11, 2001.

What else September 11th destroyed

On September 11, two hijacked planes flew into the twin towers of the World Trade Center in New York City—my hometown. When I saw the collision on network news, my first thought was, *Please, God, don't let it be Arabs.* Of course, it was.

The buildings were destroyed, along with thousands of lives and America's sense of security. A Lebanese friend noted that New York then resembled Beirut during the war—silent, empty, shell-shocked, numb. The world mourned with us; the few who added, "Now you know how we feel, every day," were swiftly hushed. But they were right. When you grieve a death in your own home, go find a home untouched by death. Good luck with that.

America's leaders chose to go to war. Somebody had to be held accountable. Somebody had to pay. Not Saudi Arabia, longtime "friend," who had everything to do with September 11th through its financing, support, and protection of extremist groups such as al-Qaeda and Da'esh. No, they chose Iraq, an "enemy" (i.e. holder of oil we don't control), who had nothing to do with September 11. Iraq, with millions of already-destabilized Iraqi citizens. These folks had nothing to do with politics, and they already hated the USA for the earlier Gulf War, as many believe the USA's radioactive bullets caused Iraq's alarming uptick in leukemia and birth deformities.

Let's take a moment here to deconstruct some of the anti-Islamic feeling in the USA and the West. Islam, Christianity and Judaism, the Big Three Religions of the Book, are all amalgams of sects and schools. Each has progressives and conservatives and everything in between. Each has power-hungry militant radicals who practice a strain of their religion so severe, so extreme that everyone else avoids them. In Islam, these folks are often referred to as *Salafi*, or more recently, *Wahabbi*.

These are fundamentalist groups who advocate a return to the most severe aspects of Islam, and the waging of *jihad*, traditionally understood to be a personal struggle against sin, but which they have made synonymous with holy war. The vast majority of Muslims shun this stance. However, Islamic fundamentalism is well-funded, voracious, and presented to us in the West as the most common point of view. The upshot of this is that we are encouraged to fear and revile all Muslims, most of whom are peaceful, kind, deeply faithful people.

As of this writing, extremism has flourished and American coffers are emptied. The extremist agenda has only been fed by our bombing. Our jobs have been automated or "outsourced" overseas. Our citizens are out of work and slipping into poverty. Our veterans commit suicide daily. Our sense of outrage, of retribution, our "War on Terror," has become a war *of* terror. We have damaged our standing in the world and lain waste to countless lives, our own and innocent civilians in the areas we have invaded, all in the name of peace.

So maybe one more death is small potatoes, but it is symbolic of a larger death—that of the American Myth, the land of the free, the home of the brave, with brotherhood from sea to shining sea. Well, that was always a myth. Racism and class warfare have long been America's dirty secrets, even as Lady Liberty lofts her torch in New York Harbor, gloriously welcoming "your tired, your poor, your huddled masses yearning to breathe free." Good luck with that, too.

Give me your tired, your poor...

Here's what happened.

For weeks following the attacks, nothing in this country moved. Goods did not travel, nor did people. Ships were not unloaded. Nobody bought anything. The entire land was in a state of shock. In this short period of time, small manufacturing in America got hit hard. Independent publishing, too. Many small businesses, deprived of those few, precious weeks of income, quietly starved.

Over the following year, the shelves of the May Store, a tiny department store in my tiny town of Lyndonville, Vermont, got emptier and emptier. The May Store was where you got whatever you needed—a kid's birthday gift, fabric, sewing notions, art and craft supplies, hardware, underwear, pots and pans—you name it, they had it.

Until, suddenly, they didn't. "What happened?" I asked. "Nine-eleven," they replied, glumly. "Almost all our suppliers are tiny independent American manufacturers, the only people who make what they do. Nine-eleven killed them." Soon enough, the May Store itself was dead—a delayed casualty of September 11th. In its place, there is now a Dollar General, selling crap made overseas. Oh, and guess who won? Big corporations with the wealth to withstand the siege. So much for competition.

What does this all have to do with dance?

In New York City, the bridges closed (Manhattan is an island, and rivers or bays separate most of the boroughs). No one could go anywhere. Most of the clubs were in Manhattan and Queens. But much of the ethnic clientele lived out of town. No one could get to the clubs. No one had the heart to, either. As Morocco points out, no one wanted to be seen as celebrating after such a horrific event, hence the music and dance shows were closed down. There was no work for the dancers or the musicians. Few businesses have the capital to withstand a siege of any length, especially restaurants. The clubs began closing.

Yes, the clubs closing was a NYC thing. Shakira was building steam with her belly dance fusion between 1998 and 2002. But clubs closed in other places, too. And with the exception of a few places, such as Boston, live music largely went away during this period. Now, when there is live music, often the band takes a break and puts on a recording for the dancer, whose show has become a choreographed parade of props. How sad is that?

And there is more. Because who hijacked those planes?

Muslims.

Who were conveniently brown, thus easy to target. Americans have long regarded Arabs as terrorists and villains. Witness the book, *Reel Bad Arabs* by Jack Shaheen. The racial profiling commenced forthwith. Anyone brown became fair game. Not only Arabs, but Sikhs, Indians, even Latin and Hispanic folks were harassed, threatened, beaten, arrested—even killed. Many folks who looked "Arab" went into hiding or left the country. Again, many ethnic clubs went down, with no audience for their offerings.

What about the dance? Most belly dancers in the USA, for example, are not Middle Eastern. Most are white; a few are black or brown, but even so, generally all-American. However, the dance itself was now painted brown.

America was at war. Her husbands, wives, and children were dying every day. People held bake sales to buy body armor for their loved ones and their vehicles, since the USA could not be bothered to properly equip her soldiers (true fact—not kidding). Veteran's benefits were cut to fund Bush's ten-year tax cut for the rich (Bush also tried to cut combat pay and his appointees obstructed research into the Gulf War illnesses). An army grown bloated in peacetime (as decent jobs were automated or sent overseas) was being ruthlessly thinned. National Guards were called to serve. Only sons. Single mothers. Who would be next? Girl Scouts?

There was a lot of justified rage among the people and nowhere to put it. Americans became squeamish about supporting an Arab dance. As one dancer said, "*Those people* are shooting at my son." Dancers all over the country saw classes dwindle, bookings evaporate, and incomes drop. They needed a plan, and fast.

What Arabs? The globalization of belly dance

When the dancers saw their livelihood shrinking and the dance they loved rejected due to racist, knee-jerk "patriotism," they realized they better do something before everyone was out of a job. They began to downplay the Eastern aspects of the dance. Dancers began repositioning their studios and schools as bastions of "world" dance. Their push to decouple from the East echoed that of the Tribal world. Belly fitness, bellycize, and bellyrobics came into the vocabulary, all to capture market share, all so soccer moms could do belly dance without feeling dirty or unpatriotic.

And then, along came the Belly Dance Super Stars.

Miles Copeland, hitherto manager of the band The Police and founder of IRS Records among many other things, is also the creator of the Belly Dance Super Stars (BDSS). Miles, who speaks fluent Arabic, grew up in the East (his father was a founder of the CIA and his mother worked for British Intelligence). Miles decided to make belly dance more accessible to Westerners. This was a great plan. He launched the Belly Dance Super Stars in 2002, allegedly calling them, "My new tool for world domination: Riverdance —with bare midriffs."

The BDSS first toured with mega concert Lollapalooza in 2003. The company debuted under artistic director and choreographer Jillina Carlano, and featured the groundbreaking Tribal fusion artist Rachel Brice.

Tamalyn Dallal, *tamalyndallal.com*, a filmmaker, world traveler, belly dance missionary, and one of our great teachers, was one of the early SuperStars. She notes that Miles' earliest concerts were soloist-based shows with traditional music. She said, "When I was being filmed for the first Belly dance Superstars DVD, we were all soloists, accustomed to improvising. They did three takes of each of our dances, expecting to edit together different camera angles. The editors had such a hard time because most of us did each take different from the others. The DVD was slower than expected to come out because they had to splice together different parts of each dance and make it look like one dance."

"It was odd when I traveled to different countries and saw groups imitating our "choreographies." These dances never really existed. If anyone was to be credited for our choreographies that were being imitated worldwide, it was the guys in the editing room."

However, as the SuperStars played bigger and bigger venues, these traditional, soloist shows simply didn't work well. Belly dance is made for small spaces. So, within a few years, the format shifted. The dancers became highly technical, tightly choreographed, wore splashy costumes, performed splashy group numbers, and favored Eastern pop music, heavy on the rhythm, and light on improvisation, heterophony, and feeling. Once they found their niche—other belly dancers—they became a hit.

A big hit.

And belly dance has never been the same.

RIP Ethnic dance

PART II
SAME BUT DIFFERENT

"The only reason for mastering technique is to make sure the body does not prevent the soul from expressing itself." —La Meri

5

TICK-TOCK TECHNIQUE

The tyranny of the visual

The current trend in belly dance is for stylized, choreographed, difficult, athletic dance. It is so controlled that you can almost hear the clicks as the wind-up dolls go through their routines. The Belly Dance Super Stars didn't originate precision movement in belly dance (Tamalyn Dallal credits Suhaila Salimpour with that), but they popularized it. How? By touring relentlessly. And though Miles wanted to bring belly dance to the mainstream, the bulk of post-Lollapalooza audiences were belly dancers. Wherever the BDSS went, they inspired controversy—feelings ranged from idolatry to rage—but everyone went to see them.

Precision and stylization are exciting. Mastery through difficulty made sense to dancers and ordinary folks alike. This is how you excel, through hard work and control. Precision was also something that driven, fitness-addicted, Western women could get excited about. And they did. Belly dance classes blossomed anew, spinning off bellycise, bellyfit, and bellyrobics ad nauseam (not to mention Zumba, which stole our hip scarves).

(By the way, Morocco credits Edwina Nearing, a dance scholar and writer specializing in the Ghawazee, with inventing the modern coin hipscarf—and Morocco went her one better (or at least quieter) with the beaded hipscarf (I still have the first one I bought, which came straight from Rocky). Both women had these made originally by Mahmoud abd-el Gaffar, whose Al-

Wikalah shop of wonders in the Khan al Khalili is a major belly dance destination.)

The SuperStars exemplify a shift that has long been occurring in belly dance, from an Eastern mindset to a Western mindset. Choreography replaced improvisation. Stylization replaced micromovement. Same replaced different. Western values that include No Pain No Gain, Just Do It, and a ballet-inspired work ethic of practicing until your toes bleed, marched in and took over. Where was the sensuality? The relaxation? The joy? The connection to anything other than a thumping bass beat?

Gone.

More and more dancers molded by Miss Suzy's School of Dance took up belly dance. Trained from the age of two in precision choreography and competition, they brought their values with them:

- Mastery = Difficulty. Combinations must be complex and difficult to show the dancer's ability.
- The most important thing is flawless technique. Stylization, precision, and repetition are key. Why? Because...
- Choreography is king. You dance what the choreographer gives you. Complex movement strings must be memorized precisely.
- Dancers are vehicles for choreographers. Certainly, dancers may be beautiful and valuable; occasionally, one or another will emerge as a star in her own right, but the choreographers, the dance makers, are the real artists.
- Group dances are favored. Troupes and student groups abound. Dance is done on the largest stage available; it is Art, therefore serious business; and the "fourth wall" excludes the audience.

Contrast that with belly dance:

- Mastery = Oneness with the music and the guests. Musicality, relaxation, embodiment, and shared feeling in the moment are the mark of greatness.
- The most important thing is the feeling. The dancer expresses what she feels from the music, physically and emotionally, in the moment.
- Technique is the servant of expression. You practice and hone your chops, not to show off your virtuosity, but to express what you feel.
- Improvisation is the standard. Never do it the same way twice.

- A modest core movement vocabulary featuring micromovement. Dancers adapt the dynamics of the movement however they choose.
- Dancers have ultimate agency; they choose their own movement in the moment.
- Solo dances are favored. Small groups may mirror or interact, but rarely stylize.
- Dance in small spaces, to close audiences. The dancer's personality and playfulness are key, and she includes the guests.

Ahhh...

Thus, a dance that exemplifies feeling, relaxation, improvisation, and close contact with the audience became a precise, technical, tightly choreographed, athletic tour de force.

Stylization, precision, choreography, athletics, spectacle, etc.—these are all great. They are important elements. People love them. They are wonderful challenges. The Rockettes draw huge audience year after year, as do marching bands. We as human beings are symmetrical. We love to see humans move in unison. However, stylization, precision, et al., are Western. And belly dance has an Eastern soul. Yes, there are lots of line dances in the East, and when people line dance, they do the same steps. But the dancers do not strive for precision—they strive for enjoyment and group fun. And line leaders improvise, bringing in their own flavor, artistry, and expression. Finally, precision movement is martial. Soldiers do precision drills. We are the opposite, bringers of love and joy.

So we have two main conflicts here.

The first is Same vs. Different. Western classical traditions largely value Same Every Time. Eastern improvisation values Different Every Time. This we began to discuss in the Music chapter, and we'll continue with that here. But there is another issue as well: valuing the External (the visual form) over the Internal (feeling and expression).

Yes, of course, it is vital to have an engaging performer, for their beauty, intensity, stagecraft, or whatever. But that performer is compelling because they have something to say. They are more than a pretty or even spectacular picture. They have depth. Feeling. Soul. They bring joy. This is what I mean by the internal. It's more than feeling that is important; it's the expression of that feeling, the shared quality—Tarab. Joy. (There is also the issue of sexuality, but we will take that up later.)

Different Every Time, *The Feeling in the Moment*, and *Bring the Joy* are the Trifecta of Oriental dance mastery. It's interesting that all of them have been rigorously co-opted and disdained by Western value systems. Stylization, choreography, rote movement, drilling, gratuitous difficulty, perfectionism, technique, and memorization as mastery—these are all symptoms of an imbalance between the values of East and West. In the coming section, we'll explore their causes—and some solutions.

You call that dance? The invisibility of micromovement

Many of the art qualities of belly dance are under-appreciated in the West, and some are downright invisible. One such quality is micromovement, which both sets our dance apart and ironically keeps it from being fully appreciated by the larger dance world.

Imagine a dancer expressing a taqsim. Her body is in complete accord with the musician's playing. The music sweeps and roils through her body, though she does not move from her spot. She may barely move at all, yet you can see every shimmer and whisper of the music as it passes through her. You feel at one with her and the music—you feel her responses in your own body, as if the two of you are one—and everyone else feels the same wonder.

Sounds lovely, doesn't it?

Yet, as Dunya MacPherson, Sufi master and Juilliard-graduate classical ballerina, has observed, to Western, classically-trained eyes, this ever-changing movement vocabulary makes no sense. There is no frame of reference. It doesn't exist. Again, belly dance gets no respect (our costuming doesn't help, but more about that later). In addition, Leila Farid points out that Eastern music is subtle. To Western ears, it all sounds the same. How can one appreciate dance done to music one can't hear?

Worse, on a big stage, you can't even see these movements. Big stage = big movements. Tamalyn Dallal notes that the BDSS's later, more spectacular shows didn't have much to offer close up, but on a big stage, they had a lot of impact. Ramzi Edlibi, *ramzidance.com*, a Lebanese artist of the world-renowned Caracalla dance company, told Tamalyn that belly dance should have no more than 100 people in the audience due to its intimate nature. A traditional nightclub is perfect for this dance—but most of them are gone.

Micromovement is the infinite variability of a given move (Same but Different). For example, consider the infinity shape ∞ (this shape is often referred to as a figure 8, but in Arabic, an 8 looks like an inverted V, so let's prefer infinity, the shape of which is the same in any language). It is often done with the hips (aka snake hips), or the chest, or any other part of the body, from the foot to the head. It's a basic, core shape. Even an undulation can be visualized in this shape (this whole concept of infinity is important later on, so make a note of it now). But this "basic" move can be adapted a thousand ways to more perfectly embody the music.

It can be done in any direction—in, out, vertically, horizontally, or sideways. It can encompass any degree of size, speed, or force. It can be done smoothly, sharply, or fragmented into stages. Moreover, these dynamics can apply to sections of the movement—part slow, part fast, smooth here, ornamented there, etc.

These principles apply to *any* move—and *every* move. AND they can be initiated from any point in the movement's continuum. We can dance an entire song with one single movement—and we can do this with any movement.

Why would we do that? One of the callings of Oriental dance is to interpret the music. One way we do this is to visually demonstrate the timbres—not only the pitch, volume, or duration of the notes or rhythm, but also the force, texture, emotional charge, etc. Each instrument in a traditional *takht* (ensemble) has its own specific timbres (sonic colors); therefore, we vary the textures, duration, size and speed of the movements to better express the sound.

However, this is *not* a common feature in Western dance, particularly in ballet (the touchstone of Western movement), or even in modern dance, ballet's rebellious child. In ballet, each move is named (Oriental dance moves have no traditional names, though Western dance teachers have lavished myriad fanciful names upon them), and each move has a Platonic ideal of its precise size, shape, etc. In ballet, a *jetté*, for example, must be exactly so, and it must be exactly so Every. Single. Time.

Still, ballet often represents the music. In modern dance, music for a piece may be an afterthought, appended to an already completed dance. It has been considered déclassé to match the movement to the music. Sure, audiences like it, and you have to do it sometimes to engage the proletariat, but it's tacky. Again, an interesting, valuable practice—but Western.

Contrast these values with Oriental dance, in which the move melts into the music, into the moment, modulated by the dancer's feeling from that sound in that moment. Not only this, the dancer is free to do the movement however she wants, every single time. Though she may do the "same" move, each time it will be different, colored by the music itself, and by the dancer's (and the musician's) feeling in the moment.

This is what folks mean when they talk about Egyptian dancers who do only a few movements in their show. These dancers often explore simple movements, enjoy them fully, and allow themselves a full range of expression without anxiety over novelty.

This is a profound difference in philosophy.

The quality of micromovement and microtonal variation sets Eastern dance and music apart from other forms. Their elasticity confounds eyes trained to measure stylized precision. It is mysterious, ineffable, elusive, defying categorization. To the Western eye, an Eastern dancer may appear to be doing absolutely nothing; whereas, to the eye trained in Oriental movement, he is in perfect union with the music.

Oriental dance evolved with a deep connection to its music. It favors close contact with the audience and smaller spaces. Though these attributes may conflict with Western dance principles, their value remains. It is wise to explore and treasure these qualities, to preserve and embrace these subtle miracles of Oriental dance. But this is not our only obstacle.

We humans tend to discount what we can't see or don't understand. It's not only micromovement. There are even more subtle things, like the use of weight and gravity, that have escaped our Western eyes, resulting in a dance freighted with muscular excess and Mastery Through Difficulty (for more about the concepts of gravity and weight, see the video course on Baladi movement and character: *aliathabit.com/baladi*).

To attain mastery in this art, we learn to listen, feel, and respond intuitively. The practice of micromovement is a big piece of this puzzle. It follows, then, that one of the more unfortunate aspects of the current trend in belly dance is the displacement of micromovement by stylization and precision. Controlling the body's organic response to the music undermines the very nature of Oriental dance. Allowing the body to move as it wishes heals us from stress and misfortune. Focusing on stylization and precision can prevent the body from entering the dance's healing state.

It's true that the execution of a well-constructed choreography is a great pleasure (as is the making of one), like a martial arts kata. When all we have is recorded music, why not record the dance? And sometimes we need to do it, for reasons from big stages and group dances to high-stakes events. I am fine with making dances—I do it myself. I teach it. Plus, for many of us, choreography is didactic, a teaching tool, a way of contextualizing a specific vocabulary or to show how movement combines with music.

But recorded dances do not help us improvise to live music. They do not give us agency in the moment. They do not instill the Eastern ethos of the dance. They do not enhance our sense of wonder.

We come to this dance for joy, love, and healing. Instead, we get a heaping helping of perfectionism, negativity, and rigid control. A dancer who spent over a decade dancing in Egypt and around the world for Arab audiences said, "I felt good on stage in front of Egyptian and Arab audiences. I feel criticized on stage in front of dancers." A glorious dance of love and self-acceptance has been locked into a cage match with razor-sharp, competitive knives.

No wonder we lose our sense of wonder.

Four problems with precision (and one solution)

The emphasis on stylization shows up in both the precision of the movements themselves, and in the expectation of drill-team synchronization of group dances. Here are four problems with precision—and one solution.

1. **It's external:** memory and retrieval vs. feeling in the moment. The focus on choreography shifts the dance from one that is improvised and created in the moment to one that is created off stage and repeated later. Yes, we have more recorded than live music, so it seems logical to pre-record our dances as well. However, pre-recording values memorization over synthesis, feeling, and agency.

This often means the dancer is not in the moment at all, but is working hard to remember and recreate a dance. Often, dancers end up dancing next to the music rather than with it. Additionally, the dance is often created by a teacher or choreographer. Thus, the dancer's agency may be stripped away as well as her discovery of, and feeling from, the music in the moment.

2. It's excessive: too much, too hard, too fast vs. relaxation and play.

With a focus on choreography, we also have the tendency to make the dance as hard as possible to show off the dancer's technique. A dance steeped in sensual abandon and enjoyment of the music has become instead a vehicle to showcase athletic ability. Expression of the feeling from the music has been superseded by the determination to articulate every single note, ornament, nuance, and trill.

Thus, the dance becomes a contest for how many moves one dancer can cram into eight counts. The guests can't relax and enjoy the dance when every moment is filled. As such, the emphasis changes from giving—giving joy to the audience—to getting—getting adulation or approval from the audience. This is a crucial difference in a playful dance whose raison d'être is expressing and sharing joy.

3. It's exclusive: step up or get out vs. welcoming and inclusive.

Valuing memory and athletic ability raises the bar for excellence to a superficial level. Because Western dancers are trained to remember choreography, stylize their movements for accurate repetition, and display dizzying feats of physical prowess, Eastern values (and dancers) are left in the dust. Visual perfection in body, face, costume, and execution become the stock in trade while richness of emotion, stillness, and simplicity are dismissed.

It's not that the dance is evolving—every living art will. The problem here is disregard for (or ignorance) of the elements that make this dance special. Our dance welcomes all body types, all ages, genders, and ability levels. Favoring Western perfectionism disdains these qualities, and turns the dance into one more competitive arena for overachievers.

4. It's extreme: make your body do stuff vs. sensual enjoyment.

And here we come to the saddest and most destructive of the new trends. One of the most brilliant, beautiful, magical elements of Oriental dance is the training of the body to respond intuitively to the music. Sure, one has to learn vocabulary, and that takes effort. But the basic vocabulary is fairly simple.

What takes one's entire life is the level of artistry that is attainable with these basic movements. To express physically the texture, pitch, speed, and emotional timbre—as well as the dancer's emotional and physical enjoyment of her body in motion, particularly when responding to live, improvised music that the dancer has never heard before—this is a stunning accomplishment. We give our lives to this.

But the wonder of our dance is more than artistry.

Current research shows that part of the trauma resolution process is in allowing the body to move as it wishes. When a dancer is in the moment, allowing the music into her body, allowing her body to respond intuitively, the dance's magic suffuses her body and soul, bringing with it healing, radiance, and joy. And these come not only for the dancer, but also for the guests, whose brains and bodies vibrate in tandem with the dancer.

Dancers are not factory robots stamping out precision parts. We are living, breathing, unique human beings, and this dance is our celebration. It is a mystical adventure, a sun boat bound for the glory of joyous connection. The hard focus on memorization, stylization, repetition, and precision movement short-circuits this magic, and with it, the mystical, healing soul of the dance.

With soul as a value, where do we put our attention? How do we aspire to greatness? There is another kind of precision on which we can focus: Timing.

Timing—musicality—is the bleeding edge of superior precision. This is what we practice to achieve greatness in Oriental dance. Yes, we need beautiful lines, posture, strength, presence, technique, endurance. And we practice them. But timing is the queen. And it must be intuitive, open and fresh, ready for anything. Our hearing is one of our fastest senses; the body can respond to what it hears almost before we are aware we have heard it. In the wild, the body's intuitive response to random rustles in the tall grass has saved many a life. In the dance, we hear the music and let the body respond; we let the intuitive body choose the movement. We practice physical skill so that the body is free to respond intuitively to the music in the moment. This is the heart of the dance.

What about a group?

Think about the Rockettes. All that stylized precision. They make a big long line and kick those legs up. They strive for unison, to look exactly the same. Ballet is like that, too. In ballet, each move has a name. It has an exact shape. The arm must be here—no higher and no lower. The leg must be here, the knee here—all exact. In most group or chorus choreographies, the goal is to be like everyone else.

Not in belly dance.

Belly dance is about individual expression cohering within a group. The musicians play what they feel. They have a melody, but everyone ornaments the music as they please. The drummers ornament the rhythm as they feel it. There is a basic rhythm, but everyone plays around with it (okay, one duff player will play the basic rhythm most of the time). Likewise, dancers dance what they feel from the music. Different Every Time. Thus, the Rockettes, ballet, anything like that are unsuitable models. It's not where we want to be.

What, then, might be an appropriate model for belly dance? I suggest chaos theory, in particular, the phenomenon known as "Strange Attractors."

What are Strange Attractors?

Strange Attractors are the tendency of random instances to group together. In science-speak, "an attractor is a set of physical properties toward which a system tends to evolve, regardless of the starting conditions of the system." This means that things tend to cluster together and create patterns. A leaky faucet, for example, doesn't drip on an exact rhythm; but over time, the drops will form a fuzzy pattern. No two drops will conform exactly, either in the time between drips or where they land, but over time, when you chart the drops, a shape forms in time and space.

How does this relate to belly dance?

Because of the principle of micromovement, a single move, let's say an infinity, will never be exactly the same—but it will be similar enough to create that pattern. The shape may never be exact, but each iteration magnifies the cluster so that a general shape emerges. Ironically, the most common illustration of strange attractors is a fuzzy infinity:

Strange Attractors

So what?

The problem comes when the general shape is stylized into an Ideal Shape, and dancers everywhere try to copy an exact yet completely arbitrary schematic, a simplistic representation of thousands and thousands of elegant, swooping, manifestations of the rich tapestry of expression.

In the West, we have all been taught to strive for the Platonic Ideal, this exact, perfect form to which we should aspire. Nothing has tortured artists more than throwing themselves against the rocky shore of formal perfection. Instead of appreciating what we have created, the Platonic Ideal has us mourning how it doesn't exactly copy the idea in our heads.

Plato was a philosopher in ancient Greece. His work is still highly regarded in the West. His Allegory of the Cave, for example, is a brilliant examination of the shifts that come when we move outside of our preconceived cultural understandings. But some of his writing is more controversial. For example, Plato wanted to ban poets and theater from his Republic as they encouraged people to glorify heroes and ideas that were not entirely (gasp) virtuous.

Now, Plato also condemned the writing of imagined dialogues with great men. Since much of his writing is exactly this—imagined dialogues with great men—it's possible that he is poking fun at a few other things (or is too conflicted to take entirely seriously). Hence the Platonic Ideal is not *our* Ideal.

Then what is?

I would submit that it is *imperfection*. I would go even further and state that perfectionism is a pernicious vice we would be well rid of. Imperfection doesn't mean we all suddenly become slipshod layabouts. It does mean we can take joy in our creativity without crushing ourselves under unreachable expectations. The relaxation and playfulness of belly dance do not mix well with the rigid control to which it has been subjected. Let's all relax and have more fun with our dance.

In Islam, for example, the only perfect thing is God, Allah. Nothing else is *meant* to be perfect. Imperfection is part of a thing's beauty. Of course, this is not an Islamic dance, but Islam does hold sway over many of its homelands, and has for over a thousand years.

There are also numerous myths that warn against attempting to create perfect things. For example, in one Greek myth, the weaver Arachne challenges Athena, the goddess of craft and technology, to a weaving contest. Athena wins; she then changes Arachne into a spider (an *arachnid*) for her hubris in challenging a god. There are Native American myths with the same conclusion. An imperfection must be included, on purpose, if necessary.

And there is more.

Is *anything* exactly like any other? A leaf? A human being? Even a vista? Nature never makes anything the same. Why should we? There is a lot of organic support for the woozy elegance of imperfection. When we embrace the principle of strange attractors, we are freed from the tyranny of stylized symmetry. When we glory in the sensual exploration of a shape, allowing the body to enjoy the journey without imposing an idealized trajectory, we connect on a deep level to the Divine.

Well, sure, that's fine for a solo dancer. But what about *groups*? If the group doesn't move together, you'll have chaos!

Um, yeah. Structured chaos. That's what we want.

Belly dance is not the Rockettes. The Rockettes are wonderful, but their aesthetic and intention are entirely different from ours. When a group moves with strange attractors, their precision comes from intention and timing. When the entire group is at one with the music, when they all hit a beat in the same millisecond, or respond with the same (or opposing, or whatever) energy to a musical moment, it is far more powerful than superficial unity.

A group can have a fantastically rich interior score. They can illustrate relationships, instruments, and conceptual content. They can have emotional symmetry—unity of intent. And even when they all do the same thing, that thing can be individually held together by conceptual content and connection to the music. This can be breathtaking. It is an area worth exploring.

We've been trained for a long time to value precision and stylization, even in belly dance. Changing our viewpoint may take some effort, but we have the power to reorganize our expectations of the dance. Remember: Beware of the Platonic Ideal. Be one with the music. Enjoy the ride. And bring your friends.

But if the dance does not inherently value precision and stylization, then where did it all come from? Yes, they are Western values. Yes, micromovement is invisible to many classically trained eyes; but as recently as the 70s, everything was improvised. This shift to stylization began long before September 11th. What changed?

6

THE FLAMING JEKYLL-HYDE OF BELLY DANCE

THE SAME EVERY TIME

The Strange Case of Dr. Jekyll and Mr. Hyde is a novella by the Scottish author Robert Louis Stevenson first published in 1886. Dr. Jekyll is a nice guy with a grim side. In an attempt to rid himself of this, he creates a potion—which turns him into a monster. Oops. We have the same issue in belly dance.

One of the main culprits in the focus on the external, the shift away from improvisation, micromovement, and the feeling in the moment is also one of our great assets: Recorded Music.

The phonograph record—plus movies, radio, and television—were all invented around 1890, essentially yesterday in the timeline of human development (photography predated these by about 50 years). Up until this time, there was *no recording of any performance, ever*, except through art—painting, drawing, writing, and sculpture—all static, silent media. Instead, *everyone* played musical instruments. And while a great musician has always been revered (Orpheus, for example), merely playing an instrument was quite common—how else were you to get any music?

Everyone who was anyone learned an instrument, if not several. The poor might have lacked instruments, but that didn't stop them—a friend recalls attending a packed Romani wedding in Spain, maybe in the 50s. The entire celebration was fueled by one guitar and one bottle of beer, but a delirious, ecstatic time was had by all. As recently as the 80s, dancers working in Egypt rarely even practiced with CDs—you hired a band for your practice. Yes, a live band, just for you.

Now, however, recorded music is everywhere. What once fit on large, heavy cylinders now fits in pockets, on phones—10,000 songs on tiny gizmos small as a matchbook—and it travels thousands of miles through the ether or jumps from one device to the next with a simple bump. We can listen to music from all over the world. Anyone with the Internet and a microphone can share their music with anyone, anywhere. It is a miracle.

But there is a price.

The Tyranny of the Professional

Music is more available than ever, yet fewer and fewer people play instruments. Fewer venues feature live music. Westerners who learn Arabic music (often coming from Conservatory training, with the injunction to play the piece exactly), struggle to internalize the richness of heterophony. And even though, for our dance, the miracle of live performance with live music is unequaled, the *opportunity* dwindles hourly, as master musicians pass away and young folks bring Western mindsets to the music or cleave to the faux perfection and ease of synthetic sounds and electronic beats.

It's that same thing with precision—we are constantly confronted with pro musicians at every turn—so why should we honk and squeak our failure, trying to play music? Yet the benefits to learning music have been studied and expounded at great length and depth, even as funding for school band programs (and arts in general) continues to shrink. Music is one of our great human joys. Dancing with live music changes lives.

Let me tell you what it's like, dancing to live music from great musicians. You, as a standalone entity, disappear. You become enmeshed in the music, in the sounds. The musicians watch the dancer; they play what the dancer does. The dancer listens to the music; she dances what the musician plays. This dynamic synthesis of movement and sound feeds upon itself—it grows, becoming something much greater than its individual parts. You dance the violin, and the passion of it is such that you begin to tremble. Some part of you notices the trembling. So does the drummer, who begins to play it—your trembling, he plays it. And you dance what he plays. And the violin picks it up —and the whole room takes off into the stratosphere.

Remember, that concept in Eastern music, *tarab*? Tarab translates loosely as musical ecstasy. It is a state shared between musicians and guests; it is the goal every musician of the culture, and also of the guests. Eastern audiences know that the evening's success is a group effort. It depends upon their investment in, their response to, and their engagement with, the artists. This is why Eastern audiences call out and engage with the performers. It's their job.

Arab audiences are not silent like Western audiences. The Arab audience enjoys its role in the success of the evening. They call out, exclaim, and exult in the music, in a well-modulated transition, in a beautiful phrase. They cheer wildly when a singer or musician executes a truly remarkable bit of magic, or gasp "Allah!" (the Arabic equivalent of "Oh, my God!"), at a beautiful passage in a taqsim. All this is part of the generation of tarab.

The artists thrive upon this. They will play a popular section over and over again (or segue into another song entirely). It's fun. Umm Kalthoum, for example, is famous for repeating phrases thirty or more times in a single song, with different timbres and ornaments each time. There is even a joke, "So Umm Kalthoum walks into a bar. Walks into a bar. Walks into a bar. Walks into a baaaaaaaaaaaaaarrrrrrrrrrrrrrrrrrrr..." If the godmother of Arabic music can do it, so can you.

Dr. Racy writes that tarab is retained in recordings. Not as strongly as the live experience, but it is there. And, you know, you can feel it, in certain recordings. Listen to a recording of a live Umm Kalthoum concert (and watch the documentary, *A Voice Like Egypt*, if you haven't yet had the pleasure). The headiness, the magic, is preserved within the quality of the sound, a honeyed rush, a thrill of exquisite mystery. The brilliance of live music is that it is ephemeral—it exists once only, and it will never be there again. Live improvised music and dance create a state of grace for the performers and the audience unequaled by anything. Recordings enable us to regain these moments, to experience them decades later, to treasure a musician long dead, and to discover someone new.

This is the blessing. But it's not all rosy bliss.

~

The ancient Greeks argued bitterly over the introduction of writing. In classical rhetoric (speechmaking, which the Greeks adored), the best speakers captivated the audience with the power of the voice. The voice is so compelling that a charismatic speaker can sway the listener by the cadence, tone, and timbre of their spoken words. The listener might not even remember what has been said, swept away by the magic of the speaker's voice.

Um Kalthoum captivated the Arab world through the radio. Every week, for many years, she gave a radio concert. Even the poorest folk knew someone with a radio—and everyone clustered around to bask in the beauty of her voice.

Then there is the other side—for example, Hitler. Another powerful speaker, he swayed an entire country, brought its citizens to commit unspeakable acts of atrocity—all through the power of his voice, also heard over that amazing invention, the radio. Let's not start on conservative talk radio—or Rwanda. You get the idea. This is the power of the human voice.

So anyway, written language began getting popular in ancient Greece. The top orators were furious. With writing, the audience could go back and look at what you said six paragraphs ago. They were no longer at the mercy of the speaker's magic. But less-powerful speakers were delighted. Here at last was their *metiér*! Those who prized subtle logic, complex arguments, they could put everything down on paper! Then the reader could appreciate their clever turns and twists. They could outmaneuver the orators. Thus was broken the spell of the speaker.

And thus was broken the spell of improvisation.

Oops...

Like the written word, recorded music is—say it with me—the Same Every Time. No matter how many times you play the recording, it will never change, not one single note.

Eastern music is the antithesis of this. Eastern musical masters, like Western blues masters, pride themselves on never making a song the same way twice. It is an ephemeral magic. It is the feeling in the moment, every moment (this is why the Grateful Dead have such a devoted following—year after year, night after night, set after set, every show was different).

Here in the West, we have few artists drenched in the culture and soul of Eastern music. Many brilliant musicians of the culture have passed away or taken other work. Recordings, however, which were few and far between in the 70s, even into the 90s, have now taken center stage. Recordings can be played in any studio or living room, no matter where it is, even in the wilds of Iowa or Albania. This is fantastic for dancers scattered far and wide, and for musicians who may not live near a decent teacher. But it has also been disastrous for our dance.

Why is that?

With recorded music, it also possible to record the dance. Every step, every turn, every wink and nod can now be laid out in advance, because that piece of music will never, ever change, no matter how often you hear it.

This has become a curse.

The problem with pre-recorded dance is that one's focus changes. Previously, the dancer's task was to be in the moment, attending to the music and reacting to it intuitively. With recorded dance, the task becomes memory—remembering the movement as a linear construct, remembering what comes next upon the line. Instead of reacting to the music in the moment and sharing that with her guests, the dancer scans the teleprompter inside her forehead, checking to see what comes next.

Of course, great artists learn their part inside out. It becomes second nature so they can express themselves within the composition. Performers, actors, musicians, dancers, do this all the time. It can certainly be learned, and it is a standard process for anyone who studies choreography. But it is hard for student dancers. And it is Western.

Again, choreography is great. But too many students *only* learn choreography, even though the whole memorization, repetition, drilling thing is anathema to Oriental dance. Moreover, students of Oriental dance are rarely taught expression, aside from some blithe admonitions to "feel the music," with little to no instruction or modeling. We can make beautiful dances that retain the soul, freedom, and agency of improvisation (see the course *CreateDanceArt.com*), but few dancers learn how or why to do this.

Instead, they are taught to copy.

Here's how many belly dance classes are taught. The students warm up—often with static stretching (which modern science has shown us is better when warm, at the end of class). Then they drill, often at high speeds. This means they practice some move or combination over and over in robot fashion, striving to do the move exactly the same every time. Stylization is the goal. The combo may then be applied to different music without adaptation, further removing it from any feeling other than the count. Then they learn or repeat their choreography.

Why is this a problem? Because the range of experience is limited. Often the students practice the same choreography for months. Months, listening to the same music, doing the same stylized moves. What do they learn? They learn how to repeat a string of pointless, stylized moves. How does this prepare students for the magic of intuitive response to music?

It doesn't.

The problem for teachers is that most of the students are not trained dancers; they can't follow anything complicated. But this dance does not require trained dancers. It requires humans who love the music and let it into their hearts. To feel the music, to find your style, to become your own true self, *you love and respond to the music.* You discover in the moment what you feel and where you feel it.

Still, few teachers take this tack. Most classes are beginner to intermediate levels. They want a product for the recital, something the whole class can do. The teacher must craft a dance that is simple to learn and do. Then they practice forever to become the Rockettes—stylized, exact copies. The teacher also may not be a trained dancer; many teachers are barely past their students.

So the predominate student choreography is some variation on four to the left, four to the right, circle, accent, pose, repeat. If it is a beginner class, maybe it's eight on a side. In the transitions, everyone gets confused, because you have to let go of the repetition to remember what comes next (and partly because transitions are rarely taught as separate steps).

The music is as simple and rhythmic as possible, to accommodate simple choreography. The students count how many more to the right while trying to remember what comes next. They barely listen to the music, which is often so repetitive you can't tell by listening where to be anyway.

If the class is more advanced, the choreography will be more complex—often extremely so. There is a sense that the harder the dance, the more advanced it is. There is pressure to use lots of difficult moves. Again, the dominant skills are drilling, stylization, and memorization. The students work the same music for weeks or months.

Nobody learns to improvise by doing the exact same thing for months. Quite the opposite: they learn that they must be told what to do and how to do it; that mistakes are bad; and that if they can't memorize, or if their line, move, whatever is not exactly so, then they are bad dancers. What a tragedy. Where are agency, interpretation, and embodiment? Right out the window.

But the students don't know. There is no one to tell them. The models held up to them are YouTube videos of beautiful, young, athletic women dancing busy, difficult, highly refined choreographies. These models reinforce students' previous (Western) understanding of trained dance in general. They have no idea of this dance's glorious heritage and all of the miracles awaiting them. While maybe it's not their fault (their teacher *is* supposed to educate them), student expectations and anxieties can influence how—and what—they are taught.

Blame the victim: How students help destroy the dance

Most folks go to a belly dance class because there happens to be one nearby. Or they have a vision of themselves in diaphanous veils, undulating seductively, and they think, Sign me up! Or a friend makes them go for company. Or they are over forty and want to do something for themselves. Or whatever. Most go to have fun. They want something fun and a little sexy. To dance for their lover. To feel pretty. To get some exercise. All these are excellent reasons. Few students go to a belly dance class to immerse themselves in a complex art from another culture that will take their entire life to explore. That comes later. For some. And that's fine, too. Fun is great. Students come back when they enjoy themselves, and this is a dance of joy, right?

So there they are, ready to have fun, be a little exotic and sexy, and what happens?

The teacher puts on this weird foreign music that sounds all out of tune. There is singing in a foreign language (remember, Arabs are perceived as terrorists; to the anxious ear, it all sounds rather suspect). The moves are much harder than they look. And everything is slippery—how you feel. The students don't like that. It is quite common to begin a new session with a full slate of students and lose two-thirds of them by Week 4. Many classes limp along with the same three to five students, month after month.

But teachers want students. So students get what they want.

- Stylized movement
- Easy music with a focus on the rhythm (even Western music)
- Drilling (which feels valuable since it is like exercise)

- Spoon-fed, repetitious choreography
- None of this scary solo, feeling, improvisation crap

And the students are happy. Note: This is why Zumba is popular—upbeat music, easy combos, sparkly hip scarves (ours), and fun, fun, fun! This is great. People get fun exercise. It's good. Anything that's upbeat and fun and gets people moving is great.

But when do we *dance*? When do we create out of our own bodies? We don't. Because improvisation is scary. So scary that many students (and teachers) have no exposure to it, and many who do dismiss it as pointless fooling around (more later).

What happened?

I was out of the mainstream raising kids between 1978-1993, so I missed the changeover. When I came back, all was choreography.

My first brush was in the mid 80s. I was in NYC to visit family and slipped into class. Bobby had recently been to see Nadia Gamal in Lebanon.

According to Morocco, Nadia's shows were tightly choreographed. Her parents were ballroom dancers for Badia Masabni's Casino Opera shows, and their shows were set down to their facial expressions. Nadia was backstage all that time, watching everything that went into those shows. She improvised when dancing casually, but for stage she choreographed.

Bobby said he watched Nadia's show every night; by the end of the week knew her entire choreography—which he was teaching in that class. It was disorienting to say the least.

By the mid 90s, I was able to come fully back to the dance. My first big event was a weeklong with Morocco, one of our great scholars and curators. Morocco teaches workshops almost entirely through choreography and her great, thorough, warmup (look for her new book *The Fundamental Movement Vocabulary of Raqs Sharqi*). She has good reason for it, as her choreographies are carefully-constructed teaching tools for specific genres. But it was a big surprise. And from there on in, it was largely choreography everywhere I looked.

Tamalyn Dallal suggests that choreography in belly dance became popular partly because the dance teachers who came from the East taught choreographies, so everyone thought that was more correct. And as we have seen above, Nadia Gamal, a major Lebanese star, danced choreography. But there is a difference of opinion as to whether or not many of the stars of Egypt in the 80s and 90s danced choreography.

Dancers in the East often have huge shows with many sections, "folkloric" backup dancers, and multiple costume changes. They have their own orchestras, often their own music. When you dance every night to the same songs, certain things fall into place. You start doing the same things to the same parts of the song. This is natural progression (and why people shouldn't stress when they make dances). Plus, the band is going to improvise within the song, and the dancer can imbue even the same step with today's feeling, so it will always be fresh. But it can look like a set choreography even when it is basically structured improv.

Of course, some Egyptian dancers did and do have set choreographies. In high-stakes performances, setting things can help make the job easier. You have a set list for your show and you know what you are going to do. Leila Farid told me that a dancer's entrance is often the only part of the performance where the dancer actually has to show off what she can do. The rest is visiting and having fun.

But there's also a chicken-egg thing going on here. If the Western dancers' perception is that there is choreography, they will ask to be taught that choreography. Then the Eastern dancer has to make a choreography to teach. And that notion spreads, meaning pressure is put on every teacher to teach choreography. There is a lot of discomfort in the West with the "follow the bouncing butt" dance-along, Eastern style of teaching, which is sad when you look at the benefits of following (more soon).

Western dancers wanted everything broken down, explained. They wanted an intellectual relationship with the dance, because that's what they knew. But it's not an intellectual dance. In addition, many of the Eastern dancers coming West to teach started as folklore dancers in the big troupes—Reda, Kawmiyya, etc. Raqia Hassan, for example. Those troupes were choreographed to the hilt, so choreography became those dancers' usual method of transmission.

Sahra Saeeda mentioned that back in the Golden Age film days, the star performers—Taheyya Karioca, Samia Gamal, etc.—were given choreographies (Mahmoud Reda and Ibrahim Akef were both film choreographers). But the cultural notion of the time was that stars did their own dance. The star dancers would learn the choreography and then go ahead and do whatever they wanted. Sahra says the main concession they made was in arm placement, holding the arms a little higher than they normally would.

Naima Akef, according to Sahra, was a different story. Akef was a circus performer from a circus family. When the circus she was with folded, her uncle, famed choreographer Ibrahim Akef, got her a job in the film industry. Because Akef wasn't a dancer in her own right, she learned and performed the choreographies assigned to her. She was a great performer and did a wonderful job, giving us delightful shows in many films (and making her uncle Ibrahim a star as well). But now we have star as vehicle for choreographer. Again, a film is a high-stakes venture—millions of people will see it, so you want everything to be right. But it's a Western ideal.

For a third thing, there is a tendency to tell the nosy anthropologist whatever they want to hear. To sell them what they want to buy. You want choreography? Sure, we got it! Why not? Tourists have money, and guess what makes the world go around. Though a few top Eastern stars do well from this dance, most dancers in the homelands struggle to make a living.

The chicken-egg conundrum is still going on. I hear top workshop teachers talk about how they are locked into teaching choreography because that is what event sponsors want them to teach—and event sponsors talk about how they can't get people to come to events unless they offer choreography. The attendees collect these store-bought dances instead of discovering their own expression of the music. It's sad.

The upshot is that dancers don't get the opportunity to develop the skills they need to present their vision of the music, their interpretation and response. They never experience the dance arising out of their own body, their own feeling. This leads to a terrible lack of confidence and dancers concerned only with technique, trapped by perfectionism (which is another word for fear).

The dance calls for confident, playful self-expression.

The dance calls for love. It calls for joy. It calls for wonder.

Belly dance transmits wonder

How do we transmit wonder with our dance?

Students new to the dance are overwhelmed by its beauty. Look at that hip drop! Oh my God, that circle! The beauty of this dance, the human body enjoying itself with the music, inspires wonder. But the wonder is soon beaten out of us. Many classes are not wonderful. They are not even fun.

At least one study has shown that wonder *decreases*—over time, dancers who regard the dance as spiritual *lose* that sense. In a small study of 35 women, queried some 6 years apart, Rachel Kraus found that women identified Oriental dance as a spiritual activity far *less* as time passed (Kraus 2014 DOI: 10.1111/jssr.12136). Why, if the dance is a venue for spiritual seeking, do people lose their sense of wonder? The dancers in the study had a range of reasons, from catty, backbiting behavior to finding activities that better filled the role of spirit in their lives. And they are not alone.

"I used to feel such awe, such amazement at the beauty of a simple hip drop. Now it's just a hip drop." I hear this over and over as students struggle to regain some pleasure in their dance, some sense of the joy that once inspired them. Far from being a community of seekers, many dance "communities" are anything but. Instead, they descend into competition, perfectionism, backstabbing, and insincerity.

Why do dance communities turn mean? What if this is related to the way the dance is currently taught?

What if our over-tech focus on spectacle, athletics, etc., burns out our ability to feel and express wonder? From abject awe for the beauty of the moving body, dancers are instead directed to relentlessly critique the stylization of their movement, to despair over their lack of perfection, and to stare fixedly at videos of other, "better" dancers, seeking an ever higher, more rigid, and superficial bar by which to measure themselves. We have an epidemic of insecurity in our dance. This is tragic when you realize that the dance's power is its welcoming, simple, open structure.

On top of this, there is money. The dance is pointed at performance rather than dancing for pleasure. A dozen dancers compete for a single slot at the local restaurant or hookah bar, or the few students they might inveigle into their classes. The dance scene becomes a turf war of self-promotion, undercutting, and character assassination.

No wonder there is no wonder. When the aesthetic is a pretty girl—when the pinnacle of perfection is stylized athletic spectacle—when the model of group choreography is rigid unison with no individual agency—when teachers bash colleagues or forbid students from studying with others—who would find belly dance to be a soul-nurturing, self-loving activity?

Yes, many of us treasure our classes and our friends there; studies show that spending an hour with a friend does more to lift depression than a week of pills. And despite everyone's best efforts, our dance retains its uplifting joy. But far too often, dance becomes another all-work-and-no-play venue to validate our failure as human beings. Since that's generally all we have in our lives, who even notices? Like *Alice in Wonderland*'s Red Queen, we run as fast as we can to stay in the same place.

Another world is possible.

We humans like to strive and succeed. We like challenges and the feel of accomplishment from puzzling through them. We love to learn, explore, and feel connected to something greater than the self. There is art to this dance—a great deal of it. We physically express the music and our feeling from the music. This takes a lifetime of connection, patience, and practice. And there is more.

A sense of depth, discipline, and spirit connection frees us and satisfies our seeking nature. It is rewarding and beneficial to explore and connect deeply. But finding depth can be a challenge. Anything labeled "Spiritual" has been rendered suspect, co-opted and drained of energy. Yet many of us cleave to this dance because we feel its mystic core. Where do we go? What if we had a different way to engage with the dance, one that frees us from oppression and comparison, one that builds a bridge to our True Self?

In our secret heart, we come to the dance for transformation.

We seek a magic carpet ride to our true self, our inner wonder, our power and glory. We want this so hard it hurts. We cry at night for the loss of the beauty, freedom, mystery and adventure to which we were born. Life is hard, and it has taken its toll. We come to this dance for redemption, to see ourselves in a true mirror, one that reflects the beauty and joy we have hidden away in our souls.

This dance delivers.

It delivers in unimaginable abundance. Everything we crave awaits us: all the joy, the beauty, the glory, hidden treasure waiting to be seen. A secret blossom trembling on the brink. A fourth doorway, a portal to the Divine, hidden from sight—until we are ready to see it. But we are afraid. Afraid of feeling our pain, afraid of shoveling through the shit of life to get to the treasure. Afraid there is no treasure. We put on our hip scarves and copy empty movement for an hour a week, pretending we are beautiful. It is an epic tragedy.

Our dance offers so much more.

How do we step through this portal to the Divine?

Well, first we have to find it.

To do that, we have to make a few changes. And that may take some effort.

Learning is hard. It aches, like an unused muscle, newly awakened. We all want to have fun, but we also want to learn. Luckily, the difficulty of learning is beautifully balanced by the pleasure of the dance itself—especially when we enjoy it within its cultural context. All of our dance's wonderful, chaotic heterophony, micromovement, improvisation, and feeling—these are not quaint traditions. They are the living, breathing center of the dance.

The dance itself is the magical doorway. It leads to a place within, a place where we recognize our beauty, dissolve trauma and stress, nurture our body and brain, feed our soul, and connect to the Divine.

This is the nature of our dance.

It is a magical transmission of wonder.

How do we transcend stylization, perfectionism, and hierarchy? How do we celebrate the anarchic glory of our dance?

The first step is to reclaim our own wonder.

We have all been brainwashed into regarding ourselves with narrow eyes, alert for any flaws or ways in which we do not fit the prescribed vision of perfection. Alas, there are many ways to miss the mark. We have all stared endlessly at YouTube videos, by turns snarking other dancers or feeling inadequate.

Let's change the rating system. Let's step back from perfection of form and the Platonic Ideal. Let's step up to shared mystery and glory. "It's not *just* a hip drop," explains the wonderful Fahtiem, *fahtiem.com*. She tosses off some hip drops and rolls her eyes, looking jaded. Then she gasps, "It's a *hip drop!*" She gazes at her own hip, eyes wide, amazed. Suddenly the move transforms into wonder—the wonder we all felt once upon a time, the wonder that drew us to this dance.

What if we dance for the joy of it?

What if every hip drop, every move, every moment of our dance were a testament to wonder? When we feel and express this wonder, our own dance becomes the doorway. It shows the way. We give others permission so that they, too, can see, feel, and live in wonder.

7
THROUGH THE DOOR

Rote movement

It's all well and good to walk through magical doorways, but many of us have classes to teach and recitals to produce. The reality of the day is that we often perform on large stages in front of many people to recorded music, plus we have students who want to dance within the security of a group. How do we reconcile these elements with a tradition of solo extemporaneous dance in small spaces to live music?

Here are some things we can do:

- Learn and teach improvisation, micromovement, and embodiment
- Favor functional movement, communication, and expression of feeling
- Focus on embodiment and timing rather than prerecorded and preconceived
- Highlight and model the sensual pleasure of the movement
- Explore the healing, curative powers of our dance
- Dissolve our sense of duality; connect ourselves, our students, and our guests, to the Divine

The dance is much more than sparkly costumes and group dances. We have this magical, healing balm, this panacea for the soul. There is much to celebrate. Despite our best effort to make it difficult and a lot of work, at its heart this dance is a physical pleasure to do, and one of the elements of trauma healing is to opt for the pleasurable—things that feel good. Why not enjoy the hell out of the dance as we sink into its sun-kissed sensuality?

This has to do with performance, but also with home dance. It is for everyone who wants to be part of a quiet, subversive, spirit revolution. Let's step back from our focus on stylized, memorized, combinations and set choreography. Let's let go of rote movement.

Wait, what is Rote Movement?

Rote means "mechanical or habitual repetition of something to be learned." Rote learning is flashcards, times tables, any kind of memorization-based learning. Rote movement applies to activities we do in a mechanical, repetitive way. Jogging, for example. Or calisthenics. Or drilling. Or choreography. Six hip drops, turn left on seven and pose on eight.

Great. Why are we doing that?

Because the teacher said to.

What did the music say?

Um... Huh?

Who can embody the feeling and nuance of the music when they are working so hard to remember and execute what comes next?

Of course, rote learning does have a place—and what it does, it does well.

The purpose of rote learning

Rote learning can stick in the brain—my mom, with severe dementia, could still recite most of the poem *Jabberwocky*. We remember what letter comes next in the alphabet by singing the alphabet song. We know how many days in a month by reciting *30 Days Hath September*, and we can do simple calculations quickly because we have drilled them, over and over, in grade school. We don't have to think or discover—we remember, because we repeated it many times in the past.

What's wrong with that?

For many things, like the times tables, French verb conjugation, or choreography, rote learning is great. For others, it's not.

Bloom's Taxonomy of Learning is the brainchild of Dr. Benjamin Bloom. He created it in 1956 to encourage higher levels of thinking in education. Bloom's Taxonomy classifies different kinds of learning according to their levels of cognition (thought). It runs from remembering knowledge (memorization) to synthesis (creation). Memorization requires a low level of cognition. Synthesis, creation, which is what we do when we improvise (or choreograph), requires the highest. But it's not the memorization factor that is the problem. Everyone has to memorize stuff.

The problem is the mindless, mechanical aspect.

When we do things in real life, our movement has purpose. It is functional. We open the door, pour coffee, etc. In the martial arts, you rarely see students run mindlessly through their katas. No, because katas are the epitome of functional movement. You are blocking someone here, punching another person there, kicking someone else through the door in the next move. There is purpose in every step, every moment.

But when we jog or run for exercise or do calisthenics, there is no real function to those actions. We do them because of some abstract goal. We run on a treadmill with our earphones on while watching TV. This is the poster child for rote movement—mindless repetition to the max. It is a withdrawal from the body, an escape. It has no meaning, no expression, no soul.

We say we need to drill stuff to get it into "muscle memory" (though all memory is in the brain). But if all we practice is mindless step sequences, when it comes down to it, the show will be mindless, too. We do what we practice. Drilling empty moves will not get us to embodied brilliance. The memorized material must be connected to function in order to blossom.

Note: We are talking here about memorizing and repeating. We are *not* talking about following. According to Carolyn Hamilton, a dance friend researching brain health, one of the most improv-helpful and brain-healthy activities we can do is to follow someone improvising or doing a *loose* choreography. Following helps us get out of our own way and follow the music. It's the reacting and spontaneity that lets the brain create new pathways. We'll look at this more fully in Book 3.

For now, let's get back to functional memorization.

Here's an example. Actors need to memorize their lines. Those lines have a function—they drive the plot forward and they reveal character. Actors must understand the meaning and purpose of their lines. If they don't embody that meaning with every iota of their being, who's going to watch them? Musicians need to remember complex musical passages—and play them with feeling, or the music is dead. By the same token, dancers need to know their choreography—but if there is no purpose or connection, nothing to express, it's lifeless.

This is the problem with rote teaching of choreography. Student dancers often have no connection to any of the things they are doing. They may not understand the relationship between the movement to the music—and there often isn't much of one, aside from the most obvious rhythmic connection by which they count. Consequently, many students of belly dance count their steps as they dance alongside the music, while trying to remember which step comes next. The upshot of this is that students always feel tentative, dependent and unoriginal. They never get to experience the joy of the dancer's connection to the music.

Over-drilling, over-stylization, erasing the motivation of the music from the move, these are how we lose the feeling. These are how we hide from the joy of dance. Making the body do stuff is another layer of control, a way to keep ourselves from feeling. Stylization is control. Unison is control. All of these are intellectual pursuits that prevent the body from directly experiencing and responding to the music—and from feeling and sharing joy.

In addition, mindless repetition is how we get hurt. Repetitive Stress Injury (RSI), anyone? Carpal tunnel? Doing things past when the body tires, over-practicing moves that in performance would only be done one or twice (knee walking and knee spins, I'm talking to you), can cause serious damage to the body.

Ballet dancers, for whom this is daily bread and butter, are not in touch with their bodies so much as they are in control. They make their bodies do things that normal bodies would not. Utter control, practicing until the toes bleed, they punish their bodies into form. We celebrate their sacrifice, but why must art include ruination?

We dance teachers can build involvement into our student dances—while defusing the impulse to force and control. Here's how:

- Allow the dance to be playful and fun. It is a dance of celebration and joy
- Drill less. It's a drag and reinforces stylization.
- Use slow motion for refining complex combinations
- Model gentle leading and following, especially with improvisation. The students learn faster, let go of the critical mind, and go with the flow
- In combinations, tie each move inextricably to the music. Include the melody. Articulate the connection. Sing the steps to the tune of the song
- Involve the students in the dance-making process. This will boost the dancers' investment and make the dance easier to remember
- Create characters, backstories, and motivations for the action of your dances so the dancers have something to feel. Engaged dancers

invested in their stories create heart-rending beauty on stage (this is a Western touch, but then, so is choreography)

The idea here is to pour something delicious *inside* the moves, so the dancers have something to express.
Give us more than a pretty container.
Give us heart and soul.
Give us art.

How meaning creates emotion

There is power in art, particularly art invested with genuine feeling, loving intention, and generous soul. When we allow these elements into our work, it changes into something real. Imagine a real smile, crinkly eyes and all. Those crinkles have a name—the "Duchenne smile." When you see a *real* smile—even a picture of one—instinctively, you smile, too, another real smile. The feeling, intention, and soul in your smile create a response of warmth. This inspires the return smile.

What does this have to do with dance?

Humans make meaning. No matter how random and unpredictable life might be, we humans are out there creating scenarios that imbue its events with meaning. It's what we do. In terms of dance, this is another blessing/curse thing. One of the challenges of Oriental dance in the West is that Western audiences expect art to have meaning. But the only meaning those early audiences could construe from the movements and sensuality of the dance was SEX—and this misinterpretation has followed us ever since. This is the curse.

Traditional Oriental dance is an abstract art form. It is not a pantomime. It does not tell stories. The dancer expresses her feeling from the music in the moment. Some of the songs have words, and the dancer may reference the words or story of the song—not to tell the story, but to express their feeling from the emotional timbres grounded in the words.

Abstraction

Here's the thing about stories.
A story is a sequence of emotions—a narrative arc is a sequence of emotional timbres. A good song, dance, story, whatever, has an emotional arc, from suspense to resolution. But the *details* of the story—the plot, the specific events—they don't matter in our dance. What matters is the emotional arc. It's the same with steps—individual step choices are arbitrary. Any step that fits the music will do. What matters is filling the step with our feeling. When we dance, we make the music visible. But—and this is important—the music exists on far deeper levels than notes and rhythm. The music has these emotional timbres. The musicians actively express their feeling in the moment in their music. We feel that, too, and channel our feeling into the movement with which we interpret the music.

As dancers who must often dance to recorded music, we have the option of harnessing this tendency to make meaning and using it to create powerful dances that affect our guests on a deep level. Rather than developing a step-based choreography, we can dance an emotional arc. A story is a series of events hung upon an emotional arc. For example, we might dance about coming to terms with loss. The details of the story (who lost what and what happened) are immaterial—everyone's story is different, but they follow that same arc. This is part of the Eastern ideal of Same but Different. When we work in this kind of archetypal way, the guests *hang their own stories* on our arc. In this way, each guest creates their own world in our dance. The dance has the power to unite.

Wait, don't we have to smile all the time?

We have all heard the admonition "You can't be sad onstage." This means that when we go on stage, we make a contract. We are in service to the guests and the joy of the evening. If we had a fight with a lover, our dog passed away, or whatever, this stays off stage. The present moment is for joy.

But what if the song is sad? The treatment of negative emotions in traditional Oriental performance is fascinating and complex. Pain and sorrow tend to be presented as things that happened in the past. The present moment is love and joy. Sad songs evoke a bittersweet reminiscence of the hard times of the past tempered by the joy of the present moment (thanks to Souzan Healy for her research in this area). We will get into this fully in the Body chapter.

So, no, we don't have to smile all the time, but we do have to love and bring our joy to the guests all the time. We do have to be engaged, authentic, and honest in our joy. If we fake a smiling face, or place ourselves in an empty arrangement, the audience will feel this dishonesty. The secret ingredient is our willingness to open ourselves to the music and to share joy with our guests.

Dance is an expressive, interpretive art. We express what we feel from the music. We interpret it through our movement, intention, and energy. If it is a joyous song, we smile. But the brilliance of Oriental music is in its infinite shades of emotion—our smile may be fleeting, but everything we express will be grounded in the joy of the present moment.

In the continuum between pleasure and pain, joy and sorrow (and every moment of song, every inch of movement, is a microcosm of this most fundamental nexus), there exists every emotion, from love to hate, anger to joy, fear to comfort. As we train ourselves to respond in the moment to these timbres, we create rich emotional tapestries. Even negative emotions have the power to unite. Most of us feel alienated and alone in our pain. We turn inwards and waste away, or outwards and inflict pain on others. When we see the pain of human existence expressed as art, we feel our connection to the world. We are not alone.

Every one of us has felt sorrow, shame, fear, loss, and grief. When we express these emotions in the context of art, when we temper them with joy, we unite our guests. The love and camaraderie of the world help us to bear our burdens, to access our buried feelings, and even to let them go. Art is a catalyst for catharsis, the "purification of emotions that results in renewal and restoration."

When we step upon the stage, we are in service to the guests and the creation of joy. We ground negative emotions in the joy of the present moment. "A long time ago, a bad thing happened. Tonight, we are all here together. Isn't this wonderful! I love you so much." We give solace to our guests through sharing joy in the moment.

What about theatrical dance?

In a theatre piece, one may express negative emotions as if they are happening right now. The rise in theatrical approaches to belly dance has taken it far afield from the dance of joy and celebration at its heart. How do we manage this?

Theatrical dance is a Western concept, but one can see theatrical approaches even in classic Egyptian films, where the story or its characters infuse the dance scenes (Tamra Henna being a good example). I am Levantine by blood, but I grew up in America. I love theatrical dance—I enjoy its artistry; I practice and teach it (see *CreateDanceArt.com*). I'm writing a belly dance musical. I am even fine with belly dance to some non-traditional music (though not so much for teaching, especially beginners), and of well-made fusion.

For me, there are three keys.

1. The first key is to ground the work in the principles of Oriental dance: The feeling in the moment, same but different, and bring the joy (theatre is a classic vehicle for catharsis). Consider Eastern movement vocabulary and music as well.
2. The second key is the venue. Are you dancing to a traditional band, or in a restaurant for civilians or people of the culture, or doing a bellygram? Then do a classic show. Are you dancing in a group show or recital, or your own production? Unless it is billed as a traditional show, you may have the option of theatre.
3. The third key is impact. In a show with many pieces, emotionally challenging or disturbing pieces may be sandwiched between things that are more traditional or upbeat. Always end the show with an upbeat, happy piece. There must be resolution so the guests can go home feeling refreshed. If you yourself dance two pieces within a longer show, one more emotionally challenging and one light or traditional, do the challenging dance last, so your own show ends with impact—as long as you are not the final dancer in the show. If you are, be sure to make a joyous finale to lift the mood.

I've seen theatrical work from accomplished artists that, on the surface, didn't look like belly dance, but brilliantly embodied its music, quality of movement, and/or conceptual frameworks. Elena Lentini is a prime example of this kind of successful fusion. I've also seen theatrical belly dance that was more about belly dancers doing theater—the belly dance qualities were gone.

I have also seen some real train wrecks. Many of these are products of youthful bravada and/or ignorance. Thank goodness we grow and learn! Our art develops as we deepen our understanding of the form. This is why we seek to educate rather than to shame. Shame is highly destructive, there is far too much in our world, and it rarely helps anyone do better (more about this in the Body section).

As dancers, we are in service to art, in service to love, and in service to the world. We make the party. We give our guests permission to enjoy themselves. We make space for emotional release, help our guests resolve pain, and open the way for joy and love. This is our job as artists—and it is particularly our job as Oriental dancers. Though our art may be ferocious, when we present it with humbleness and in service to love, we help ourselves and others feel connected, release pain and suffering, and walk in love.

This is our highest calling as human beings. But how do we get from here to there? How the heck are we supposed to learn how to do all this stuff?

We need models *and* permission.

The place of copying

When you learn something new, you copy. When you learn to draw, you look at a lot of art and a lot of things. They become your models. You draw the models. You may copy a still life or a cup on the table. You may trace photographs, drawings, or reproduce paintings to get the technique. Hopefully, you seek quality feedback in any of these endeavors. When you learn to write, you will read (and copy) other writers.

Heck, when you learn to write, literally, like in grade school, you certainly copy. Right? When you learn to play an instrument, you copy the placement of the fingers, the shape of the mouth, and you play the notes as written. In martial arts, yoga, ballet, etc., etc., you copy the teacher as she shows you the movement. When you learn a new move, you copy the new move, and so on.

When does copying stop?

As soon as possible.

Whatever Lola Wants is a charming 1998 film with great messages, if rather lackluster dancing (though fine choreography from Morocco). The song

"Whatever Lola Wants" by Adler and Ross is originally from the play *Damn Yankees*. Gwen Verdon's performance of this song is marvelous (and choreographed by Bob Fosse—search YouTube to find it). Anyway, after the Arabic singer Natacha Atlas covered *Lola*, her version of the song got picked up for the film. The film's trailer, which features Atlas, is a lot of fun.

In the film, Lola, an American postal worker, goes to Cairo in search of her Egyptian boyfriend, with a side mission of locating Ismahan, a famous Egyptian dancer who retired in disgrace after a mysterious scandal. After much effort, Lola finds Ismahan, who reluctantly agrees to teach Lola to dance. During the lessons, Ismahan sits in her chair, instructing Lola. Lola complains bitterly that she doesn't get what Ismahan wants her to do. Couldn't she demonstrate? No, Ismahan replies. "For then you would only see how *I* do it. You must discover how *you* do it."

There is a lot of room in the world of belly dance for folks to discover their own style—how *they* do it, how *their* own bodies respond to the music. As a cartoonist, when I don't know how to draw something, I go find a picture (or the real thing), and I copy it. I copy it to get a feel for it. Once I have that, then I can draw it myself, without copying, and I vary the object to fit my wishes—because it's ART. I'm not a plagiarist or a forger. Nor am I a ballet dancer or a martial artist, for whom exactitude is vital. Or a competitive ballroom dancer. No.

I am a belly dancer. And the Eastern mark of mastery is Different Every Time. Improvisation. Feeling. Expression. I want my art to represent *me*. I want folks who see my cartoons to know *I* drew them, without even seeing my name.

It is a recursive process. You copy to learn something new, and then you internalize it—you make the new thing your own. Now you can bend it, stretch it, and play with it. Then you copy to learn something new...

But in belly dance, a lot of us *only* copy the work of others. We are often afraid of (even actively discouraged from), creating anything of our own. Many of us never improvise because we have no idea what to do—nobody ever showed us. Besides, it might not be (gasp) perfect! A lot of fixed mindset, fear of failure, fear of making a mistake has invaded belly dance. And for a dance of joy, there is an awful lot of cattiness and disdain going around. Dancers are terrified that the Dance Police will cart them off to belly dance jail if they throw in so much as a Roman hip bump or Persian gesture while wearing an Egyptian dress.

Why do we feel the need to point out every flaw? Understanding the lineage of dance is important and all, but really. Like grammar pedants sneering because a writer used *who* instead of *whom* (I teach writing), we are missing the big picture. Let's focus on what's best *for the dance*. Dancers need to feel confident. They have to present themselves with flair and joy. When we get to that place, a lot of issues fall away. Of course, there is a place for correct usage (and spelling). There is a place for technique. I see the same crap you do. But when crap is *all* we focus upon, we harm the dance.

Critique

One of the more dysfunctional attitudes with which I was raised was the dismissal of anything done well, and a focus only on what was broken. For example, growing up, I never heard, "Oh, honey, four As. Nice work!" Nope. All I got was, "What the hell is this B?" So this was how I did things, too. But it didn't work. In child-rearing, the productive model is to tell the kids what *to* do. Instead of saying NO all the time, you say YES. Instead of "Don't touch that!" you redirect the kid to what is okay for them to play with. This was a big shift, and over time, I brought it into my teaching.

I taught myself to focus on the students' success. In addition to dance, I have been a teacher at some level since the early 80s. I worked first for Headstart and later as a Speech Language Assistant in the public-school system. I have taught English Composition at the college level for over 20 years. I often teach three sections of comp, which means around 50 students. I do a *lot* of critique.

It was a hard job to change this in myself, but it mattered. I knew I was on the right track when a writing student told me I was the only teacher in her entire life to ever say anything good about her writing. I learned to emphasize what students did *right*. And I went one step further. When we discussed what needed improvement, I framed it as an action step—what *to do* in the next paper, instead of what they had done wrong. For a dance example, to the student with sloppy hands, I'd say, "I'd love to see you bring more energy into your hands. What if you extend your energy out past your fingertips?" This builds so much more joy and confidence.

We have been brainwashed into thinking that we have to be perfect or stay home. Women especially are tyrannized by the expectation of perfection. Perfection is a myth designed to keep us powerless. Life is not about being a perfect copy. It's about being you, 100% yourself, with all your beauty, variety, and personality. The world needs your individual glory. Yes, there is a lot of crappy dance out there. But shaming dancers isn't going to change that. Confidence and enjoyment help a lot more. When dancers enjoy the pleasure of the movement and the moment, when they have something to say, their technique improves organically.

Let's all reinforce the good, critique wisely (*aliathabit.com/for-dancers/focus-on-the-feeling*), and model Eastern dance principles before we start randomly tearing down strangers for their hand placement, hairstyle, or how they tuck their hip-poofies.

Nothing is perfect. Everything evolves. Martin Luther said, "This life is not being, but becoming." We learn, we grow, we change. Otherwise, we are dead. Perfection is death. We copy to learn, we take classes, study others, and practice. But there comes a time when we must hop out on the branch, flap our wings, launch ourselves, and fly. Taking such risks benefits us in many ways, some understood and others yet to come.

Will our first efforts suck? Of course, they will! Growth and learning include failure and revision. That's how we learn—through trial and error, persistence, feedback, and trying again. We embrace the challenge. This is one place in the dance where the pain of struggle does equal the gain—of skill, ownership, and confidence.

We can even like ourselves!

But what about group dances?

Group dances are here to stay. How do we adapt them? How do we make group dances that aren't about copying, stylization, and precision? How do we represent the dance yet give people what they want?

One way is to engage the students in the creative process.

I was lucky—I had the benefit of a superlative dance education through several years with Ibrahim Farrah, one of the most highly regarded teachers of his day, plus his protégés, Jajouka and Elena Lentini (my long-time mentor and the goddess of this dance). Even though I had little conceptual knowledge, I understood the dance *in my body* thanks to Bobby's teaching—

modeling, ever-new combinations, and improvisation—so that is how I taught.

But this didn't always fly with my students. A few started asking for choreographies, something they could take home and show off. And we had recitals, shows. So I made dances for them. Because the students were beginners, I looked for simple, repetitious music. Do you know how hard this was to find? These days, there is plenty of Egyptian pop and Western fusion music (much of which is synthetic repetition). Back in the 80s and 90s (in a small Vermont town, before iTunes, Amazon, or Internet shopping) it was almost impossible to find a song that kept the same structure all the way through without multiple taqasim. I looked for repetition because, being a self-taught choreographer (as most of us were), and lacking any conceptual understanding of the values and principles of Oriental dance and music (ditto), I didn't know any better.

I did make some charming dances for my students. They tended to have folkloric structures and to match the structure of the song, with verses being different from choruses. And they tended to have backstories, emotional and narrative elements that arose for me from the music. Plus I made space for little solos, even from the beginning, because the fun parts of the song, the taqasim and whatnot, always seemed a crime to set.

As my skills improved, my choreographies became more interesting and fun. I still improvised my own solos, and I encouraged my students' creativity as well. It was important to me that their own voices come through, that they be creators in their own right. People who came to our shows often commented upon how unique each dance was, how different each dancer's style—and they were. But we still kept at those group dances...

Over time, I noticed something.

The minute I started teaching choreography, the students' creativity levels dropped like mercury in a polar vortex. Suddenly, they became anxious, careful, and narrowly focused, where before they had been open, graceful, and free. They couldn't remember, they were overly focused on symmetry, and they argued about their stage positions. Their own dance suffered, as did the overall easygoing atmosphere I treasured in the classroom. Moreover, I felt pressure to dance choreographies myself—there were opportunities for presentations, performances with students, and teaching outside workshops. What did those students want? Choreographies! So I made solo dances. And then danced them in the shows. But there was a problem. I often felt stilted, disconnected, and self-conscious.

Just like my students.

This had to change.

So, I thought, why can't the students make the group dances? All my students make their own solo dances. They often told me that when they performed at outside events (I encourage them to travel to workshops), other students were amazed that they had made their own dances (and more amazed when they improvised). Even my beginners are trained to improvise and encouraged to make their own dances.

I set out to include them in a group creative process.

I began by having each student choose a move that went with the music, which they then taught to the other dancers. I sequenced the steps, often in the same order as the students presented them. We let the music decide how many times to do each move.

SHAZAM! Suddenly I had fully engaged students who remembered the moves, counts, and transitions, came up with floor patterns, and filled in any blanks without even being asked. Our focus was on feeling and expression rather than stylization. We had far more elaborate and complex interactions than before. Cooperation soared. The dances were great. And everyone was learning and doing all the time. It was a miracle.

I began using a lot of conceptual and team-based models for making dances, both for myself and for the groups, and I extended this to other arenas. In 2003, Stewart Hoyt and I made the show *Oriental Splendor*, composed of duets we (only half-jokingly) called our "three-minute psychodramas." These story-based compositions allowed us to have freedom in the moment and avoid both setting steps and dancing in unison (our styles were so different that any attempt at that quickly fell apart). This conceptual model worked perfectly for us. We toured the show all over Vermont and in neighboring states. Its success emboldened me to try a more ambitious project.

In 2004, I applied for and received a Flynn Center "New Arts Space Assistance" (NASA) grant to explore the development of a collaborative, improvisation-based approach to group dance-making. Our group gathered seven dancers from three states, and resulted in the show *Jeweled Splendor*. We presented in January 2005 to an SRO audience at the FlynnSpace (at the time, the largest crowd ever for a NASA show) then toured in several venues.

The strategies we developed now form the basis of my work with groups. These include composition, improvisation, use of teams, and story development. It works. It's great. I continue to develop ways to make dances that honor our dance's soul (I present these in the course How to Create

Dance Art, *CreateDanceArt.com*). My goal is an improv-based company. And we can do it.

I love making dances. I love to share and encourage creativity. I love my happy, productive, creative, engaged students. And the results are stunning. My community college classes of absolute beginners compose a fun, engaging dance—in about an hour. The following week, they perform it—with confident, happy smiles (and they can improvise, too).

WIN-WIN.

~

We've covered a lot of ground examining causes and solutions. Let's do a quick recap. There is a trend away from improvisation. Precision movement, unison, and exact copying have risen in status. These practices reflect Western rather than Eastern values. The rise in pre-recorded music has contributed to this rise in pre-recorded dance. Currently we have a highly critical culture focused on choreography, stylization, athleticism, and perfectionism.

But belly dance is a magical transmission of wonder—while form is important, the feeling in the moment is the most important thing. Let's focus on the feeling, encourage success, and celebrate what's good about each dance.

Traditionally, the Oriental dance experience is shared with musicians and guests. The dancer makes the party. She gives the guests permission to enjoy themselves. She is the über-woman—in Egypt called the '*Alimah*—learned, magnetic, fascinating. She cleanses the souls of the guests through art, beauty, and joy, to free them from pain and suffering, if only for an evening.

The dancer shares her felt experience with the audience. Through the miracle of mirror neurons, the guest experiences the acceptance, love, and joy the dancer pours out. Guests feel renewed and refreshed, soothed and nourished. It's nice to see a spectacle, but it's a lot nicer to feel loved and loving.

Okay? So far, so good. But there is an elephant in the room, something we haven't yet addressed.

Sex.

How has the objectification and sexualization of the dance, and of dancers, coupled with the demonization of women's sexuality and agency, has skewed our response to (and understanding of) the dance?

Come hither...

8

SEX

The transformation

Oh, the wonder of belly dance costumes! They fill our imagination with silk, jewels, and incense. It is a miracle to me how simply changing my clothes transforms me into a glorious, powerful being. It happens every time, and I'm not the only one who finds this. Other people remark upon the change, and most notice it for themselves. Michelle Forner, a longtime dancer and performer, was one of the first to get a college degree for her study of Oriental dance. Part of her 1993 landmark Master's thesis, *The Transmission of Oriental Dance in the United States: From "Raqs Sharqi" to "Belly Dance,"* examines this quality of transformation. It is some of the most accessible magic in a deeply magical dance.

Our costumes come in all shapes and colors, from glam and bling to muted organics with shells and coins, from skimpy two-piece wisps to loose, full-coverage robes and dresses. Dancers express themselves in part through costuming choices. They also influence the impression the outside public gets of the dance and of dancers. Don't worry, I'm all for fun, blingy costumes. But there are some things going on here, and, in that what-were-you-wearing, blame-the-victim sort of way, our garb has taken some flak.

The history of the spangled two-piece costume as seen in golden age movies is fairly short. Back in the not-so-distant past, performers wore the same clothes as everyone else, though theirs may have been fancier, because, hey, performers are fancy. In Egypt, for example, according to dance scholar and teacher, Sahra Saeeda, the Ghawazee (dancers who performed outdoors), wore the same clothes that regular women wore—a vest or long coat over a sheer tunic, with voluminous pants gathered at the ankle and a couple of hip scarves (hip scarf = dancer).

But regular women wore these outfits *indoors*. No "decent" woman would go out without being covered in her outdoor drapes—except those Ghawazee, who thronged the streets and coffee shops, wearing outfits meant for the privacy of the home. (Kathleen Fraser in her excellent book, *Before they were Belly Dancers*, explains that the Ghawazee were a guild of "outdoor," public dancers, lower status than their "indoor" sisters, known as *'Awalim* (learned women, masters). So they may not all have been of *Sinti* extraction, as Ghawazee was a performer class).

Anyway, our bad reputation started a while back.

A woman's reputation is generally understood to involve sexuality. From this perspective, women are either good or bad; there is no in-between, and one's state can flip in a single moment (usually downward). A woman seen as sexually available, one who consorts with men other than her husband (or has no husband), who goes out and enjoys herself, she acquires a bad reputation. *Even if she does none of these* but has been sexually attacked or otherwise compromised, she is now "tainted goods" and has a bad reputation. Even if she has merely declined the advances of an admirer she is at risk. This perspective seethes in the East and is shockingly active in the West.

Worse, that bad reputation is then co-opted into a license for sexual aggression. That is to say, if a woman is dressed in attractive clothing, out having a drink, she is a target. Heck, she doesn't even need the clothes or a drink. All she needs is to exist—to be in a woman's body or present as a woman. To even exhibit "feminine" behavior puts one at risk. It's crazy.

It's an interesting facet of patriarchal culture, the notion that women "ask for it" by virtue (or lack) of their quantity or style of clothing. Any woman not wearing a full suit of armor is generally suspect, guilty of arousing male lust, and must therefore be punished, preferably with rape. Except for one thing—statistics regularly show that clothing (or its lack), has little bearing on whether or not someone is raped.

Fear of rape is a problem for all women (in fact, for all humans, but women are especially at risk; statistically, men are most likely to rape and women most likely to be raped). The sexual politics of patriarchy is such a rabbit hole I could write a whole book on the topic; for now, let's move forward.

Warning: I'm going to make lots of generalizations about Men and Women in this section. We are all different, but we are also shaped and conditioned by our culture, which is historically patriarchal. That is what I want to address here, as patriarchy seems to me the root cause of a lot of our problems with sexuality and this dance (and general othering, hierarchical thinking, competition, and even perfectionism). So I'm talking big picture, general forces I see affecting all of us. I am *not* calling out individual humans. A lot of what I say is my own observation, underpinned by decades of reading and conversation, so it lacks attribution. Any errors of fact or interpretation are my own. I've also noticed people flip out when anyone talks about this stuff, so buckle your seat belt; it's a bumpy ride.

What is patriarchy?

According to the Oxford English Dictionary, it is "a system of society or government in which the father or eldest male is head of the family and descent is reckoned through the male line," and a system in which "men hold the power and women are largely excluded from it." We have both, in the West and in the East.

Though there are a few women in government, and some of them in high roles, it is still largely an old boy's club. Women still earn less than men, and women of color earn even less. But it is not only the state that controls and shapes us. There is also the church, and in many cases, the church controls, or at least heavily influences, the government.

Religion may be the opiate of the people, but it also tends to be the jailer of women, especially the fundamentalist versions of the Big Three religions of the Book, Christianity, Judaism, and Islam. Why do fundamentalists of all three of these heavy hitters have it in for women? Maybe it's the exodus from the Garden of Eden (Islam blames Adam and Eve equally, but the others just slam poor Eve). Maybe it's the power of women, which is far too dangerous and must be contained at all costs.

Maybe it's property, inheritance, and the patrilineal line. If you don't know which kids are yours, who gets your stuff when you die? How do you continue your empire? According to Gerda Lerner's *The Creation of Patriarchy*, economics, property, has a lot to do with this. Ibram Kendi, a leading scholar on racism, agrees. Kendi finds that self-serving economic decisions come first (for example, with slaves I can get more work done for less money). Racism is how you justify those decisions (those savages deserve to be slaves).

Dehumanizing the victim is a classic strategy. Maybe misogyny is a justification for the self-serving economic decision to own women, thus protecting a male's investment. I don't know the answer. In any case, the oppression and blaming of women continues in all three religions.

Fundamentalists often frame women as dangerous agents of chaos who distract upright men with their seductive, sensual ways. They must be corralled and controlled by marriage, transformed into property, protected from any rival attention, and discarded or punished (or both), at the first sign of waywardness. Basically, men punish women because they find women both scary and attractive. *What?* Yes. Because it's the woman who chooses. And if she doesn't choose you? How do you live with that shame? You must co-opt her choice, her power, her agency, to protect your pride.

Men are historically afraid and angry with women. I'm just going to say it. Women are mysterious, erotic, insatiable, bleed without being wounded, make babies, *and* feed those babies out of their own bodies. That's power. On top of that, women cause erections. Men can lose control of their own bodies around women. They feel helpless in the face of woman's erotic power. But our dominant cultures say that men are top dogs. They can't be afraid of weak, stupid women. That psychic dissonance breeds rage. So women are subjugated and shot down at every opportunity, framed as weak, emotional, deceptive, and frigid, slutty, or both.

Women are also afraid of and angry with men, conditioned to want and need them and furious at this reaction. In the short term, women are maybe even more afraid and angry, because of the threat of violence, but also because patriarchy favors men. Sort of. It gives them far more power and influence, but it does exact a price for that power. Men's hearts and souls are coopted by the injunction to be strong, fearless, never cry, and generally act like machines, stuffing all emotions except anger and lust (because emotions are for those weak women). As you can see, this creates problems. The result is an epidemic of sexual rage and unhappiness.

We're going to talk more about women here, as the vast majority of dancers are women, but men who dance (or who are tender, loving, and kind), face a lot of the same issues women do, since they risk being seen as feminine. This is a particular issue in the West. No matter if they are gay, straight, bi, or other, being seen as feminine puts a big target on their backs. The whole deal is wrong from one end to the other. It's time for equality. More on this soon.

∽

One big issue in the world of dance and sex is *misogyny*, the contempt of and prejudice against women and "feminine" behavior. People get all down on the misogyny of the East; this is a red herring. We have plenty of misogyny in the West. Rape culture is alive and well, and every woman who has ever felt afraid walking down a dark street—or in a bar or a coffee shop, or on the corner, or in her home, or any place, any time—yes, she knows all about it.

Of course, the higher your socioeconomic status, the more peaceful your area, the less danger—or so we are told. The fact is, however, that sexual abuse and domestic violence cut across all socioeconomic lines. Violence against women and children (and there is a lot of it), most often comes from family, "friends," or lovers. This sword of Damocles hangs over every woman's head at every minute of every day (gay and trans people face the same harsh reality).

So why put on costumes that expose us to more judgment, fear, and danger? Because dance releases us from fear and stress. It gives us access to our glory and wonder. This is odd, since it can also place us smack in the middle of sexual judgment.

It is this dialectic that is at the heart of so much confusion and disagreement about this dance. Is it a sexual dance done for the titillation of men, or an empowering dance, done for the joy of the dancer and her guests? Is it a dance to be done at home, either alone or with family and friends, or is it a performance dance to be publicly presented? Is it a dance for human beings to connect to each other and the Divine? It depends upon whom you ask, who is dancing, the venue, the audience, and the dancer's intention.

Dance in general is an age-old activity that connects humans socially and brings joy. Ours is a particularly age-old dance. It is, therefore, puzzling and suspicious that religious fundamentalists, be they Christian, Muslim, or Jewish, tend to despise dance and forbid it as sacrilege. This means they find it threatening to their world order—an important element to the above mix. Let's untangle some of these knots and see what we find.

Shifting sands

Home-style belly dance is a playful dance of joy. It expresses the dancer's feeling from the music, both physical and emotional. It is often done in groups, because in the East, several generations may live in the same household and the women (who do most of the dancing), prepare food and do household tasks together. The focus in this case is on the inside—the participants' joy and the sharing of this feeling. The audience is more of a participatory group, since all may dance, and anyone may be dragged, pushed, or wheedled into the center to strut her stuff for the joy of the group.

This group feeling pervades *haflis* (parties) etc., where everyone is there to have a good time. At a party, the line between audience and dancer is permeable and ever shifting; anyone may be in the center of the dance circle at one minute and a witness the next. Though skill and beauty are always welcome, the main focus is fun and pleasure. Even when you had, for example, outdoor coffee shop performers, the dance was still a dance of joy. Seeing dance uplifts the heart; participation releases stress and brings joy via the magical healing qualities of music and mirror neurons.

But somehow the dance became conflated with sex.

What happened?

Women still dance together in all but the most religious of homes, so that hasn't changed. Fundamentalists have frowned on dancers for ages. Within Islam, there is a long-standing religious objection to female performers. It is not so much the kind of performance—it is the problem of a moving female body (even fully clothed). A female singer is regarded as bad enough—her voice is a problem, but at least her body can be hidden behind a screen. But a dancer reveals her body to the eyes of men who are not part of her family. This was and is *haram*, forbidden. The dance itself wasn't the issue. Only the female performers themselves were regarded as rather slutty. So that hasn't changed, though it has gotten louder.

When did the dance itself come under fire? There may be a watershed moment that helped influence some of the changes:

Westerners began seeing the dance.

I am guessing here, so bear with me.

Why might this be the moment? As Dr. Nagwa Adra points out, Westerners expect meaning in art. Yet Oriental dance is decidedly abstract, a representation of the music and the dancer's feeling from the music. It doesn't tell a story as such, though it may reference the words of a song. For most dancers, it's celebration, stress release, and a form of play. Of course, for professional dancers, the only kind any Westerners could get to see, it is more than play—it is their livelihood. So they might put more pizzazz into their dance, since they have to separate themselves from the crowd, but still.

In addition, the pro dancers (such as the Algerian Ouled Naïl), did many kinds of dance; not only did they perform dances that might have been varieties of belly dance. And some were rather racy, such as the infamous *Dance of the Bee* (or wasp or whatever—there were versions of *the Bee* in many lands, including Egypt, so the idea got around). The dancer pretends to have a bee caught up in her voluminous clothing, *all* of which must be removed during the frenzied hunt for the creature. The Ouled Naïl were famous courtesans; such dances probably helped move the business along.

However, dances such as *the Bee* seem to have been invented for Westerners. In *Flute of Sand*, Lawrence Morgan's lovely 1956 memoir of his time with the Ouled Naïl, Morgan reports that during the Dance of the Bee, the Arab musicians had to play with their backs turned, and that as he became closer to the women, they required Morgan, too, to turn his back. Morocco cites Flaubert, who reported that when he made the famous courtesan Kutchuk Hanem dance naked for him, she obliged her musicians to be blindfolded. Therefore, naked dance was clearly developed to please the foreign trade (nice dance; can you take your clothes off?).

Westerners were used to there being meaning in art, whereas Eastern art was primarily decorative, functional, or designed to entrain meditative states. Most Westerners would not know this (or care). They saw the swaying bodies, the sensuality of the hips, and they thought, SEX.

So that became the meaning of the dance—it was a representation of sex and sexuality, and *therefore immoral*—which fit perfectly with the Western image of the Sensual East, the harems, and all that Orientalist jazz. Hence, we get origin stories of the dance such as women used it to compete for the Sultan's attention. They may have, but, as Morocco notes, they are more likely to have used it to amuse themselves and each other, as women do all over the East, rather than for sexy dance-offs to catch His Majesty's eye.

Islam is traditionally fine with sexual pleasure within marriage, and fine with women's sexual desire—again, within marriage. Ali ibn Abi Talib, the cousin and son-in-law of the prophet Muhammad (peace be upon him), and leader of Islam in the late 600s, has been famously quoted as saying that, "God created sexual desire in ten parts; then he gave nine parts to women and one to men." This is pretty accurate. Human women have a capacity for sexual pleasure that is rare in the mammalian world. Women don't need to be fertile to desire or enjoy sex. They can have multiple orgasms. Women can come all night and still be ready for more. Yowza!

But this is part of what makes women scary, because what if you can't keep up? How do you satiate this paragon of desire?)

Ali ibn Abi Talib spoke in the early days of Islam, when women gained many rights compared to pre-Islamic times. Many of those rights have since been eroded; women veil to "protect themselves" from the gaze of men, female genital mutilation (FGM) took over Africa (Egypt has an astronomical rate of FGM), and sex outside marriage is judged severely, even if the woman has been raped. It is so harsh that a woman who engages in any way with a man not of her family can, in some parts of the culture, be regarded as irredeemably tainted, and her own family may kill her for this transgression—even if she did not initiate or welcome the contact.

We don't have quite these strictures in the West, but we are not innocent, either. Sex in the West is and has been decidedly problematic.

Smash…

Western cultures tend to be mired in sexual conflict. In the USA, we have this ongoing madonna/whore divide that comes straight from our Puritan forbears. People feel guilty about taking pleasure in the body. It's quite tiresome. We have historically been fascinated by sex, yet also ashamed of it, viewing women's sexuality with suspicion even as we are tormented by desire.

In the West, we have long been told that women don't like sex but they have to put up with it—because children, and hey, men have needs (anger and lust, remember? If they don't get to satisfy the lust, they get angry). Women have been routinely shamed and punished for expressing their sexuality or for being nonconformist. This is so common that attributing sexual behavior is a go-to terror tactic—from high-school slut-shaming to rape apology, it is all the victim's fault.

Did Western sexual disgust (coupled with our vaunted superiority) infect the East and push them to view their own culture with dismay? This is my guess, and it wouldn't surprise me. Many colonialist views, including homophobia and racism, have tainted the East's relationship with its own culture. For example, the East was historically pragmatic and even agreeable about same-sex relationships, particularly among men; now this is a moral crime—and the colonizers certainly viewed it as such, even as they sought out boys for their own pleasure. The same could go for that other reluctant obsession, sexy dancing girls. Shame is hidden; thus, it festers and grows more toxic.

I wondered about this. I asked, but no one knew.

Finally, I got an answer.

I met Dr. Mo Geddawi, *drmogeddawi.com*, in 2017 at Yasmina Ramzy's Blossom Festival. Dr. Mo, Egyptian born and raised, has an historical understanding of Egyptian culture. He is a co-founder of the iconic Reda troupe and an expert on Oriental dance. He loves the dance so much he snuck into a nightclub as a child to meet Taheyya Karioca.

I asked Dr. Mo if British colonial attitudes towards sex had fueled the Egyptian love/hate relationship with the dance.

Absolutely, he replied.

Dr. Mo explained that the masses never had a problem with the dance itself, even though the ruling class, religious view had a moral issue with women dancing in public. However, the British *saw the dance itself as immoral.* Their colonial disdain indeed became internalized by the ruling and upper classes. Hence *the dance itself* became a problematic activity. A perfect storm of "public dancers are slutty" became conflated with the Western "dance = sex." Thanks, British colonialism, for this little gem. It's painful to realize that we in the West started this problem all by ourselves. But it is so. And it is sad.

This shift highlights a few things that have long plagued the dance, one being the sex aspect and the other equally insidious—something that has reached dizzying heights in recent times: the valuing of the outside (the visible) over the inside (the feeling).

Focus on the outside

Traditionally, the dancer's ability, musicality, knowledge, beauty and joy were all highly valued. However, if sex was the main meaning of the dance, the dancer's appearance became the most important thing. If the purpose of the dance is a sexual thrill, then it matters that the dancer is beautiful (anything else reflecting poorly upon the viewer's taste). Skill in dance was still important, but the dance was put in service to the viewer's fantasy.

This sexualized view of the dance came with it to the West, was encouraged by the choice of the term belly dance, and firmly plastered into place by an impresario's decision to put the dancers in a tent and declare them too raunchy for delicate female eyes. There followed a stream of Little Egypts, hoochie koochie dancers, and Salomes, all clearly understood to be sexualized, naughty, and titillating. The nudge-nudge, wink-wink has followed us ever since.

Dance was frowned upon in the West in many circles as well—especially in America, which was founded, let us remember, by Puritans, religious extremists who were not allowed to practice in their home country. Plus, misogyny is alive and well all over the world. The ensuing disdain is so pervasive that it is no wonder this view now infects the dancers themselves...

Our baggage

It's a funny thing to be a belly dancer.

We wear revealing, blingy costumes and then get huffy when anyone looks at our breasts or expects us to be sexual (and sometimes if they don't). Question: Why are you wearing that if you don't want attention? Answer: I can wear whatever I damn well please. Who are you to police my choices? One male friend, at his first-ever belly dance event, looked around the room full of women in every shade of sexy outfit and said, "Oh, I get it. This is not about sex at all. It's about expression."

Boom.

On the one hand, Western dancers tend to feel balky and suspicious when anyone (even a lover) expects them to dance as foreplay. The dance does not feel sexual to them. On the other, we have a greater public that equates belly dance with stripping—the purpose of which they also believe is sexual arousal. It's funny that neither strippers nor belly dancers see their dance that way. But the expectation creeps in anyway, to all kinds of havoc.

One thing that happens is that dancers divorce themselves from the sensuality of the dance. They present a whitewashed dance devoid of lusciousness, earthiness, or *dala3* (playfulness and sexual confidence), even though they are clothed in a two-piece bling-fest that emphasizes their breasts and hips. Then there is the opposite pole on the spectrum—a hyper-sexualized dance, complete with "porn face," lip-licking, and come-hither seduction.

Neither approach helps our cause. The Western obsession with sex (coupled with the demonization of women and women's sexuality), pushes us to take sides—good girl or bad? It's important for us to reject this dualistic trap. Bodies are inherently sexual. All of them. It's not a big deal. We are humans, and we have bodies. If you don't like it, don't look. A shocking number of people let their children watch traumatizing bloody violence on TV or in films—but wring their hands over the wonder of a beautiful moving body. They have worse problems than we do. But I digress...

Sure, dancers' styles vary; this one more serene and that one more passionate. We are all different. But when the focus is on the feeling, none of that matters. The dance is still in service to the music and the shared experience of joy. It's a benediction. When the focus changes to the *outside*, our interest turns to how the dancer looks. And what the dancer does. The dancer —and the dance—become objects.

Suddenly a lot of other things change. There is now more pressure on the dance to be whizz-bang—and more pressure on the dancer too. This is *not* a difference between Art and Entertainment. Both suffer from the same issue. This *is* a difference between Us and Them, between a shared experience and objectification. It's also about social mores and internalized oppression. When society says over and over (and over) that the dance is about sex, that women are either madonnas or whores, that clothing defines the woman, and that women who have or enjoy sex are sluts, it puts a lot of pressure on everyone, both dancer and guest.

Belly Dance and the Male Gaze

A little recap: In the conservative Eastern view, belly dancers are regarded poorly because they show their bodies in public (this is sadly common in the West, too). This is a religious concern. Historically, this public visibility is the problematic part (and the two-piece costume only makes it worse. Even appearing fully clothed is a problem).

Professional dancers are the antithesis of a "good" woman—they show their bodies, boss men around, and generally act like men rather than women. However, Western influence added a new layer of shame—that *the dance itself* is sexual—the dancers move their bodies in seductive ways and the *purpose of the dance* is male arousal. As we have seen, this wasn't the deal before. Being a *dancer* was bad—but the dance *itself* wasn't inherently dirty or bad—look at all the dancers publicly performing at weddings, in streets, and at *moulids* (Saint's Day festivals), not to mention *millions* of women dancing at home. Nobody hid their children's eyes when the dancer came on. The whole family enjoyed the show—unlike here in the West, where I know at least one person whose mom hid his eyes when dancing girls appeared in those Biblical epics. And his family was not even religious.

The dance itself has important social functions—as a social ritual it is highly valued. Does this distinction make sense? It's important. Professional *dancers* were disdained for showing their bodies. It's okay to watch them and you need one at your wedding, but you wouldn't be one, marry one, let your son marry one, or let your daughter become one. But dance performers as part of celebrations were important, and dance *per se* brought no shame.

Western dancers, of course, think that demeaning dancers is a disgusting point of view; many don't even want to dance for a Middle Eastern audience. The popular touch point is, "Why would I want to dance for someone who thinks I'm a whore?" And really, why would you? (NB: This disdain of the Eastern audience is a sad change, as in the West, it was the Greek, Turkish, and Lebanese clubs that kept the dance alive, kept the music and the musicians alive, and wholeheartedly supported dance and dancers. Many dancers had excellent, respectful relationships with these long-standing clubs.

This is part of what September 11th killed, but also times have changed. It's not so easy to run a club, and everyone has become more jaded. I was thrilled when lovely Australian dancer Rachel Bond, *inspirebellydance.com.au*, brought me to Tony's Family Restaurant, a Lebanese supper club in Sydney that still keeps the old school model—tables of excellent mezze, main dishes at midnight, live music, a dancer, entire families out late enjoying the fun.)

Sadly, the common Western view of belly dancers (and women is general) is not much better than the Eastern. It is maybe kept a bit more tightly under wraps, the veneer of civilization may be a bit thicker, but underneath, it is just as bad. Many people still see belly dance and stripping as having the same purpose—the sexual stimulation of men. This is why feminists used to be against belly dance—they thought the dancers were sex slaves to the male gaze.

Why do people confuse belly dance with stripping?

Maybe it's because there are a lot of similarities. Belly dance favors small spaces, intimacy, and close contact with the audience. Just like stripping. Dancers are tipped—including on the body, in their costumes, and with money showers. Just like strippers. They have stage names. Just like strippers. So we have to constantly prove we're not strippers. We have often done this by shaming strippers—because strippers are dirty and do what they do for sex—

and by "stripping" the sexuality from our dance. We don't do it for sex! We are not all about sex! Those dirty strippers are nothing like us!

Are they?

Dr. Judith Hanna, *judithhanna.com*, a researcher and author, specializes in dance as communication. She has often served as an expert witness in strip-club court cases, defending strippers as artists in their own right. In her book, *Naked Truth*, Dr. Hanna explains that strippers generally don't think that what they do is all about sex, either. They don't appreciate the idea that they must be prostitutes because they dance. They don't want to be ogled, pawed, or any of those other things. Strippers have to hide the work they do or face public recrimination. In the East, belly dancers have this same problem (as do many belly dancers in the West).

What's more, the prevalent perception is that stripping and strip clubs increase sex crimes, degrade neighborhoods, and cause a general rise in crime. But Dr. Hanna shows that all of these accusations are outright lies fabricated by the radical Christian Right (who have their own law schools to teach their flock how to attack strip venues, among other things). Instead, well-designed studies show repeatedly that the presence of "Gentlemen's Clubs" mean safer, more peaceful neighborhoods and higher property values. Dr. Hanna's book, *Naked Truth* is a fascinating, recommended read that documents this massive fiction. In addition, she cites studies that find men who watch women dancing sensually are mellower and more relaxed than men who don't. Maybe belly dancing (and stripping) are public services.

Stripping is a public service?

Surprisingly, your average gentleman's club (or wedding, or moulid), models a sense of respect towards the dancer. When fundamentalists intentionally destroy this, such as the shocking disrespect and gang violence against women fostered by the Muslim Brotherhood in Cairo in the wake of the 2011 revolution, it's another, much more dangerous, story. And it gets creepier.

Leila Farid, an in-demand professional dancer in Cairo and the world Arab community for over a decade, mentioned to me that since the revolution, there had been a lot more belly dance on television in Cairo. But unlike the classic black and white films available before, it was highly sexualized. She wondered why the Brotherhood would allow that to be shown. I suggested that the idea was to degrade the very idea of dancers and the dance, to make them easier targets for cleansing, and she stared at me in horror. I may be jaded, but it would not surprise me in the least. This is the scariest way that belly dance is like stripping: they are targets of religious fanatics.

A friend of mine used to be a stripper. The guy who hired her showed her the ropes, how to handle a feather boa and take off her gloves, and sent her out on stage. She loved it! It was fun; she felt sexy and powerful. The guests respected and adored her, and she made a lot of money. What's not to like? Little by little, however, the situation changed. More and more, her power and choice were stripped away. Soon enough, she was expected to simply go out and dance naked. That's when she quit. Where's the fun in that?

There is a fairly constant pressure on us as belly dancers, even in the West, to do the equivalent of dancing naked. As the culturally-aware audience has faded, we have become sexy wallpaper for hookah bars and corporate events. It becomes less and less about the art, the fun, the joy, and more about being a trick pony in someone else's sideshow, doing what we're told rather than glorying in our own agency.

Stripping is not to blame. Strippers are under this same pressure. It is a patriarchal power play designed to make us conform to their rules, feel ashamed of our own sexuality, and frame us as disreputable harlots who get what they have coming to them.

The Christian Right, certain ultra-orthodox Jewish sects, and fundamentalist Salafist Muslims like the Taliban, Da'esh, and the Muslim Brotherhood are all on the same page. Among their other crimes, they are weapons of patriarchy who deprive men of their feelings and keep women in their place as submissive breeders, servants, and property. Patriarchy, religious fundamentalism, misogyny, homophobia, and racism are all connected and have done immeasurable damage to humans, men and women, worldwide.

You would think that women—who go through this stuff and know how bad it feels—would be more considerate.

You would be wrong.

We beat up ourselves—and each other

Internalized oppression

This is the tough one. When people are oppressed, they often take on the characteristics and opinions of the oppressor. They don't even realize it. This, for example, is why there is color discrimination (aka "light" privilege), in the black community. Even in Egypt, which has a wide range of skin tones, light-skinned dancers are more popular and respected than darker dancers, such as Mona el Said. According to Morocco, Mona had to become *very* popular in the UK before she ever got a five-star job in Cairo.

Women are not immune to internalized oppression. For a long time, prosecutors of rape cases didn't want women on the juries. Why? Women were far more likely than men to blame the victim for the crime. What were you wearing? Why were you walking there? What did you do to make this happen? We women are so used to blaming ourselves for unwanted attention, we do it in our sleep. With good reason.

A woman I know was raped at the age of eleven. The (male) judge *let her attacker off*, calling her "preternaturally seductive." At *eleven*. And this was over forty years ago. I'm sorry, but eleven-year-old girls, no matter what they do or wear (or not), don't know any better. They are too young to understand the gravity of their actions. Grown men are supposed to.

Girls today are often expected to have sexual relations with their boyfriends or risk losing them. How is this liberation? The message here is that all the rest of us better wrap up in our burqas, because men can't help it. It's all our fault, and we better get used to it. What, and you *dance*? That dirty dance that's all about sex? In *public*? In *that outfit*? You clearly deserve what you get.

∼

Women may live with fear, but that doesn't stop us from adopting the oppressor's values and practices. Woodrow "Asim" Hill, *raqsstorm.org*, is a male belly dancer. He's straight, by the way—not gay. He told me of the indignities he endured, the objectification, the sexualizing, the panties thrown—by women dancers. Yeah. The same women who fume on social media about (Western) men's unwelcome sexual advances. It became so confusing and difficult for him that he gained a lot of weight and stopped dancing.

He is quick to point out that what he endured pales beside what women endure on a daily basis, but that didn't make it any less traumatic. He also described the strip club in his former hometown. That club has a ladies' night. On the men's nights, the place is quiet, respectful, and relaxed. On ladies' night, it's like the Wild West, screaming women rushing the stage, grabbing dancers, the works.

You might say that he lives in a strange place, but this type of behavior is quite common. So this whole confusing dialectic is far more pervasive than we might imagine or like to think. During the presidential primaries in 2016, the USA became mired in an ultra-right-wing "Christian" conservative race to the bottom, to see who could promote the most reactionary, rape-apologist, woman-hating, sexist agenda, and they were all winning. It's not an isolated problem.

So how do we push back? Or at least sidestep? Because you get what you pay attention to, so ignoring the whole mess may be the best defense.

At the end of this chapter is a list of ideas. Before we go there, let's take a look at how the dancer's sensuality, sexuality, and personality are expressed in the East.

Sex and dance

Back in the 70s, a gal in one of Bobby's classes bemoaned her boyfriend's antipathy towards her dancing. A tall, willowy blonde, she was torn because her boyfriend so hated that she performed. But the boyfriend had no job and they needed money (at that time in NYC, you could make a living dancing in clubs). The issue was sex (to be more exact, jealousy). There she was, putting her body on display for other men. I was mystified by this response. I later saw the woman perform and was even more mystified. She was the Ice Queen. How could anyone regard what she did as sexual?

I was only a teenager then. I would have my own experience with that mindset later on. And many of us have struggled with this conundrum. Our partners abhor our public dancing, yet we feel called to dance. The dance gets the blame. Belly dance may well have wrecked a few marriages, but often because it undermines patriarchal control. The dance gives us a sense of agency, freedom, and connection (not to mention joy) that is rare in our culture.

However, in attempting to bridge the gap between our desire to dance and other people's perception of it, we often resort to ridding our dance of its sensuality and sexual confidence. We become prim and proper. We hate on other women's sexuality as it may reflect badly upon ourselves—or the dance. This also connects to our issues of perfectionism and self-denial.

The other side of this coin is an in-your-face sexuality bereft of playfulness or joy. This may manifest as a directness designed to intimidate or by becoming the expectation of the "sexy" dancer. There is also plenty of confusion. For example, skimpy costumes paired with a nervous rejection of sexuality. We can do much better.

Many, many dancers perform with confidence, openness, and joy. They neither push what they have, nor do they hide it. They enjoy the dance, their guests, and themselves, radiating confidence and playfulness. It is this happy medium to which we aspire. In that vein, let's take a look at how the dancer's sensuality, sexuality, and personality are expressed in the East (remember, by East, in this book, we mean the lands of this dance's origin). By understanding the cultural context of the dance, we can find clues for how to let go of our baggage and open ourselves to our own beauty and power.

Eastern dancers, in general, display playfulness, humor, and sexual confidence. They interact with their guests and enjoy themselves and their dance. This runs the gamut from the audacious Turkish dancers Asena and Birgul Beray to the sweet, demure Golden Age film stars, Taheyya Karioka and Samia Gamal. Birgul lusts after guests, adjusts her bra on stage and generally shows that she is more woman than anyone in the room can possibly handle. Asena strides around her stage clearly not giving a damn about what anyone else thinks. Samia is the epitome of kitten-like playfulness, while Taheyya exudes quiet joy. And this is not limited to women. Bobby Farrah, Tito Seif, and many other male dancers, also show this warmth, charm, and confident playfulness. Though different from one another, all exhibit the Eastern concept of *dala3*.

Dala3 (دلع)

Dala3 (aka dela', dallua, dallal, and other spellings) is an Arabic word usually translated as flirtatious, or as treasured, pampered, or spoiled. It is often referenced in Egyptian belly dance as sex appeal. It is pronounced da-LA; the 3 represents the Arabic letter ayn (ع), which sounds like a little growl, so you want to close the throat at the end of the word. Dala3 is related to several English words; for example, *adore*, ('dalaal, dallal (v) 'to treat kindly, to pamper'); *Dally* and *dalliance*, ('dalliance, loving treatment' or dalah 'love'); and *dear*, (from the Arabic dalaal 'endearment' or dalah 'to go mad in love)' (Jassem 2013. doi: 10.11648/j.ijll.20130104.13, and a fascinating read). These words evoke the loving sensuality of the dance, and the pleasurable relationship between dancer and guests.

Does dala3 mean we have to be twinkly and sweet all the time?

Of course not.

In the West, dala3 has often been reduced to an array of mannerisms supposed to be cute and flirtatious. These may even be choreographed into a piece to be repeated precisely. But dala3 is not necessarily cute and frilly, and it is certainly not carbon copies. Look at the dancers mentioned in this section. Their styles range widely. Dancers may be commanding, coy, or anything else, depending upon their intention and personality. What all these dancers share, however, is a grounded, sensual confidence. Let's get a little more deeply into this concept of dala3 and open it up into something more genuine.

Dala3 is not a bid for approval. It is not about being seductive, sexual, or cutesy, or making an effort to please.

It is a statement of innate adorability. Dala3 bespeaks sexual confidence, a playful, flirtatious quality. A confident, playful dancer, in touch with her body, expressing joy in the moment, has dala3. According to Sahara Saeeda, the 'Alimah, or learned woman, is seen as the über-woman, so drenched in her femaleness that she is irresistible. She may not smile, but she knows her power. She certainly has dala3.

A different example is Taheyya Karioca in the 1946 film 'Lea'bet al Set' (The Lady's Puppet لعبة الست). She condescends to dance while rolling her eyes and chewing gum. Her character does not need to dance to the song, or to get any approval. She is not being sweet, cute, or eager to please. She is, in fact, bored. But she has confidence, allure, no matter what she does. She displays dala3.

We are not talking a few gestures here. Dala3 is an attitude, an ethos that permeates the dancer and makes her delicious. It evokes the confidence and playfulness of one who is treasured and expects to be treated lovingly. It evokes the safety and special nature the dancer brings to any event—she is there to make the party and to bring everyone together.

When we have dala3, we are beautiful (no matter what we look like). We are glorious, sensual beings. We enjoy that. We revel in it. It is a quality that infuses every step we take. We have the confidence to play—to joke even about ourselves and to create that warm, enchanted space where everyone feels special. It is attitude that makes a dancer irresistible. Not her looks, nor even her skill. It's personality and charm. It's the love she brings to the table. It is a laughing acknowledgment of all the above.

I've got a secret...
When we have dala3, we have a lovely, joyous secret. It surrounds us wherever we go, trailing after us like the *sillage* of an expensive perfume. We can turn it on and off, show it or not, but it is always there. It is our secret. Because of it, we do not have to push. Our existence is enough. The Eastern dancer excels in this resting place of glory. She expresses this mystique in her oblique presentation. She casts sidelong glances and presents herself on the diagonal. She recycles her energy, extending it outward only so far before pulling it back into herself.

Morocco observes that female dancers of the culture almost never start their show on stage facing the guests, as that would be uncomfortable for the guests. Instead, they tend to start on a diagonal, with the back to audience, or come from offstage.

Amity Alize observes that Eastern dancers tend to keep their fire on the inside. They choose when to show it, to whom, and how much. Eastern dancers pull you towards them. In contrast, she finds that Western dancers often have their fire outside, on all the time, gusting at the guests, amp turned up to eleven, pushing rather than allowing, "Look at me" rather than "Here, have some joy." Morocco notes that as her own dance improved, she stopped dancing to get the audience to like her, and began dancing so the guests would have a good time.

Is this magnetic quality a cultural thing or a personality thing? Certainly, it is an Eastern cultural value. But anyone can cultivate a delicious quality of "I've got a secret." I have long tended towards that, but I also had good teachers. In any case, I have intentionally built that quality into my dance for years without having a sense of it being Eastern per se because it suits me and I like it.

Dala3

What drives this quality of dala3?

Perhaps Eastern dancers express themselves indirectly because it is too dangerous to do otherwise. Their level of personal danger due to cultural taboos and restrictions is much higher than that of most Western dancers. This may be true (most women on the planet must be careful), but there are further elements that inform the Eastern dancer's allure.

Eastern women understand that the sight of them is so powerful that it entrances men. This is the flip side of that double-edged sword. On the one side, there is that "men can't help themselves so you better cover up" trope (which insults all humans, but whatever). On the other, being magically irresistible by your very existence carries a *lot* of power. It has nothing to do with being pretty—it is all about being a woman. As women, we hold a heaping helping of sexual power. It's a conundrum.

In the West, we've been fed this same garbage about men—they can't help it, and if only we had worn something frumpier, or better yet stayed home, we wouldn't be in this mess. But we were never given any sense of power. We take no glory in the marvel that we are, only shame. We are instead told that attraction is a function of physical beauty (focus on the outside), *and* that we are never beautiful enough (thank you, endless ads for beauty and weight-loss products). We are also pitted against one another, for beauty is framed as hierarchical—we are more or less beautiful than others.

Thus, we waste our lives in constant competition for approval. We have to put ourselves out, tart ourselves up, and generally abase ourselves to get approval from the über-Daddy. Girls are still told to act like adoring twits or boys won't like them (and if boys don't like them they are nothing). We are responsible for the happiness of everyone around us, but nobody is responsible for us. We internalize all this liability of being women, but *none of the glory*. Where is our glory? Where is our rich thrill for the wonder of being born a woman?

In the West, we are pushed to be sexual on demand (and reviled if we do it on our own), but not permitted access to confidence or glory. Our value, based upon our attractiveness, is never enough. The sexual rage of the West is as confusing and dangerous as that of the East, even though (or because), it is more hidden. We don't have honor killings in the West, for example, yet alarming numbers of women are battered or murdered by intimate partners every day. Yes, these numbers have dropped in recent decades, but they are still far too high.

We don't have to settle for this.

As we open up the word dala3, we find a trove of riches. It's more than a few flirty gestures lifted from dancers of origin. This playful behavior expresses a place of love and an expectation of loving treatment. It speaks to dearness, a delight that we have been forbidden from lavishing upon ourselves or accepting from others.

It's time to love and accept ourselves, to accept our glory and power. Many of us think of power as power over. This is power *of*. We have the power of love, of courage, of joy.

Consider the constraints on Eastern women. The danger in which they place themselves as performers is incredible. Their courage is humbling. It's a miracle they can be playful, loving, or kind. Yet they are, despite huge odds.

We, too, can do this.

We have all been treated badly at some time. Both women and men, we have all felt helpless. We have all lived a portion of our lives in fear. This is human. To let go of fear and pain, to treasure and love ourselves, to have compassion for ourselves and for those around us—a heart-opening stance.

It's time to come from a place of love. It's time to find our joy, our center, our balance, as men and women. To be so confident, loving, and strong that we can afford to laugh and tease—this, to me, is the essence of dala3. This is where we want to be.

Solutions

How do we bring these concepts into our dance? Here are some ideas...

- Let go of being "sexy." When we put on a "sexy" show because we think that's what's expected of us, we play right into the hands of those who would destroy us. Instead, allow yourself to genuinely enjoy your own dance and share that joy with your guests.
- Cultivate dala3. Embrace the dance's playfulness and sensuality. Have fun. Flirt. Engage with people. Treasure yourself. Let your body enjoy the dance and the music. Love yourself. Let it show. Share joy with the guests. "Aren't we all having a wonderful time!" Each of us can be herself. This is our true style.
- Radiate love and compassion. Love your guests. Include them in your radiance. Dance is a healing force in the world. Bring this joy into the every day. Let your light shine.
- Love your sisters. Strippers are our dance sisters. They have it a lot rougher than we do. Let's not add to it. Besides, when the Right has finished them off, who's next? "When they came for the strippers, I did not stand up, because I was not a stripper…"
- Occupy Belly Dance. In the parlance of Occupy Wall Street, to occupy something is to inhabit it with political, economic, and social consciousness. Bring your consciousness to your dance. For more on this idea, see *occupybellydance.com*.
- Bring men into the dance. It's good for everyone.
- Lead by example. When you do the right thing, you give others permission to do so. One person makes a difference. Stick to your principles and be matter of fact about it. Some of us live in areas where this is extremely difficult. Tread softly, and take comfort knowing we are all with you. As we each create a cell of good living, we create ripples in the pond. Those ripples travel ever outward. Slowly, more of us make ripples, then waves.

We change the world, one undulation at a time. One of the ways we do this is by letting go of our preconceived ideas, patterns, and stylized responses—both in dance and in life. This is how we find our true selves in the dance, our personal style—by discovering how our own body feels, understands, and represents the music.

Yes, improvisation.

PART III
BRING THE JOY

"I looked in temples, churches, and mosques. But I found the Divine within my heart." —Rumi

9

IMPROVISATION—THE BELLY DANCE BÊTE NOIRE

Why all this fuss about improvisation?

I came to belly dance in the early 70s, in the heyday of the NYC nightclub scene. The snazzier nightclubs had big shows with live orchestras and several dancers per night, booked for months at a time. Elena Lentini told me that each dancer had his or her own music; that same music was played for them every night for months. Yet the vast majority of dancers improvised. Why?

Partly because that is how the dance was done—but also because all the music was live and the musicians improvised, so they played the same song, but different every time. You danced your feeling from the music. Your dance may have had similar elements over time, you might set some of the structure, but the dance was never exactly the same, because the music was never the same and neither were you. The whole thing was quite glorious, a heady experience for dancers, musicians, and guests.

Improvisation has a lot going for it—yet it has fallen out of fashion in the West, in a big way. In a little while we will look deeply at its benefits. But first, let's dissect some of the more insidious myths that have pushed improvisation off the table—that it's not art, that it's laziness, that it takes "natural talent." Then we will examine some surprising reasons for these beliefs. There's also a whole series about this on my blog, *aliathabit.com/enjoy-practice*.

1. The first myth is that improvisation is somehow less artistic then choreography. Real art is in composing a piece and fitting it all together,

making a beautiful piece of jewelry out of carefully chosen beads of movement; whereas improvisation is merely scattered beads rolling around on stage.

Of course, choreography is an art. But improvisation is also an art—a generous art, as it willingly gives itself up, dance after dance, never to be repeated. It is art created in the moment, a unique expression of the artists and guests, channeling everyone's feeling into one shared experience. A good dancer embodies an entire madly improvising orchestra, expresses through movement the emotional timbres that she feels in the moment, revels in the sensuality of her movement in a beautiful way, and shares all that with a room full of guests. If you think such an accomplishment is a lesser art, I invite you to try it.

2. The second myth is that improvisation is lazy. Choreographers work hard to compose durable works of art; improvisers throw something together after they get on stage. Well, yes, they might. But that "throw something together" has a thick cushion of effort and focus behind it. It takes high levels of skill to open the body to the music and express something real and beautiful. There is a lot of practice behind that effortless flow.

As with the musicians, technique is the servant of expression—dancers open themselves to the shifts and nuances in the music, as musicians open themselves to the dancer. And, while most dancers work with recorded music, bringing something fresh to a recording takes skill. It's not easy—good dancers make it look that way.

3. There is also the conflicting notion that improvisation is too hard. It doesn't come easily, as it seems it should (since it looks so easy). Highly skilled dancers who have been trained to copy and repeat choreography may be left flustered and adrift when there is no pre-recorded movement string. They stumble—and they don't like it.

Improvisation is a skill.

It can be learned. And real learning (as opposed to the amassing of information) is generally painful and unattractive. Everything we already know is easier to do than learning a new skill. So, for a dancer raised in choreography, stylization, and repetition, yes, it's going to be challenging—at first. And that's okay. We have all learned to welcome the discomfort of muscles given good use; we can learn to welcome the discomfort of our brain learning new skills. Most things worth learning involve challenge, stepping outside our comfort zones. The important thing is believing that it's possible. And it is.

The next set of obstacles includes the fixed mindset that equates mistakes and difficulty with failure and the subsequent desire to destroy the evidence (those grapes were sour anyway). When people don't understand the mechanisms of learning, or don't understand how to learn (or teach) improvisation, they tend to dismiss it out of hand rather than risk the shame of failure. Improvisational ability may then be disdained as something that can't be taught. It requires "natural talent," which one is born with.

No. Modern learning science simply blows this out of the water. Skills are acquired through deliberate practice and systematic application of effort. Look at the history of anyone with "natural talent," those prodigies who are fantastic at their craft from a young age. You will see a monumental application of effort that took place long before you and I were plunking out a few keys on the piano. (For more on mindset and learning science, see *bellydancesoul.com/resources*. For more on learning improvisation, see *aliathabit.com/effortless*).

Those who excel in choreography have put in many hours learning how to copy, repeat, and remember movement strings. We forget how hard it was to learn this—partly because the learning happened when we were young, and partly because once we master something, we can't remember what it was like before we did (biological fact).

It is humbling, scary, and painful to be a beginner again—but that is what we must be, over and over, when we want to embrace our best selves, adventurous, curious, and free. Learning something new takes a lot of effort and concentration—it literally makes your brain hurt—but intelligence has been clearly shown to be malleable. Learning new things literally increases our intelligence and capacity to learn even more things. Any investment in genuine learning thus pays off in miracles down the road. Let's get started.

The Benefits of Improvisation

Improvisation is not merely a quaint thing that people do in traditional belly dance. It is a powerful tool with far-reaching effects. Because we turn off the scurrying, thinking, judging aspects of our minds, improvisation allows us to access deeper layers of creativity than we can when in editor mode. We get these benefits (and see improvisation in action), in any creative enterprise, be it writing, painting, music, or movement.

But there are some special benefits to improvisation coupled with Oriental dance. In this section, we will look at the benefits of improvisation for the mind, body, and soul, especially when coupled with the music and movement of Oriental dance. Up first is mind, the effects of improvisation on our brain and thought processes. There are some dang good reasons to gird up that hip scarf and enter the improvisation fray. Among them are increased intelligence, ongoing brain health (of the first magnitude), and heightened creativity. Not bad, eh?

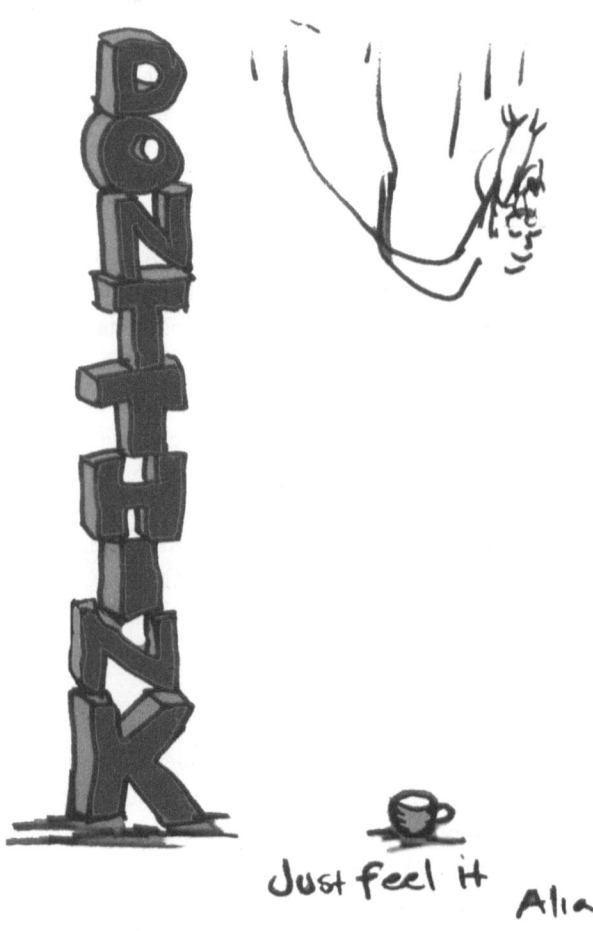

Don't think...

10

MIND

Dancing makes you smarter

Back in college, I took a piano class. I had often plunked around on a piano, but proper keyboard technique, even which keys corresponded to which notes, was a mystery to me. In the class, I learned how to find the notes, make chords, and play simple songs. It was unspeakably, shamefully difficult—to remember, to execute, to do anything at all. I totally sucked at piano, a beginner in the worst possible way. It literally hurt my brain.

At the same time, I was teaching writing at the college level. Ah, the irony of being simultaneously a beginner and an expert. I viscerally understood how my writing students felt, being asked to do hard things with which they had no experience, feeling stupid, slow, and clumsy. This is how everyone feels when learning challenging new skills. It's hard. It hurts. It's infuriating, and you feel like a chump. Why bother, we think. This is dumb and I will never be any good. Why bother?

The more challenging the material, the worse we feel. But there is a secret thing happening when we feel this way. The secret is this: difficulty and frustration when learning new skills are *signs of neural enhancement*. They are *not* symptoms of failure, but success.

Wait, what?

Many of us believe that we are born with a certain level of smarts, talent, or whatever, and that's it. If we are smart, talented, etc., a task is easy. If we are not, it's hard. If something is hard, we are not smart enough. Except, surprise! That's wrong. Advances in neuroscience show us that intelligence is highly malleable. We *increase our intelligence* by learning new things. The brain, like a muscle, grows more powerful with use. It *literally* changes overnight as we learn new skills. This has been observed, studied, and documented.

Many of us suffer shame when confronted with difficult tasks, avoid anything that might make us look awkward or stupid, and turn away rather than face failure. But the fact is, when we struggle, we exercise the "muscle" of the brain. Like any exercise, it hurts at first—one feels sore and tired. But muscles develop and get stronger, and so do the neural pathways in the brain—plus, the brain makes new neural pathways when we learn new skills.

Learning new skills is one of the best ways to keep the brain in good health (and true learning comes only with effort). Learning develops new neural pathways. Repeated practice wraps these pathways in *myelin*, a white, tape-like structure in the brain that reinforces neural pathways. Dementia, Alzheimer's, Parkinson's and several other diseases destroy myelin. They are diseases of *demyelinization*. We forget how to do things and what things are. Pretty soon, we are loading the laundry into the freezer and brushing our teeth with face cream.

My Mom has dementia. Day by day, her memories and skills unravel. She can no longer make a phone call or a cup of coffee. She can still use a toilet, but at some point, that will go, too. Her myelin is peeling off and falling away in ragged tatters, like some apocryphal Abstract Impressionist painting made with house paint.

It's too late for my Mom. But the rest of us, the more we consistently learn and problem-solve in the moment, the more myelin we produce, the more we strengthen and protect our brains.

~

What is exactly is myelin, and how is it formed? How does it relate to belly dance? When we learn a new skill, we create new neural pathways. These pathways are like maps of the new skill in the brain; they are the route the brain takes when we execute the skill. At first, with only a few scattered neurons, the pathways are faint and we stumble often in our execution. But as we practice skillfully and eliminate errors, as we learn to balance on our two feet or our two-wheel bike, those neural pathways get reinforced. Each time we practice, we scatter more neurons along the path. Once we have a critical mass, the brain realizes the new pathway is here to stay, and wraps it in myelin.

Myelin sets skills in place. The more myelin we have wrapped around our neural pathways, the stronger our skill sets (Einstein's brain was thick with myelin). But there is a catch: *whatever* we repeat over and over will get wrapped in myelin—the brain is not picky. This is why it is so hard to *un*learn something or change a habit (better to simply overlay the existing habit with something new).

We produce most of our myelin as children, when we grow our huge skill sets of being human—walking, talking, learning to read, do math, etc. However, myelin production continues at a good clip our entire lives—as long as we continue to learn. Continued learning is a key to brain health. And learning makes you smarter. Myelin literally equals smarts.

So, what's a great producer of myelin—and how do we protect the brain from Alzheimer's?

Dancing!

But not just any dancing…

Stanford University did a 21-year major study, reported in the New England Journal of Medicine, looking at how well leisure activities, both cognitive and physical (from reading to swimming and everything in between), protect the brain from dementia. Frequent dancing topped the list, reducing the risk of Alzheimer's by 76%. That is a *lot*. It was the *only* physical activity correlated to a reduced likelihood of dementia—and it had the greatest risk reduction of any activity studied, cognitive or physical. Here's a link to the study: *nejm.org/doi/full/10.1056/NEJMoa022252*.

The study didn't look at different kinds of dancing—but Richard Powers, a ballroom dance instructor at Stanford, examined the cognitive activities that were most protective and collated the findings with several other studies on brain protection. His advice is, "Involve yourself in activities which require split-second rapid-fire decision making, as opposed to rote memory (retracing the same well-worn paths), or just working on your physical style."

Split-second, rapid-fire decision making. Yes, we are talking about improvisation—and improvisation to live improvised music doubles the payoff. When we improvise, we make innumerable calculations and adjustments in the microsecond. We are not even aware of them. But they add up.

Powers further predicts that, of the couple in a ballroom dance, the one who gets the most benefit by far is the *follower*. That's right. The leader can resort to well-worn patterns in which there is no spontaneity, only repetition. The one who benefits is the one whose dance is spontaneous—the one who listens, intuits, and goes with his feeling in the moment. Hey, that sounds familiar (imagine the benefits to duet and group improvisation...)

Powers explains that, "One way to do that is to learn something new." Anything. Learning new skills will make everything else work better. And taking a dance class can be highly effective, as dancing "integrates several brain functions at once — kinesthetic, rational, musical, and emotional — further increasing your neural connectivity." This is also a good reason to study with many teachers, as the learner navigates a variety of movement patterns, music, and methodology.

Powers further asserts that a leader who embodies these same principles can find as much benefit as the follower, which has a lot to say for improvised duets and group dances. "Spontaneous leading and following both involve entering a flow state. Both leading and following benefit from a highly active attention to possibilities... That's the most succinct definition I know for intelligent dancing: a highly active attention to possibilities." You can read the full text of his article here: socialdance.stanford.edu/syllabi/smarter.htm.

It is in improvisation that we make these rapid-fire decisions, that we develop Powers' "highly active attention to possibilities." Dancing in restaurants, at parties, and in odd spaces we have to be awake—especially with live music. It's Different Every Time. But repeating choreography? Drilling established, stylized steps? Doing the same thing every time? Not so much. Repeating what we already know does not help us.

And there's more.

Dr. Marilee Nugent has been studying neuromuscular control and the stages of learning—how one goes from beginner to advanced. She presented on this in 2014 at the Sahar conference in Vancouver, BC. As she applied her research to belly dance, she found that each individual movement has an arc from beginner to expert—and the arc for each move is different. Learning one belly dance move (for example, a hip drop), does *not* prepare us to learn another. The learning curve for each is unique and distinct. Even going from one version to another, for example, from bottom-up to top-down infinity, can challenge new students (and doing that with an undulation can challenge advanced students).

What Bobby Did

Ibrahim "Bobby" Farrah had a deep understanding of the soul of this dance. As a dancer of the culture, he realized the dance is about expression of the dancer's feeling from the music, embodiment, and timing more than specific steps. He encouraged personal expression and style in all of his classes. But he did much more.

Bobby's classes in the 70s were models of learning science. One of the hottest concepts in learning today is *interleaving* and *varied practice*. This means that rather than sticking with one thing until you get it, you keep the brain always reaching. You do different things so the brain never knows what to expect. You cycle through things randomly so they are different every time. I went to Bobby's classes up to three times a week for two hours at a time. He never repeated. Never. Every single time, he did something completely different: combinations, ideas, music, everything.

There was a consistent format of options—for example, an extended combination, traveling across the floor, following Bobby as he improvised—but it was never the same combo, the floor crossing was always different (and sometimes different for each person), and the improvisation—well, that was crazy wild, and different every time, even to the same music. Carolyn Hamilton notes that, "Following someone who is improvising or doing a *loose* choreography is the most beneficial in terms of brain health. Not even the person doing the leading gets as much benefit as the follower... It's the spontaneous reacting that causes the brain to create new pathways."

Because we constantly re-encountered moves we knew conjoined in new ways and with moves we didn't, we continuously re-contextualized every move. This sort of constellation-making is another facet of high-level learning, as we encountered the familiar and the unfamiliar in multiple frameworks, different combos with different transitions to different music. We engaged in ongoing problem solving as we figured out how to do all these things within our own bodies--Bobby only broke things down if he had to, after we had struggled with the movement for ourselves, another plus. We learn more durably when we struggle to figure something out.

We were encouraged to do things differently from him and each other, to add our own style. He had other students model the combos, so we could see them on different bodies. We constantly learned new things, saw new ways that moves fit together.

The result of this multiplicity was that we learned. Fast. We learned how to marry movement to music, combine steps, and follow the music without question. We learned musicality, how to transition between moves, how to improvise, how to interpret music, how to compose, how to use a stage—without him ever saying anything about it. And we learned how to present ourselves, even though we giggled to see Bobby swan across the floor, beaming at himself in the mirror.

All the music was recorded. We had no live music in class—back then, we danced to vinyl records. But lo, when I performed, I was able to connect to the music and allow it to move me. And when I finally danced to a live band, it was like coming home. So it is more than possible to teach students how to do this. But first we have to learn how to do it ourselves. And we have to value it.

Back then, we valued improvisation. Everything was improvised. That was normal. We've looked at how and why that changed; the question is what can we do about it now? This is the question that needs answers. This is what we have set out to discover. The answer, I believe, lies in the myriad benefits of improvisation within this dance form.

However, there is a caveat: If no one eats meat or milk, soon there will be no more cows. We take care of cows because they provide us with a benefit. For improvisation to be valued, people have to discover its benefits. And to do that, they must practice. In practice, its benefits become clear.

It's a steep learning curve for folks who have been trained to copy and stylize. But it's worth the frustration. The neurologist who diagnosed my Mom's dementia told me that one third of us are expected to develop Alzheimer's. *One third of all of us.* That is a staggering amount of people. At the time of this writing, there is no cure. There is little anyone can even point to as protection. But we can dance. And when we do, we can improvise. And we can teach it to our students. Knowing that our struggle is an genuine investment leading to increased skill is half the battle.

So there you go for increased intelligence and ongoing brain health. Now let's look at heightened creativity...

The diffusion factor

Have you ever had an idea or answer come to you out of the blue? Like in the shower? You aren't even thinking about anything but enjoying the hot water raining down, and BOOM. Yet when you think and think, no answer comes. This can also happen walking along a path in the woods. Exercising, freewriting, daydreaming, or "sleeping on" a problem or decision can also have this effect. This is the power of *diffuse thinking*.

We humans have several kinds of thinking. Among them are focused and diffuse. Focused thinking is when we actively try to solve a problem, to come up with an answer. We weigh and measure, poke at all the holes, use our analytical skills. In this organized, structured, mode of thinking, we explore ideas, understand concepts, and get a lot done. But sometimes we hit a wall. We don't know the answer. We don't know how to proceed. We are out of ideas. We flounder.

That's when it's time to step back from the focused mode. It's time to let the unconscious mind have a crack at the problem. This thought-break can happen in many ways, from going for a run to taking a nap. But one great way is through improvisational dance.

When we dance improv, we let go of our constant thinking and controlling. We let the body call the shots. It's moving meditation—we clear the mind of its constant scurrying, busy chatter. We focus on the breath. We step back from the mind and into the body.

This state allows Diffuse Thinking. In diffuse thinking, the brain makes much more random connections. Our unresolved questions are still floating around, but we do not actively dig at them. It's like a dreamtime. Fragments and wisps arise and mingle. We don't seem to be doing anything, but the powerful brain always seeks organization and resolution. Behind the scenes, it processes all those bits and fits the missing pieces into the puzzle.

We may get only refreshment from our break (the mind needs and enjoys breaks in the routine far more often than we might think, as we are so used to pushing ourselves endlessly). But quite often, after such a break, we find answers to our questions, new understandings of our ideas, and wholeness, where before we had only broken bits.

Rather than controlling a systematic exploration, diffuse thinking makes a space for something unstructured to arise. Rather than determined digging, we let the rain wash away the dirt. It's so valuable a process that I keep a notebook handy when I dance, as ideas sometimes come in floods.

∽

A couple of years ago, I wrote a novel for National Novel Writing Month, *nanowrimo.org*). In this challenge, one commits to writing a 50,000-word word novel in thirty days. That's 1,666 words a day, if you are counting. Well, time passed. I did not write those words every day. I had no support or other people with whom to write. Work was intense; I had no time, blah, blah, blah. Resistance had a hold on me. And I had to hurry, as the month was nearly over.

Resistance takes many forms…

Finally, Thanksgiving vacation arrived. For that week at the end of November, I wrote six to eight thousand words *a day*. This was a novel that had no pre-planned structure—I had no idea what was going to happen next. I had one angry, unhappy character when I started, and that was it. How did I do it? I interleaved half-hour writing chunks with ten-minute dance chunks (thanks, Chris Baty!).

I did this in two-hour blocks, three or four times a day (with a couple hours between each block). I even used an app called Time Out—it greyed my screen after half an hour and opened it back up after my ten-minute break. Each of those dance breaks gave my brain the space it needed to approach the next batch of the story.

Before the end of November, I had a complete novel. *Before* the end. Usually, I would be updating my time zone to Hawaii for the extra hours as I desperately hammered out my final pages. I was done and well over the 50,000 words necessary to win—*two days* in advance. This was a first. I could never have done it without dance.

Improvisation gives us a vacation from focused thinking. It makes space for ideas. It allows creativity to blossom through unstructured, diffuse thinking. It gives the brain a rest and refreshes the body. Of course, other activities also do this (like showers), but improvisation takes little space, can be done wherever we are, and doesn't require hot running water.

On top of all this, it may help protect the brain from dementia and

Alzheimer's. And on top of that, it actually makes us smarter—the learning and problem-solving of improvised dance increases myelin and thus our overall intelligence—as well as makes it easier for us to learn other new things down the pike. And it's beautiful.

That's a lot of benefit.

So why do we still push improvisation away? Why are students afraid of it, and why do teachers prefer canned choreographies? Maybe it's our mindset.

Changing your mind(set) & learning how to learn

When I was a kid, people believed that one's level of intelligence was fixed—you had a certain level of smarts, and that was it. If you were smart, learning came easy. If learning *didn't* come easy, then you weren't smart enough. And if you weren't smart enough? No soup for you.

As we have seen, that view is dead wrong. Learning makes you smarter. It grows the brain's capacity and measurably increases intelligence. The more you learn, the smarter you get—and no one has found an upward limit. But facts have little power against beliefs. And when we believe that we are not smart enough, pretty enough, or whatever enough, that's when we run into problems. As Henry Ford said. "Whether you believe you can *or believe you can't,* either way, you're right."

That belief—that you can't? The researcher Carol Dweck, *mindsetonline.com*, calls that a *"fixed mindset."* A mindset is a set of beliefs that we have in any given area. The understanding that skills and intelligence grow through challenge, learning, and problem-solving, Dweck calls a *"growth mindset."* It is common to have a fixed mindset in some areas (I suck at math), and a growth mindset in other areas (If I practice with this new brush a little longer, I will get it).

Mindsets can be changed, so be on the lookout for areas in which you feel helpless or hopeless (like math—or béchamel sauce), and start turning them around by challenging your mindset. Dweck's groundbreaking research, the basis of the mindset philosophy and practice, is outlined in her excellent article, "How to Raise Smart Kids." Originally published by Scientific American, it is now available all over the web (check out *bellydancesoul.com/resources*).

Mindset shift is quite the light bulb moment. And it doesn't stop with kids. We grownups can apply the same strategies and increase our intelligence, too. Of course, we are all born different. Genetics and luck play a big role in our initial equipment. Along with the resources (or lack thereof), with which we are raised, they may help or hamper us. But any one, at any age, can improve their intelligence, skills, and abilities—just by learning and problem solving on the fly.

There's one teensy catch. Learning isn't easy. It isn't all that fun (especially when you first start). In fact, it often hurts. This is one reason why we have so much resistance to learning improvisation (and, for those who improvise, the same goes for choreography). The discomfort of doing something new, the fear of failing, of looking stupid, of being judged or shamed, stops us in our tracks. We avoid challenging new material because of this and stick to the same safe stuff that we have already learned and know we can do. There is a difference between collecting new information, which is a breeze, and learning, which takes effort.

But here's the kicker: The frustration we feel from learning is a normal, even desirable, sign of progress. Understanding this gives us the freedom to explore and challenge ourselves. Over time, we come to associate this discomfort with new and increased skills and abilities. We recognize it, value it, even welcome it. This is a great feeling.

Yet for many, there remains an abiding resistance to improvisation...
Fear.
How do we get past it?
For that, we have to look a little deeper.
Right down into the Body.

11
BODY: THE LOCK

IMPROVISATION AND FEAR

Once upon a time, I was in a deeply troubled long-term relationship. I finally got out of it—but it wouldn't get out of me. Every time I talked, wrote, or thought about it, suddenly the room got ice-cold and I started shaking. It took a while for me to realize that it wasn't the room that got cold. One night, well over a year later, I saw my ex in the local pub. My body backed out of that room, ran upstairs, and hid. Without any help from my conscious mind, suddenly I was one flight up, cowering in a little gallery, peeking out from cover to check on him—only to realize it wasn't even him, but some guy with a similar shape.

The sharpness of that response dulled over time, but it didn't leave. It took me years to drop the restraining order. I got shaky if I drove by his house—even though he had never violated the order or threatened me again. It took a long time (and much work), to feel safe—even relatively. And I was lucky—many people never feel safe. The past can haunt us. We may relive horrors for weeks, months, years, even decades. We may live in fear.

Remember the book *Dune*? Fear is the mind-killer? It is, for real. Fear causes us to blank out and freeze. Or we may go through the motions or everyday life, but we are not present—our Self has retreated far back into a cave of safety while our body proceeds on autopilot. *This is a biological reaction to unresolved trauma.*

Fear and freeze are the body's way of keeping us safe in the face of inescapable danger. We are talking lizard brain here, instinctive, prehistoric responses from before the advent of language or reason. Fear is completely separate from the conscious mind. Logic doesn't help. Talking about it doesn't help. Knowing why it's happening doesn't help. Speech and reason are functions of the conscious mind. Fear is of the body, an instinctive, hair-trigger response. The fear connected to improvisation, performance, etc., often has deep and surprising roots.

Improvisation is risky and thrilling all on its own. It can be a glorious, adrenaline-fueled joyride. But current situations can trigger a body-memory of previous events. The chemical rush of thrill and risk can trigger old fears, which throw us back to when we were helpless, defenseless, shamed, or blamed. The body senses danger, and *all those feelings rush back*. We were helpless then, and we feel helpless now.

Being trapped in this loop is the definition of trauma. It is like an old wound that gets bumped, and all the pain and fear come flooding back. Until the wound is healed, the pain continues.

How do you heal the wound?

The trauma process

Let's take the wound metaphor a little further. Imagine you have a sharp thorn buried in your toe. It's infected. It throbs. It hurts so much you can barely live your life. And when something presses against it? Wow. Worse, it's invisible. No one can see it. Yikes! Is it all in your head? So you go to therapy. You talk about that thorn endlessly, where it came from, how it feels, what it means. Does it help? No. The thorn is still stuck in your toe. Now let's make it a little bigger. What if you have a slavering lion on your back, its claws dug into your flesh, its teeth in your neck? All day long. Forever.

Trauma is a beast (copy of Stubbs' Horse Attacked by a Lion)

This is trauma.

Trauma is a beast. It is primitive defense impulses that become trapped in the body when self-defense is thwarted, when fight or flight is not an option. It is entirely subjective—something that seems quite small to one person, like a growling dog, might devastate another. The key is feeling helpless in the face of danger. We've all been there, and if not ourselves, then our loved ones.

Let's take a look at how trauma occurs, how to get rid of it, and what it has to do with belly dance.

Fight or flight is the first level of the body's biological response to perceived danger, and it has a hair-trigger. Any suspect rustle flickering through the grass (*Lion!*) and fight or flight is ready to go. Our hearing is our fastest sense. The body reacts instantly. Adrenaline and related chemicals flood the system, blood rushes to the extremities, and, in extreme cases, the bowels evacuate. Before we are even sure there's a lion, the body readies us to meet the danger head on or get the hell away from it.

We're not afraid—yet. Rather, we are primed for action, our senses on high alert. This adrenaline high can be great as we face the glorious risk of improvisational performance. But many of us skip this stage or misperceive it—and go straight to freeze.

Freeze happens when we can neither fight nor flee. When we are trapped. It is the next level of response and far more primitive. This is when fear may kick in. The body senses that it has no options, and we freeze like a deer in the headlights. This level of the response system isn't as glamorous or well-known as fight or flight, but it's equally important—and stunningly powerful.

How does Freeze work? Think of a mouse caught by a cat. Trapped, the mouse cannot fight or flee. It is helpless, immobile. In the cat's clutches, the mouse "plays dead." But it isn't playing. There is no choice here. The body is in control, doing what needs to be done to protect the organism.

Freeze is a biological state. If the cat loses interest, preferring live food, the mouse may awaken from the state of freeze and attempt to escape—or attack the cat in a "murderous rage" (yes, that's the technical term. It is another biological protection device). If the mouse escapes, it will shake off the freeze instinctively and be on its way. If it doesn't escape, the mouse will sink deeper into freeze, until it reaches Collapse, a semi-conscious, coma-like state designed to protect the organism from the horror of the moment.

It's the same deal for humans.

In the state of Freeze and its endpoint of Collapse, we feel helpless, hopeless, defenseless. We may become motionless, numb, and dissociated from the body. Our bodies still endeavor to protect us, but we are *biologically immobilized*—physically unable to fight or flee. There is little option or choice here.

Those who have been traumatized by unbearable events may come out of Freeze feeling anything from murderous rage to debilitating guilt and shame. We didn't fight back, didn't protect ourselves, didn't protect our loved ones, didn't, didn't, didn't. We may even blame ourselves for the event. Yet the reality is that we were—and often are still—held hostage by the processes that protect us. It's not that we didn't fight back—from a biological perspective, *we couldn't*.

Freeze and Collapse are automatic defenses. When we are under inescapable attack, ancient forces go into action. Understanding this is the beginning of healing. Freeze and Collapse, like breathing, are largely out of our control, the body's protection from unmanageable experiences. The body tries its mightiest to protect us. It tries so hard that even as we enter this frozen state, it bombards our muscles with neural impulses of fight-or-flight. Trauma pioneer Peter Levine describes the effect of Freeze/Collapse on an impala caught by a cheetah:

> *"From the outside, [the impala] looks motionless and appears to be dead, but inside, its nervous system is still supercharged at seventy miles an hour. Though it has come to a dead*

stop, what is now taking place in the impala's body is similar to what occurs in your car if you floor the accelerator and stomp on the brake simultaneously. The difference between the inner racing of the nervous system (engine) and the outer immobility (brake) of the body creates a forceful turbulence inside the body similar to a tornado. This tornado of energy is the focal point out of which form the symptoms of traumatic stress."

— Peter Levine, Waking the Tiger.

Trauma results when this chemical tornado continues *after the threat ends*. In the wild, animals instinctively shake off the effects of an attack—literally. They blow out big gusts of breath, leap, and shake. We "civilized" humans, on the other hand, have lost touch with this instinct. Our lives are so much more intense than what we evolved to manage in terms of day-to-day stress that we would have to shake and blow constantly. But we can't do that—we have to get to work, pick up the kids, placate our boss. The constant barrage of self-defense chemicals never ends.

Every one of us has experienced traumatic events. Most of us still carry their residue. Imagine a child, trapped in an abusive relationship. The child is small. The adult holds all the cards. The child, unable to defend himself, falls into a frozen state during the abuse, like the mouse does with the cat. After the immediate danger has passed, the child is left to manage all those freaked-out, conflicting impulses on his own—and the abuse happens again, and again, and again.

Trauma can come from big events. Car wrecks. Witnessing horror or violence, even in films. Medical procedures. Rape. War. A soldier, driven by murderous rage, may commit hideous acts of retribution. It can also come from chronic stresses: Abusive relationships. Chronic pain. Bullying. The endless micro (and macro) aggressions of systemic racism. Poverty. Single parenthood.

Trauma can *also* come from seemingly tiny things. A house fire down the street. A modest fender-bender. Even scary news on the TV or in the papers. A kid caught stealing a pack of gum can be traumatized by feelings of helplessness and shame. Suddenly they are acting out, and the parents are mystified. What should simply resolve may be driven like a thorn deep into our flesh. Left to fester, it poisons our lives from that moment on.

How do we heal this?

The usual answer is talk therapy. But talk therapy, for all its good points, rarely dents trauma. Trauma is physical, not mental. The body *enters* the state of Fight-Flight-Freeze easily. Any loud noise or dark alleyway can do this. The problem is when it doesn't *exit*. There is actual physical residue from the chemical bombardment. It's as real and physical as a thorn.

We can talk about an infected thorn all we want, but talking does not remove thorns. Talking may help us realize what is going on, but it takes tweezers, fingers, physical action, to remove a thorn from the body. In the same way, the short-circuited impulses of Fight-Flight-Freeze need to be integrated, reabsorbed by the body, their energy expended.

Here's the good part: when the traumatic residue is released and integrated, when the body completes its process, the disorganizing event is properly filed under Memories, and the trauma is gone. Yes, gone. Forever.

The gift of resolution

The body wants to heal. It is on a constant quest to return to regulation. How do we help it do that?

How trauma is resolved

Until recently, modern medicine believed that trauma was irreversible. But enterprising researchers have found ways of helping the body in its natural quest to regain balance. One such researcher is Bessel van der Kolk. I highly recommend his comprehensive book, *The Body Keeps the Score*. It's an overview of the history of trauma research and many of its options.

Another pioneer researcher is Peter Levine, author of *Waking the Tiger* and *In an Unspoken Voice*. Levine became curious as to why humans were devastated by trauma, yet animals in the wild seemed unaffected, though subject to repeated attack by savage predators. Levine discovered that animals in the wild literally shake off trauma. When they survive great danger such as attack from beasts of prey, they go through a specific set of physical responses—that shaking, jumping, and forceful expelling of breath. When they *don't* go through this process, they sicken and die. It's as simple as that.

For humans, however, it's a slightly different story.

Humans have more insidious stresses than being attacked by lions. We have myriad modern "beasts of prey" against which we feel helpless. With trauma, as with dance, it's all about the feeling.

Trauma is subjective. What traumatizes one person may not even jostle another. Worse, we have lost access to that set of responses with which our wild kin shake off threats. Trapped in trauma's dysregulated state, we see everything through its lens. This means that we interpret what happens to us *now* as though we were still *then*, in that state of crisis. We relive the body's desperate attempt to save us, *because that desperate attempt is still happening*. Alone and hurt, we live our lives in depression, fear, mania, and rage.

It doesn't have to be this way.

Here's the amazing part: The same processes that help resolve trauma also help us develop improvisational confidence. Releasing ourselves from traumatic responses frees us to trust ourselves, to interact fearlessly with the music in the moment. This is what I discovered by entering into the healing process. Step by step, as my healing expanded, so did my ability to be present with the music in the moment.

How I got into all this

I began my research into trauma resolution to help myself recover balance. That troubled relationship I mentioned earlier left its mark upon me, and the fear still affected me twenty years later. In the fall of 2011, I went in search of release. I found a local therapist who specialized in trauma resolution. Among other modalities, she practiced Eye Movement Desensitization and Reprocessing (EMDR). I was immediately struck by how EMDR connected to Oriental dance.

The two prime connections are midline crossing and eye movements. For example, in EMDR, while processing a traumatic memory, one moves the eyes from side to side and down and up. Midline crossing helps bring both sides of the brain together—it helps bring the sense memory into the conscious mind. These eye movements perfectly coincide with belly dance's flirtatious gaze. We glance from side to side, drop the gaze demurely, then look up through lowered lashes. We are constantly giving sidelong glances, looking down and looking up. Doing this feels good—mischievous and happy (try it).

Other methods of midline crossing in EMDR include tapping or electrical impulses to integrate both sides of the body. There are *countless* examples of midline crossing in belly dance. Our smoke-like hand gestures, circles, shimmies, and infinities, the playing of finger cymbals—almost everything crosses the midline, which means it engages both sides of the brain and helps to unite them.

I asked the therapist what she thought about using belly dance to help resolve trauma. What if you held the trauma in the mind's eye, I asked, as one does with EMDR, while moving in the self-loving, pleasurable way that is belly dance? Could that help to release it? As I spoke, I danced. She stared, entranced. "I don't think I could feel bad for one minute, moving like that," she said.

The quest was officially on.

Combing the Internet for books on trauma release brought me to *Waking the Tiger*, the classic by Peter Levine, *traumahealing.org*. I saw he had a brand-new book, *In an Unspoken Voice: how the body releases trauma and restores goodness*, so I ordered that. I devoured that book, stunned by its revelations. I learned how small things can be traumatic, how trauma is stored—and what it can do to you. I realized that not only myself but also everyone I knew had been marked by trauma.

This was in early 2012, during the heyday of Occupy Wall Street—I saw clearly how police violence had traumatized my OWS allies. Many turned harder, colder, more militant. Others left the movement, unable to continue. And these were mostly middle class white youth. Look at the communities of color, for whom police abuse and fear is a daily event. Few of us can imagine the stress of inner-city poverty. It is a war zone. You are never safe. Home may be as dangerous as the street. Poverty, oppression, and desperation mix into highly combustible cocktails of rage and violence.

Endless studies show that violence is connected to unresolved trauma. Police officers are not immune, and their culture of toughness makes it difficult, even impossible, to manage their own feelings of fear and dysregulation. So trauma is perpetuated. All over the world, where there is conflict, where there is violence, there is trauma.

～

I was so galvanized by Levine's material that I wanted to know more. In his practitioner directory, *sepractitioner.membergrove.com*, I found several therapists in Santa Barbara, where I was at the time—one was also a dance therapist. Bingo! I called her up. "Hi, I just read Levine's book, and I'm in town for another three days. Would you see me?" To her credit and my good fortune, she said yes. Her name is Shira Musicant.

Our first meeting we only talked—each of us needed to be sure that the other wasn't some nut (in my experience, finding a quality practitioner is half the battle). We agreed to meet again and do the work. I was reluctant to attempt my big issue in such a short time, so we agreed to see what arose.

The next morning, I sat in Shira's lovely courtyard awaiting my appointment, wondering what to address. Suddenly a memory surfaced. Glassy and fetid as a bubble of swamp gas, it burbled up into my solar plexus from deep in my past: a botched abortion at the age of fifteen, and the weeks of fear and pain following that secret, desperate act.

In an hour, that buried tragedy was gone—for good.

That was in April 2012. As of this writing, three years later, I've learned a lot and experienced a range of trauma resolution strategies, from Somatic Experiencing® through Bio-Dynamic Cranial Sacral work—and belly dance, in particular through its practice as Sufi dance, exemplified by Dunya McPherson, Sufi master and founder and principal teacher of Dancemeditation.

This trauma resolution journey has brought significant, lasting shifts that have profoundly affected my self-image, self-compassion, and self-respect. Negative self-talk has decreased, and its power to wound has been largely nullified. My breathing literally changed as of the first session, coming from my belly instead of my chest. After the session, I simply noticed I was breathing differently, through no effort of my own. And I kept on doing it. Amazing.

My initial issue, that previous relationship, took a little more time and self-preparation. Conversations with friends (especially the remarkable Dee Powers of Maine), yielded leads, and leads yielded results—in my case, with Roger Gilchrist, a biodynamic cranial sacral therapist, *wellnessinstitute.net*. By then I was ready. I trusted Roger, the process, and myself.

I was in an altered state during much of the session (Roger takes a hands-on, body-work oriented approach). I felt a lot of strange feelings and began to cry at least once (when Roger, who was gently shaking my shoulder, explained that he was telling my shoulder it was okay to communicate with some other body part), but my memory of the session itself is hazy. Though I didn't feel the hand-tingling or other markers of departing trauma, I did feel awakened, lighter, and more real, like a lead blanket had been removed from my heart.

However, the session was not yet over.

The next day, I was driving to Vermont with Tamalyn Dallal. We were stuck in traffic in New Haven. Suddenly, I felt this congestion gathering in my chest, like thick, cold, black smoke. I became alarmed. What was this? Was I having a heart attack? In traffic? In the next few moments it intensified. I kept my eyes on the road and my hands on the wheel, but my body was freaking out.

Suddenly I heard Shira Musicant's voice ask, "How does it want to leave? Trauma always wants to leave the body." Steadied, I asked my body, how does this—whatever it is—want to leave? The answer came back: through the mouth. I opened my mouth and exhaled, slowly and deliberately. As I did so, I realized, with utter clarity, this is my ex. This is him. He's ready to go.

I exhaled him. Every shred. And he was gone. Gone. I no longer felt the anxiety that thoughts of him brought up. I no longer felt anything much at all. He was gone. He's stayed gone. And my life has been so much better. I like myself. I used to hate myself. Now, I like myself. I see video of my dancing and I no longer cringe. I like my dancing. Sure, I see where I need work. But there is no longer that constant squeeze of shame and self-loathing. I have perspective. I know what I bring to the table.

I'm more in touch with my feelings. The Bad Voices still come, but rarely, and with much less power. I see them as symptoms, not truth. I have more compassion, for myself and for others. I see my path now. I know which way to go. The trauma-clearing potential of belly dance is part of it. This has captured my attention since 2011.

Am I perfect now? No, of course not. Do I have more to resolve? Yes, absolutely. Can I totally eradicate my old trauma? I may not need to.

More important than totally clearing the past is a way, right now, to exit from the sense of threat. Ancient body systems don't change. Maintenance continues. Like dirt or thorns, stress doesn't disappear. You still need a shower once in a while. But we can learn how to help the body finish its processes so we don't get stuck in trauma-land. This is much better than being driven by invisible demons (again, I *strongly* recommend working with a professional therapist for long-term, deep, or frightening issues. Levine has an excellent practitioner directory, *sepractitioner.membergrove.com*, and many work with long-distance clients).

My trauma resolution journey has been a rewarding endeavor, for myself and for many dancers who have changed their lives and found joy though our dance. Because of their success, I knew that the dance had this potential. Still, the specifics of how belly dance helps healing remained hazy. I craved a deeper understanding—and I knew where to get it.

Before moving on, let's recap the trauma process. In the face of danger, our first response is fight or flight. The body floods us with adrenaline to facilitate our defense. When we are unable to fight or flee, the body protects us with Freeze, its last-ditch effort. Remember the little mouse? When it couldn't run, it froze. When the cat caught it, the mouse went limp, unable to move, dissociated from its body. This inability to fight or fly in the face of perceived life-or-death danger doesn't stop the cascade of neurochemicals from fight or flight—the bombardment continues.

Once we survive the danger, we must expend this chemical overload though activity—classically, shaking, jumping, and expelling breath. When we are unable to do so—because we don't know how, the stress is chronic, or we are somehow restrained—then we get trauma.

Eek, a cat!

According to Steven Hoskinson, trauma is a symptom of unintegrated resource. Our neurochemicals, body, instincts, whatever, helped us withstand the threat, thus they are a resource. However, the neurochemicals were not properly expended or reabsorbed at the end of the event.

Think of a bruise. After a bad bang (also called trauma), sometimes there is bleeding beneath the skin, which forms a discolored spot—a bruise. Over time, the body reabsorbs the blood, and the bruise goes away. In order for trauma to be healed, the trapped impulses—this chemical residue—must be reabsorbed. This is normal body activity. However, in the case of trauma, it has been put on hold—often for decades, during which we continue to suffer. When the mouse finally escapes from the cat, it accesses its natural ability to shake off trauma. Humans have forgotten how to do this.

It's time to rediscover our trauma resolution process—and one way is through belly dance.

12

BODY: THE KEY

BELLY DANCE? REALLY?

It may seem far-fetched that sparkly little belly dance can dissolve years of misery and pain, yet I have seen it happen repeatedly, in particular during the 90-Day Dance Challenge, *aliathabit.com/90days*, in which participants—mostly belly dancers—dance freeform improvisation with a focus on breath integration and slow movement for twenty minutes a day. Each time we run the 90 Days, folks report solace and major change through this simple practice. Here are a few of the many messages dancers have sent me about their experiences.

Well, the past couple of days I was dealing with some emotional stuff. Without consciously intending to, I organically found myself dealing with my sorrow and other feelings through my dance practice. My movements became the expressions of these deep emotions, and it felt so amazing and powerful. Like a wordless ritual of comfort for my soul. Wow. —NS

Thank you, thank you for this practice. It has helped me more than words can express. I found the courage to leave my husband of 28 years and finally start living for me. This practice has helped me work through everything that this entails, and started me on this journey. I have clung to this practice and your notes like a life raft, and am starting to peel my fingers away and swim on my own. The water feels great! Each daily note has always seemed to have the perfect message for me. —DE

This 90-day dance party came at the right moment for me. A friend of mine who is a recovering alcoholic once told me "the body is the final frontier." That when we heal, the body is often the last territory we reclaim. I have never been able to allow myself to wear bright colors, to lose weight, to not blend in with my environment. To be noticed was too dangerous when I was a child.

I recently started hoop dancing classes, and for the first time I didn't mind making mistakes. I could laugh & keep going. Hooping made me happy. And my willingness to make mistakes flowed into my belly dance classes...and I got better. This past month, I have hooped a half hour a day, danced 20 and walked 30. And I've lost 5 pounds & a clothing size. For the first time, this doesn't scare me. I like feeling stronger, feeling the upper & lower halves of my body connected strongly together, and not feeling so scared all the time. —AB

There are many, many more of these letters. This is the biggest gift of the work, seeing folks release suffering and enter into joy.

But I must qualify my definition of belly dance.
The way belly dance is usually taught does not focus on healing or meditative states. As we have seen, it's often more about memorizing steps and choreography, or being a pretty girl in a pretty costume. It's about performing, looking outward, and being the center of attention. This is a Western focus. In the East, belly dance is a social dance of joy, something done together with friends and family. But there is also something else—something deep and liberating.

As we will see in the following chapter, Sufi *dance* (not whirling) uses the same movement vocabulary and the same music as belly dance. The same—but with a wildly *different* focus. Sufi dance has the intention of connection with the Divine. For many of us, this is already our true focus. We dance for the dissolution of the *I* and an integration into something more universal. Traditional belly dance is a playful dance of joy. The Sufi connection brings it into a spiritual, soul-healing domain.

For those whose only experience of the dance is to collect steps, memorize choreography, or shake it in a sparkly costume, this may seem odd or even alarming. The pain of life may feel too deep to touch. That's okay. Come when you are ready. Others of us prefer an easy, simple relationship to the dance. That's fine. It's a folkdance. It's fun.

For the seekers among us, however, this approach to belly dance may feel like coming home. Sufi dance is the key in our felt relationship to the sacred nature of this dance. In the next chapter, we will look closely at this practice. For now, we'll open up the relationship of trauma healing and Oriental dance.

How does an ancient folk dance cure the blues?

Let's hear from an expert.

I met Cynthia Merchant through Dunya McPherson. Cynthia is a somatic psychotherapist who specializes in the treatment of trauma—but she is also much more. She has co-facilitated trainings of Dr. Peter Levine's Somatic Experiencing® all over the world; she has also worked with its more recent evolution, Organic Intelligence®, developed by Levine's protégé, Steven Hoskinson. She is a friend, student of, and collaborating teacher with Claudio Naranjo's Seekers After Truth (SAT). Naranjo is an internationally renowned pioneer integrating psychotherapy and shamanism with spiritual traditions. Cynthia also has experience in Sufi dance, and knows Dunya's work well.

My interview with Cynthia (listen at *bellydancesoul/resources*) confirmed many things I had been thinking and gave me the steps forward in this path. Over the course of our conversation, we discussed the myriad ways in which trauma enters our lives. These may happen before we are even conscious, which means we can't remember them. This is important. *We don't need to tell our trauma stories to heal—or even to remember them.* As we note our feeling in the moment, we use breath, movement, tracking, and here/now spatial orientation to reintegrate our bodies with the present.

Cynthia points out that when we successfully fight or flee, we usually come out okay. "Fight and flight are the responses in which the organism has a greater sense of agency, and if successful it usually means that we're not overwhelmed and we can integrate the experience. There's a sense of, 'I was endangered. I ran away or I fought, and I came through successfully. Yay for me; I've integrated a higher level of capacity to respond to life-threatening stress. Woo-hoo!'" In general, our systems work well. We were endangered. We escaped. Yay! Done.

Like the learning we discussed earlier, each time we survive a threat, deactivate, and reset the nervous system, we increase our capacity for integration. However, sometimes even when we survive the threat, we don't fully deactivate—the alarm bells keep on clanging. Which means the nervous system doesn't reset. Which means we get stuck in trauma-land.

For example, we may survive a car crash, but there we are, shaking uncontrollably on the street corner. We have to go to work, pick up the kids from school, or whatever normal daily action. There is no victory lap, no slap on the back. There's just us, alone, deeply shaken, wondering why we feel so freaked out when we are apparently unharmed.

"After a traumatic event, people are shaking, or they're suddenly weeping and turning to jelly. When somebody slaps them in the face and says, 'Get ahold of yourself, man!' that completely interrupts the organism's natural capacity to deactivate and discharge the excessive arousal that it no longer needs to survive. If that arousal is not fully deactivated, if it's clamped down, you'll end up with a residue that can be somewhat disorganizing."

The body's organic response to traumatic events has long been poorly understood. Because we have little control over it, it is alarming both for observers and for those going through it. Consequently, those involved will often try to shut down the response. Even in the medical world, people are often prevented from going through the shaking and other expressions of deactivation. However, it has not always been so.

Consider Steven Pressfield's book, *Gates of Fire* (the story of 300 Spartans who held the pass at Thermopylae against the entire Persian army). *Gates* is a meticulously researched historical novel—Pressfield devoured classic Greek texts for years before beginning the two-year research/writing phase of *Gates*, and the Greeks wrote brilliantly (and often) about war.

In the novel, Pressfield details the Spartans' post-battle behaviors, which, he explains, all warriors knew and understood as necessary. They are precisely the shaking and turning to jelly Cynthia describes, the "deactivation and discharge of excessive arousal." Clearly this knowledge is not new; indeed, it is thousands of years old. It has simply been forgotten. Besides, before we get to this deactivation stage, there may be a few obstacles.

∽

Cynthia explains that, "When people try to fight or flee, sometimes they don't succeed. Maybe they're trapped, or beaten, or end up unconscious, or they're robbed or, God forbid, they're raped. Any number of things can happen. The next level of response is to go into freeze … Freeze is a dissociative state that's highly protective. It can reduce pain. It can reduce the emotional impact of things. It can even make us amnesiac: we don't remember what happened."

Remember the mouse? When in the clutches of the cat, it went into freeze. This can happen to us over and over again, from situations of chronic stress (poverty, injury, or bullying, for example), to overwhelming, dire events. Freeze can feel variously "floaty" all the way to "immobile." It's important to remember, Cynthia warns, that freeze states *disguise and represent* extremely high states of nervous system arousal—generally *beyond* that of fight or flight. If we do not fully metabolize a freeze state, even if it was life-saving at the time, we may remain dysregulated and disorganized, physiologically, emotionally, and cognitively—in short, trauma.

The body can fully recover from freeze states as often as it needs to. Animals in the wild do it all the time. But *when the body does not get to recover*, when we are pushed back into freeze before coming out of a previous episode, it becomes more difficult to return to regulation. Cynthia explains, "There are lots of different levels of possible dissociation, from total and complete amnesia to a mild sense of disconnectedness or emotional numbness."

Freeze is a function of the dorsal branch of the nervous system. Freeze is far older and more primitive than fight or flight. It is ancient and implacable. We don't choose freeze—the body overrides every other impulse. The purpose of freeze is to protect the body from the careening redline of fight or flight and from the horror of the moment. Levine says it's like having the accelerator *and* the brake both pressed to the floorboards at the same time. We are biologically prevented from any other action until the body perceives that the threat is gone. And as we have seen, our *sense* of threat can linger long past the actual threat. The results can be devastating.

The Zombie Apocalypse

"Unfinished freeze states can be severely dysregulating for the nervous system, which I think is why we see zombie films being so popular these days. They reflect our mass state of freeze. We have masses of people who are in some variation of dissociation and freeze, walking around like zombies. It's called functional freeze. They seem to be doing life and able to do lots of things, but..."

But we only seem okay, in that "functional freeze." We are not all there, not able to be fully present. We are going through the motions, wondering why we bother. And this is not the only effect. Illnesses such as addiction, asthma, anorexia, chronic fatigue, fibromyalgia, schizophrenia, depression, and dementia are now being considered for possible connections to unresolved trauma. Still, it's not *all* bad. Even in this thundercloud there is a silver lining...

The dorsal nervous system controls our capacity to go into Freeze, to conserve energy, and to survive life-threatening situations. The dorsal branch of the vagus nerve is far more primitive than fight or flight, so freeze is a deeply primal response. Under conditions of health, the dorsal system only comes online when fight or flight fails, and it has remained unchanged for millennia. *When the dorsal system is dysregulated,* we tend to bypass fight or flight and go straight to freeze, no matter what the trigger is, no matter what the appropriate response might be. This is why those of us who are already anxious often to go straight to freeze, and often stay there (for more on the dorsal system, see *stephenporges.com*).

However, *even while stuck in freeze,* we may discover intellectual and creative treasure. "People who have a lot of dorsal dominance in their system often become very, very, very intellectual, incredibly bright, while others become intuitive and visual, symbolic, a lot of imagery. There are many ways it can manifest, and not all of it is negative." And we can bring that treasure back with us.

Treasure!

Cynthia explains that when we complete our "dorsal state" (i.e., integrate the traumatic residue and return to regulation), we "become more embodied again and reclaim a lot of other elements: vital energy, emotions, physical sensation, a greater sense of engagement and connection with other people socially—all things that can feel dulled down by functional freeze states."

For many folks, the trauma experience brings to light rich creative material, which can be a boon to artists. However, artists often subconsciously fear that their artistic inspiration is linked to their pain, that if the pain is lifted, the art will go away. And that can happen. Case in point: Antidepressants can dull *all* our feelings, forcing us into a superficial state of medium nothing, cut off from inspiration along with everything else. Fearing the side effects of medication, yet unable to bear the pain of existence, many of us turn to self-medication: alcohol, heroin, etc.

Might this be why so many of our best and brightest drink or drug themselves to death? We attempt to dull the pain without killing the goose that lays the golden egg of art. But so often, in our depths of despair, we go too far.

It is a profound relief to know that we can release pain, return to life, and bring our creative gold back with us into the bright world.

So what is trauma exactly?

Cynthia explains that, "Trauma is any experience that overwhelms the human nervous system's capacity to respond *and then return to its original state of regulation*. It leaves the nervous system dysregulated in a chronic way." Sounds a lot like daily life, doesn't it? An endless, overwhelming torrent of stress. Can chronic stress be traumatic? Poverty? Parenthood? Work?

It sure can. "We weren't organized evolutionarily to be at acute levels of stress for an extended time. The way the average modern person lives, they subject themselves to acute stress, freeway-driving commute to work, pound down several espressos, work all day, work through lunch, go, go, go, horrific commute home, lucky to get home with one's life intact, race around, do all the work one has to do at home, fall into bed exhausted, and get up and do it again, day, after day, after day, without real flow and modulation."

Slings and arrows...

Sound familiar?

Wouldn't it rock to feel like a whole person? With so many layers of disruption, childhood abuse, destructive relationships, accidents, and even daily life, how do we begin to approach healing? Must each layer be individually peeled back, like an endless onion of trauma? Or is there is a magic key that you can turn and all of the layers fall away?

Cynthia replied, "It's interesting. In a certain way, I think the answer could be 'both and,' or the answer could be, 'If you're lucky and the stars line up right.' Or it could be only the latter. All organisms are brilliant and wise. Our unconscious is always trying to organize us one way or another toward healing and wholeness. There's an impulse toward wholeness."

Let me repeat that:

"All organisms are brilliant and wise. Our unconscious is always trying to organize us one way or another toward healing and wholeness."

The body wants to be whole and integrated. The body wants everything to work. The more often we release the threat and return to regulation, the more capacity we have to do so. This is key. Our bodies are there for us in ways we cannot imagine. Yet we spend our time ignoring our bodies, hating on them, and forcing them to do things while cursing them for failing us.

Cynthia agrees. "Yes, often the body has been a source of displeasure and discomfort because what one felt in the body was overwhelming... The body was overwhelmed in some way. It was an inescapable attack. If we think of the modern version of inescapable attack, it is the car accident: a high-speed impact where you don't even know what hit you. Something comes at you from behind that you're not even aware of, so you don't even have time to mobilize a response."

"That's sort of the modern-day example of failure of fight and flight because you were down before you even knew anything was coming. If we look at the statistics for how many people have had high-speed accidents, that's a lot of failure of fight and flight out there."

And we often take that failure personally.

Somewhere deep down, we believe that we are (or someone is) at fault because we didn't fight or fly, because we lost the battle, because we were hurt. We blame ourselves, immersed in shame for the evil that befell us. Or we blame others, inflicting our rage upon the world around us. We push the body away, ignore it, punish it through eating, exercise, drugs, abuse—whatever dulls the pain of living, or hurts enough so that we feel something.

In reality, the body tries its mightiest to protect us, in all the ways it knows how. These methods worked perfectly on the veldt, but we have walked far away from our wild roots. Our civilized veneer blinds us to the powerful forces of the body. We are surprised when children subjected daily to the unbearable stress of racism or inner-city poverty turn to drugs, crime, or violence. We are shocked by the savagery of people in wartime—or any time.

Where there is chronic shame, cruelty, or violence, there is trauma. We need a broader understanding of our formative body processes, an awareness of how to heal, and availability of resources and practitioners to help us resolve this rollercoaster of shame, rage, and despair.

My quest has been to understand how our dance might be part of this healing process.

How belly dance facilitates trauma healing

I asked Cynthia, if one wanted to use Oriental dance to resolve trauma, what sort of things might one do to assist that healing process?

She first cited the work of Bessel van der Kolk, one of our foremost researchers on trauma (his book, *The Body Keeps the Score*, is highly recommended). She explained that among the things that van der Kolk studied was how mind-body practices affect trauma. He studied subjects practicing yoga and tai chi, comparing them to control groups of people working out in a gym or doing other kinds of exercise. Van der Kolk found that folks who engage in traditional movement practice that has varying levels of intensity (modulation), made far greater strides than those who did psychotherapy alone.

Cynthia explained the arc of modulation: readiness → arousal → peak → resting down → deep rest and integration. Belly dance is the queen of modulation! Fast, slow, faster, super slow—both in the big picture and in the individual movements and combinations. We can easily adapt a resting piece into our classes. So we're good—given van der Kolk's findings, there is certainly potential to resolve trauma with belly dance (and I have seen it happen in my work). Yay!

But I still had a big concern. One of the dangers in experimenting with trauma resolution is that getting close to the damaging events can trigger all those feelings all over again. Instead of resolving the trauma, this can reinforce it. Re-traumatization is common in talk therapy, when one revisits traumatic incidents, and it is common in everyday life, whether we dwell on the chaotic memories or encounter events that trigger our traumatic states. This potential is real, and quite unpleasant. I mean, none of us wants to cower in the corner crying, right? How do we maximize the healing and minimize the danger?

Titration and Pendulation

Somatic trauma resolution is grounded in the concepts of *titration* and *pendulation*. Titration means you add a tiny bit of something, drop by drop. It's a chemistry term for how to combine two substances with volatile potential. For example, in standard talk therapy, one often dives into recounting (hence reliving) the traumatic event. This flood of sense memory can be emotionally overwhelming and also re-traumatizing. However, the titration model barely approaches activation. A tiny drop (rather than a flood), makes it easier to manage *pendulation*.

Pendulation means to move away and come back, like a pendulum. We get a little bit close to the trauma (that tiny, titrated drop of activation), and then back away again. We counter the drop of activation with *resources*—things that are soothing or pleasurable, or orienting to the safety of the present moment. And then we rest and digest. We can do this over and over. This pendulation teaches the body that it's okay to approach the trauma, because it can escape. There is the safety of a back door. In essence, it gives us back the agency of fight or flight and gives the nervous system a safe space in which to deactivate and reset. Over time, we regain our equilibrium and sense of safety.

In concord with these basic concepts, Cynthia focuses on three main principles to help us stay safe in our practice:

- Orientation and Stabilizing Blue;
- Modulation, which includes titration and pendulation; and
- Rest and Digest (from Kathy Kain, *somaticpractice.net*).

Orientation & Stabilizing Blue

Orientation is about grounding ourselves in the here and now to sidestep downward traumatic spirals. *Stabilizing Blue* (a concept developed and taught by Steven Hoskinson), is a focus on soothing, positive, and pleasurable elements, both in the present moment, and in our explorations of the past. Here is an overview of these elements and their connection to Oriental dance.

ORIENTATION

"To stay *oriented* means to be connected to the external environment through the senses, primarily through sight because we are two-legged creatures that walk upright; so, sight is very important to us, but also sound." Bessel van der Kolk defines trauma as an inability to be in the here and now. Sound, sight, touch and our other senses help ground us in the here-and-now.

"Trauma draws us inward into overwhelming internal experience, so we have to stay outwardly connected to the external environment, to be present to the here and now if we're going to be processing anything that was at one point overwhelming to us." When we have been traumatized, we tend to live in a place of *there and then*, the time of the trauma.

Trauma keeps us spinning into our disorganization, dwelling on it, reinforcing its pathways and the production of brain chemicals related to wherever we may be on the fight-flight-freeze spectrum (which may be anywhere, from aggression, to running, to lethargy). The antidote to this is to connect to the present moment (the feeling in the moment, anyone?). Grounding in the here-and-now gives us the safety and security to finally release our old response.

"The more anchored we are in the here and now, the less overwhelming the material will be, because *it's not actually happening in the here and now*. In the here and now, I'm sitting in my living room. I see the fireplace. I see the blue sky, with a smattering of clouds out the window, and the flowers in the vase; it's quiet and peaceful here." Think about this for a moment. Look around.

What Cynthia describes is a framing device. In writing, an author presents past events from a place of perspective—the narrator looks back at a previous time with the wisdom they have gained since the past event. In trauma therapy, we look back to our suffering past self from our current place of safety (which may only be the therapist's office). From our safe space in the here and now, we reach back in time to give succor to our bereft previous self—the love, comfort, and understanding that we did not get at the time. We give love, acceptance, and forgiveness to our past self from the relative strength and success of our present self.

You are safe now

Love and compassion are crucial. Studies of returning child soldiers and war vets clearly show enormous trauma recovery upon receiving welcome and forgiveness from the tribe. Trauma reduction directly equals a reduction of violence and suffering later on.

What I find fascinating is how this mirrors the presentation of tragedy in traditional Oriental dance. In the dance, we may make a song that is deeply tragic, but in our performance, we do not present the tragedy as if it were happening now (though we might in a theater piece). Rather, we frame it with the joy of the present moment. We tell the audience about the sad thing of the past, but from a safe place of, "Here we are together; I love you so much."

You see this bittersweet compassion beautifully expressed in the work of the Egyptian dancer, Tito Seif, *titoseif.com*, particularly when he dances on tarab songs. So we have a clear model in the dance for grounding the pain of tragedy in present pleasure. This is, in fact, a hallmark of the dance and the music. It modulates past sorrow with the joy of the this beautiful, uplifting, pleasurable moment. Speaking of pleasurable, one surprise for me in this conversation was the idea of Stabilizing Blue and opting for the most pleasurable movement.

STABILIZING BLUE

Stabilizing blue is a focus on soothing, positive, and pleasurable elements, both in the present moment, and in our explorations of the past (this comes from the work of Levine's protégé, Steven Hoskinson). *Blue*, Cynthia explains, is all of what is more in the direction of coherence, of greater wellbeing. *Red* is anything relative to *blue* that is less so. In simple terms, "blue" is more pleasurable and "red" is less pleasurable.

"Blue is anything that is more pleasurable. "For example, if you were engaged in movement, I would encourage you always to go toward the movement that is more comfortable rather than the less comfortable. Go toward the more pleasurable because, as you stabilize into what's arising, that is the pleasurable side of things. It builds the container to hold everything else because every painful experience has a blue side to it. It's like yin and yang; you can't have one without the other." So even in the red difficulty of trauma, there is a blue side. And that's where we want to put our attention.

As you develop your practice for trauma healing, pay attention to the pleasurable quality of the moves and opt for the things that feel good, relaxing, and easy. The more *blue* we stabilize, the more joy we find in exploration and discovery.

It's interesting that current belly dance tends to focus on what is hard and difficult—to be advanced, we must do technically difficult things. It may be to our advantage, as well as the dance's, to explore a more nuanced interpretation of "advanced," wherein the artistry of musical embodiment and soul connection for both dancer and guest is valued more highly than technical difficulty. This pleasurable aspect of the dance activates its healing potential and unites dancer and witness in a healing state.

Cynthia continues, "Steve Hoskinson defines trauma as *unintegrated resource*. We survived whatever we survived because there were resources that helped us get through, but for the most part, because of freeze and dissociation, those resources remained unconscious... By tending all this 'blue' that we often overlook or devalue, we are in fact doing the work of integrating the unintegrated resource." As we move towards health, we *actively elevate these blue elements of our experience.*

In our traumatized state, we only see the horror. That's all that we have access to. But there is a positive side as well. We have resources within us that saw us through. We may not feel them or recognize their value, but they are there. They got us this far. Determination, perseverance, sheer cussedness— We tend to focus, in dance and in life, on what we are doing wrong, on our weakness. We forget our strength. We forget our power. We forget all that makes us unique and special. But it hasn't gone anywhere. It is patiently waiting for us to see it, recognize it, and celebrate it.

Cynthia puts it this way: "We didn't integrate the goodness, the power, or the whatever it was that got us through—and it *did* get us through. But it wasn't sufficiently integrated for our system to return to modulated regulation again." We want to always be in search of the delicious, leaning in to what feels good, what is pleasurable, what makes us happy, what the body likes— laughter, love, and joy. This, too, is a hallmark of traditional Oriental dance.

One of my great dance revelations came from David Badyal, *davidofscandinavia.com*, who mentioned that the Arabic word for feeling, *aHsas*, refers not only to emotional feeling but also to physical feeling (just like the English word. In hindsight, it's like, well, duh! But there you go). So the "feeling" in Oriental dance, always cited as the most important thing, is also attention to, and enjoyment of, *our physical sensation of the movement* as we respond to the music. We want to lean into the elements that feel good because that's going to create stability and wellbeing that can hold other (less pleasurable), things that arise.

Think about this for minute.

Our physical interaction with the music is pleasurable in and of itself. And the more connected we become, the better and more beautiful and delicious it feels (and looks). Who among us practices expressly to enjoy the physical pleasure of moving to music? Few that I've met. We practice to better our technique. We work. What if we danced instead for the pleasure of the movement? That sounds radical, doesn't it? Dance for the physical pleasure of the activity all by itself. But it is an important element to reclaiming wholeness.

Think how lovely the dance could be with our attention on enjoying the sensuality of the moves and their relationship with the music. What a wonderful definition of mastery. We place an enormous emphasis on performing, on looks, in our dance. In its cultures of origin, few ever seek to perform. It is a playful dance of joy. What if we relax and enjoy our dance? It is through joy that we heal...

Finding and removing the thorns

Cynthia explains that, "Once there's enough orientation and enough stabilized blue, when other material begins to arise you can tell the difference. It's not frightening any more or horribly overwhelming. It becomes kind of more curious. It's like, Oh, interesting. There's this sort of funny tightening. There's this tightening of my left hip or my left shoulder."

Very slow movement (about which you will hear more shortly), allows us to access these "funny tightenings," hitches, thorns, freezes, whatever you want to call them. When we move at speed, we rush right over them. We have walled them off for so long, we don't even notice them--but when we slow everything down, they suddenly become available. We can explore them, gently, slowly, often without activating pain, fear, or rage—and when it does activate, we can back off, exhale, pendulate into a more oriented state, and let the feelings integrate, gently and safely. Ahhh....

Cynthia's other focus is on what she calls the *"orientation architecture,"* which is the shoulders and above—neck, eyes, head, etc. In the case of threat, the first part of the body to mobilize is the orientation architecture, as we instinctively look and listen, searching for the source of the threat, the escape route, and any available resources to aid in the process of fight or flight.

Because these areas come online first in the defensive process, they are often less connected to the residual trauma (as that often has to do with later physical defenses). This means that activating these parts of the body can help to gently activate low levels of arousal with less involvement of, or resistance from, freaked-out, frozen parts of the body. It's not a given, since that top area of the body may also have been involved, but it can be a good area to include in slow, gentle movement.

Cynthia explains, "When you move a part of the body really, really slowly, if there is material stuck in little freezes along the way, *tiny little movements of the head and neck can bring up arousal.*" Bringing up arousal refers to those concepts of pendulation and titration. Once you find a "freeze," which can present as a little hitch or stuck place, tiny little movements of the head and neck can initiate arousal—the traumatic response. But only a drop, remember? Titration. Then pendulation—you take a break, ground, exhale, take a nap, to let the arousal deactivate (rest and digest).

～

What Cynthia describes here connects deeply to the Sufi dance practice of Slow Movement. In Slow Movement, one moves in what Dunya describes as "glacial slowness." What happens in this state is that established patterns dissolve, as the body is allowed to find its own path. At speed, we whip through our ingrained movement pathways—be they picking up a cup or dancing an infinity—in a fairly consistent fashion. Any skips or mistakes are hard to isolate and remedy when we are on autopilot. To make changes, we proceed with deliberate attention.

Top-level musicians use a variation of Slow Movement to learn difficult musical passages. They isolate their problem bits and play them slowly enough to play them correctly, and they repeat until they integrate the correct physical sequence of the section. Slow Movement is also an excellent way to practice anything physical that one must learn and remember, or to find and eliminate errors in a sequence (such as choreography). It is far more effective than drilling at speed.

Additionally, through Slow Movement, we are able to sidestep the activation of chronic pain. How is that possible? In glacially slow motion we can see the pain activation coming long before we actually enter into the nexus of it. This gives us time to stop, back off, relax, realign, and slow down even further before re-approaching the pain crystal. When we go slowly and gently enough, we can often go through a range of motion that would normally activate pain—without pain.

Research shows that chronic pain is often a short-circuited distress signal endlessly trumpeting its panic sirens long after the damage has passed (huh. Just like trauma). But once the pain is alleviated, the body can finally turn the signal off. *By moving through the nexus of pain activation, yet slowly enough to not activate the pain, the signal has a chance to turn off.*

Breaking up pain response patterns gives chronic pain the potential to evaporate in the same way the slow movement in trauma resolution allows small residual freezes to release—and chronic pain may coincide with trauma freezes. When we are stressed and in pain, everything in the body tightens up to protect the damaged spot. Even when the original issue is resolved, those tightened spots don't always get the memo. They stay in lockdown until directly released.

Body: The Key | 165

I used to think if I waited out injuries, they would heal. But many of them didn't. According to every health care pro and body worker I have asked, muscle spasms, for example, don't unwind all by themselves. They can stay knotted up forever—until they are manually unkinked. Entrenched trauma also requires intervention.

Slow movement allows these areas to drain and breathe. Adding tiny little head and neck movements can help. Adding side-to-side eye movements and long, slow exhales can help, too. And let's not forget the relaxation—part of this activation and relaxation cycle is modulation. Each element has a purpose.

Fight or ...

MODULATION

Modulation refers to variation in speed, effort, volume, texture, intensity, etc. There are waves of faster/slower, relaxed/intense, active/resting, etc. Modulation also refers to self-regulation as we move between states of arousal and relaxation, as the nervous system activates and deactivates in response to a threat and the withdrawal of the threat.

In a healthy organism, these things happen fairly automatically. Modulation in terms of practice and therapy has to do with the selections that we make (for example, the music we use, the space in which we work, and the structure of our practice), and how they affect us. Remember Cynthia's arc of modulation: readiness → arousal → peak → resting down → deep rest and integration. This is what we want. In our talk, she returned again to Bessel van der Kolk's research in yoga and tai chi.

"Over time, folks who engage in some kind of traditional movement practice that has modulation to it (meaning that it isn't blowing your socks off all the time, like intensive martial arts, or crazy workouts at the gym), that modulation actually works over time to reestablish the natural, healthy rhythmicity of the nervous system, and that helps the person become more resilient." Developing a practice rich in modulation helps the body to regain the ability to modulate on its own. In a traumatic state, this ability to both engage and relax gets stuck. We may live our lives on super high, super low, or alternate between them in huge swoops and crashes, with little to no middle ground.

As we develop our ability to shift between engagement and relaxation, we reestablish the body's ability to do this on its own. As we then face smaller challenges from more resilient places, we build up the capacity to successfully face larger stuff. "It turns out that if you're doing yoga or tai chi you're participating in a kind of ancient holistic wisdom tradition of movement that is actually working to modulate the nervous system."

"A good traditional yoga class or tai chi class is going to work up and then work down, and do that two or three times in an hour and a half. Every good yoga class has *shavasana* at the end, where we adjust time and space for the system that has been stimulated in a modulated way to reintegrate and to digest and absorb what it has learned." We dance folk often close our classes with a cool-down or stretch. It is a simple adaptation to include a comparable period of complete rest at the end.

Cynthia once observed to me that Dunya's music choices in a session were beautifully suited to natural waves of activation and deactivation. "One of the reasons I love Dunya's Sufi work (Dancemeditation) is that, given that it's been passed down through centuries, it embodies an affinity to our natural organismic rhythms. Most traditional music has that, where there's a flow warming up, and then often a building up to higher intensity, a kind of a climax, and then some form of denouement that comes down again to a quieter resting state, and a period of integration before the next wave of mobilization arises again."

This is exactly the model of classic Arab songs. Both classical and dance music from the culture tends to include this modulation within it, with shifts of tempo, intensity, and focus, from a verse sung with great passion by the singer, to the comfort of the chorus, the introspection of the taqasim, and the rousing nature of the orchestral sections. Much other music lacks this internal modulation: be careful to include varied musical choices.

Modulation appears not only in traditional dance and music, but is also a feature in the old-style Five-Part Routine. Such a show starts out fast and upbeat, drawing everyone into the happy mood. In the second part, the music slows down to a bolero for the veil section—a dreamy, inward phase. The middle part is often an upbeat folkloric section, faster than the veil, but more relaxed than the opening. This gets everyone clapping along as the dancer often visits tables or comes closer to the audience for more personal interaction.

The next section is floorwork. In this part, the musicians play taqasim as the dancer sinks to the floor for an intensely introspective, sensual journey. The drum solo that follows the floorwork invokes a redemptive quality as the participants come out of floorwork's altered state into the percussive frenzy of controlled abandon. The joyous finale integrates the journey in a victorious celebration, as the room melts into delirious joy. Then everyone relaxes and rests--eats, drinks, and maybe dances.

Rest and Digest

Cynthia explains Rest and Digest as part of the modulated sequence of arousal and relaxation. In this sequence, there are, "waves of mobilizing into movement slowly, building up to a higher level of arousal, hitting a threshold or climax, and then easing slowly back down until the organism comes into a natural resting state—rest, integration, digestion." In Cynthia's trauma resolution world, this phase is called "Rest and Digest," a term coined by bodyworker Kathy Kain, *somaticpractice.net*. (In Dancemeditation and Spiritual Bellydance, Dunya calls this part of the wave "Relaxation and Integration.") It is a soft, dreamy space between periods of activation, during which the body rearranges its response patterns.

If we always keep going, there is no housekeeping period for digestion, integration, etc. When we have this rest time, then we can get up and dance again—or go on to other activities. "After the resting period, the readiness wave arises again and there's a readiness to mobilize again. It's a healing, organizing rhythm—and beautifully expressed in the modulation of Dancemeditation."

Buddhists say that even if all the dharma (Buddha's teachings), should disappear from the earth, one person could stumble upon a bit of bone, and in contemplating it, all the teachings would reveal themselves to her. It speaks to the essentiality of these principles of modulation, arousal, rest, etc., that we find them in such diverse systems as yoga and Sufi dance—and thus in Dancemeditation. Cynthia observes that, "When organisms begin to oscillate in the work that we do in a more organic, intrinsic way, those same kinds of rhythms begin to show up." It's an organic, natural process. It's what the body does. We're active, and then we rest. Only we have largely forgotten how to rest...

The phase of Rest and Digest is one of the most vital elements of a practice designed for healing, and one of the most easily overlooked. "We finish our practice and run off to the next obligation of our unmodulated go-go-go lifestyle." Instead of dashing off, we can build in ten or fifteen minutes for lying on the floor, covered with a blankie or veil, resting—even sleeping.

Those who have done Dancemeditation or Sufi dance will have experienced this as part of "Relaxation and Integration." The deep, black sleep we find after such a session envelops us completely; we awaken refreshed, recharged, renewed. In a class, we might follow this by pairing up for conversational reflection. At home, we can write for ten minutes in our journals. Move, Rest, Reflect.

We have now seen the wisdom of allowing slow movement to help us locate and release the little freezes of trauma residue, and of titrating the arousal by opening up the orientation architecture of the head, neck, and shoulders. We've also examined the concept of Stabilizing Blue to help us hew towards the more pleasurable, focus on the soothing, and nurture our bodies with comfort and wellbeing. We've explored the benefits of Modulation, in both our lives and practice, how alternating between activity and rest, intensity and relaxation, helps the body self-regulate, feel safe, and turn off the air-raid sirens.

We've also discovered the essentiality of Rest and Digest, of taking the time as part of our practice to *lie down and rest*, giving all the swirling feelings and understanding that our practice has set in motion a chance to integrate, absorb, and realign.

We explore these ideas further in the section on Soul, as we see how Dunya's integration of traditional Sufi oriental dance and modern somatic understanding connect to mind-body health.

13

SOUL

Windows...

THE SOUL OF BELLY DANCE

I first met Dunya McPherson, *dancemeditation.org*, when she was a guest at one of Elena Lentini's week-long workshops. Amazed by the liquid quality of her movement and the depth of her engagement with it, I regarded her with awe. Later, as we all dressed for the show, I gazed in dismay at my reflection the mirror, bloated and frizzy in NYC's epic summer humidity. From behind me, a wistful voice said, "You have the perfect body for this dance." I turned; it was Dunya. It had never, ever occurred to me that I had the perfect body for anything, much less something I loved as much as Oriental dance. Maybe she was okay.

That night she danced. She didn't bother to wear a costume—just a tiered black chiffon skirt and simple white crop top over a bodystocking—and she danced in a way that surprised me. Not that it was strange, more that she was not bound by anything—her dance flowed out of her, her eyes were often closed, and she did this hand-jive thing that I had never seen from any belly dancer. At one point, her skirt slipped down a bit on her hips. I could see her notice it. She put her hands to her skirt as if to tug it up—and then she *pushed it further down on her hips.*

I was in love.

That was around the year 2000. I began attending her workshops. Each one was a fascinating journey into something I didn't understand, but that I knew was important for me. Dunya wielded a high level of personal power with humanity and humor. She was dead serious about what she brought to the table, but then she wore fun shoes or a super-stylie jacket. Fascinating.

Her classes were equally unusual. At the beginning, we worked on the floor, following her as she oozed and shifted in slow motion from one stretch to the next; then the pace might pick up as we did faster movement, sometimes standing, but still in place on our mats. Then she would say, "Close your eyes and do your own dance; let your body move as it wishes." When did anyone ever say that in a belly dance class? None that I ever attended.

I have never seen anyone teach so much by saying so little. Dunya rarely spoke, except to murmur, "This time…" as we shifted our stretch. There were few words of instruction for an exercise—if you mistimed your bathroom break, too bad for you. One of my favorite visualizations, "Blue Rope," came from such a mistake. I knew what our goal was (activate the interstitial spinal muscles), but missed the instructions and visualization. In the end, I invented a whole exercise for myself to accomplish the goal. It became a great tool that I've used ever since.

The big shift for me came at a weeklong she did in NYC. This was in the fall of 2007. I had recently come through some changes in my life, both good and bad. Maybe I was ripe, I don't know. Or lucky. But in this workshop, she focused a lot on breath, specifically, a practice she called Rhythmic Breath. It was like a door opened in my brain. I got it.

As a dancer, I have always reached for a particular place in performance, an effortless place where *I* dissolved and became one with the music. I think of it as the Zone, but it is better known as a *flow state*. I knew it existed—I had been there often enough—but I had no reliable way to find it. Like Harry Potter's Room of Requirement, it was a fickle, unpredictable state. Too often in my dance, I felt trapped by my thinking, going through the motions, unable to reach this place of joyful flow. But with Rhythmic Breath, Boom—I was there. It was a miracle. It was at this point that I became a devotee. I have been one ever since, and the rewards from this approach have not only continued to come, they have magnified, for my dance and my soul.

Over time, I learned that Dunya's approach to belly dance came from her experience with Sufism. Her Sufi teacher danced; therefore, his students did, too. Since she was a trained dancer (Juilliard-graduate ballerina and choreographer), this spoke to her. Through deep study of Sufism, art, somatics, movement, our dance, and its music, she has refined this system for connection to the Divine through Oriental dance.

Many of us yearn for the spirit connection our souls feel from this dance. *Here it is.*

Sufi is often translated as "free thinker," but it actually means 'woolen-clothed' in Arabic. '*Tasawwuf*,' or Sufism, is the path of the woolen-clothed. Sufism is the mystic, poetic heart of Islam. It is widely thought to be far older than Islam (as is our dance). Islamic conservatives despise Sufism (and our dance), which makes me like it even more. Of course, you will find discord and sectarianism among Sufis—some are religious and devout, some aren't; some maintain that their way is the only true way, some don't. We aren't going there because it doesn't concern us.

What does concern us is Sufi mysticism, which has nothing to do with religion. Mysticism is a personal connection to the Divine. Sufi mystics are called Dervishes.

You may have seen Whirling Dervishes in life or in video or pictures. They are usually men in long robes and tall hats, the palm of their right hand facing up to the sky, the left facing down to the earth, as they turn to the left for what seems like a blissful eternity (Elena Lentini told me that when she went to the Rumi festival in Turkey, it blew her mind to see many different kinds of people—young, old, men, women—all whirling in their own way, all at once). Whirling is wonderful, and Dunya teaches it, but it is not our subject today. We are concerned with Sufi *dance*.

The dance we're going to look at is different—and not all Sufis or dervishes do it. Sufi dance uses the same movement vocabulary and the same music as traditional belly dance.

The same movement vocabulary and the same music.

The same.

All the foundation movement, the undulations, circles, S-curves, shimmies, accents, and infinities (the infinity symbol, or *lemniscate*, ∞, describes many of our movements, and is itself an ancient and powerful symbol). I know, right? Already this is interesting. But why not? Sufism and belly dance come from the same regions. If belly dance, so ubiquitous that it is "the dance without a name," is the basic home-style dance of that region, it makes sense that folks whose homes were within its region would dance this way.

However, Sufi dance has two important differences—intention and attention. Its *intention* is union with the Divine—in Sufi terms, the Beloved. The seeker is characterized as the lover, and the Divine/God/Whatever as the Beloved. The lover's eternal desire is union with the Beloved; this metaphor informs much of Sufi poetry and thought. Its *attention* is pointed inward. Pointing oneself inward (*interoception*), rather than outward is huge. Interoception means we focus on—surprise—the interior feeling of the body.

Most of us learned belly dance (or any dance) as a performing art. Our intention is engagement with the audience. We pay attention to the outside of our bodies, how we look. Dunya remembers, "Because I was already a professional dancer, always looking at the mirror, thinking how I looked, and dancing for an audience, the stunning difference for me was closing my eyes and looking in. What is the world inside my body and where does that take me?"

This one tiny flip of focus is a major paradigm shift. Suddenly the dance changes. Rather than a way of pleasing or entertaining others, it becomes instead an interior exploration and integration. Dunya defines her signature approach of Dancemeditation as "a query into relationships of self-to-self, self-to-other, self-to-greater self, and self to the divine through movement, through embodiment." In this paradigm, the dance becomes a seeking, for our place in the world and ourselves, a centering, a way of coming home to the Beloved. It centers belly dance movement and improvisation as a healing, spiritual medium, both for the self, and, in performance, for the guests, becoming a healing and benediction for all who witness it.

How can an inward-facing meditation be interesting to spectators?

In performance, we include the guests, as do the musicians, bringing them with us on our journey. Because our dance is real and imbued with intention, such a performance can be fascinating, healing, and marvelous. Is this practice all you need to be a skilled performer? Of course not. However, instruction in performance skills is widely available—engagement with our bodies and the music is not; I find this an acceptable trade-off. Besides, I will happily overlook some stagecraft for shared joy.

In addition, far too many of us are pushed into performance. This is culturally a social dance of joy. Performance is uncomfortable for many and its focus can encourage socially destructive competition and perfectionism, which pushes people away from the dance. But many of us are professional dancers; the fear that we may alienate or bore our guests is a real concern.

How do we focus inward yet bring the guests with us?

Here's how I do it.

First, I took the time to learn and practice this inward-facing model. The positive changes in my dance made it worthwhile: for example, I was reliably able to go into a zone, I became more relaxed, and my dance became more spacious.

After I felt comfortable with the process, I began to practice maintaining my engagement with open eyes, flirting and gathering all my guests in a warm embrace—consciously radiating joy. Like an actor who includes the audience even when his back is turned, I deliberately practice enveloping us all in a warm radiance of love. Dance is about communication—with the self and with the guests. I'm an introvert and this was (and is) challenging for me. It is a vulnerable place. But it is in everyone's best interest, so I push on.

If my goal is a joyous connection to the Divine, then my goal as a performer is that my show be a benediction. I am there to bless the guests, to bring them love, compassion, and joy, to take away their fears and cares and leave them feeling refreshed and renewed. Some of my work is theatrical and my themes are not always cheerful, but I still have this intention. There is always a layer of "Here we are together, and I love you so much."

I hear those of you feeling a little twitchy. Isn't all this "connection to the Divine" stuff kind of New Age?

No.

New Age thinking is an eclectic esotericism that arose in the 70s. Many Westerners became interested in Sufism during the experimental 70s—but Sufism predates the New Age by centuries. Sufism is a mystical tradition within Islam (and has long been a thorn in its shoe). Sufism is old—clearly traceable to the times of the Prophet Muhammed (peace be upon him). Existence at the birth of Islam indicates that Sufism is even older than we might think. According to Dunya, "Early Sufism (Rabia, etc), was austere and had commonality with early Christianity in its asceticism. This is hundreds of years before the birth of Islam."

According to Inayet Khan, a Sufi master and Indian classical musician who brought Sufism to the West in 1910 (and father of Pir Vilayet Khan, another well-known Sufi master), "Every age of the world has seen awakened souls, and as it is impossible to limit wisdom to any one period or place, so it is impossible to date the origin of Sufism" (sufiway.org). It is the sense of seeking, of mysticism, of spirit connection that is the soul of Sufism. Sufism transcends Islam as it transcends the everyday—as our dance transcends the notion of performance for the other. Sufi dance is a bona-fide connection to belly dance as a mode of spiritual homecoming.

Am I suggesting we all become (or call ourselves) Sufis?

No. Though if we seek a spiritual connection to the Divine through this dance, perhaps we already are. I *do* suggest that we infuse our dance with a deeper intention and practice shifting our attention to the inside of the body.

Will we do this well (or even properly), on our own?

No. We all run the constant risk of going off the rails. Find a good teacher—none of this works properly without a teacher. A friend taught himself French from a book, and then proudly spoke it to a French friend. She apologized, saying she thought her English was better, but she had not understood a word he said.

A book is not enough. Videos on the Internet are not enough.

Find a teacher. A good one.

How it works

My teacher in this work is Dunya McPherson, who has devoted herself to bringing this practice into our modern times and making it accessible to all. Dunya has spent most of her life in this seeking. She highlighted the healing, meditative qualities of Sufi dance, infused kindred elements from her long, deep, exploration of art, somatics, and movement, and presents this in an egalitarian way.

You don't have to be Sufi, or even religious. You don't have to be a belly dancer, or even a dancer at all. Yet it provides a true spiritual connection through dance, a connection to forces greater than oneself. It aligns perfectly with trauma healing and the other benefits discussed in previous chapters. Dunya's teachings, expressed in what she calls Spiritual Belly Dance and Dervish Dancemeditation, form the basis of this chapter.

One thing that always surprises me about Dancemeditation and Spiritual Belly Dance classes is how good I feel afterwards. By the end of most daylong workshops, I am exhausted and hurting. Workshops are work! You have to follow, remember, and execute complex combinations. My body always complains, even if it isn't that strenuous. The floors hurt my feet; I'm sweaty and gross, blah, blah, blah. But after Dancemeditation classes, I feel great—energized, pain-free, and happy.

Why is that?

Dancemeditation is receptive. A regular workshop is head down—one squints and works to re-create the teacher's movement. Dancemeditation is body up. Dunya explains that, "It is very different to close your eyes and to follow your own movement, body up instead of head down. You can use the same vocabulary, but if you do it from the head down it will not have the same effect as listening to your body and following the body. The reason you follow a teacher, to a large degree, is to learn to follow, period, so that when you dance, you're following your body--you're *following* the movement, not moving it, not telling yourself what to do."

This concept is huge. This is the basis of Eastern teachers follow-me method of teaching as well. Just follow. Get out of your own way, thinking and naming, and let the body follow. I focus on my breath and allow my body to move, to follow the music without judgment. I am not drilling or repeating movements over and over, trying to make them all the same. If I repeat a movement, I am exploring it, deepening it, engaging with it, seeing how it feels, and how its variations feel. It's a radically different perspective, and a radically different experience.

Going to a Dancemeditation class is like going to a spa. It's a day of drenching oneself in the senses, of gentleness and relief. Part of this may be how much we sleep. After each major segment of the day, we lie down on our mats, pull up our veils and blankies, and pass out cold for ten or fifteen minutes.

On occasion, I've wondered vaguely if I were getting my money's worth, as I passed out for the third time in one day. For the first day or so of a weeklong, it seems like all we do is sleep. But that isn't all we do; It only seems that way. And I have come to look forward to the rest periods, to cherish them. Sufi 'rest' is more than a nice little nap. This is sleep like no other—deep, black, full. I mean, people snore.

The only sleep to which I can compare it is the 3pm naps an acupuncturist once prescribed to heal my ravaged adrenal system. As I started paying attention to this, I realized that on the dot of three, I was overcome with fatigue. Even when driving a car, I learned to pull over, lie back, and crash out for ten minutes. This sleep had the same kind of black, healing depth. From these naps, as from Dancemeditation rest, I awaken refreshed and energized.

Rest is one of the hallmarks of this approach. The work causes a lot of internal activity—I was going to say, on both the physical and mental levels, but the mental is profoundly the physical. Emotions are physical. Many disorders of the mind are rooted in the body.

The brain *literally* changes while we sleep. This has been documented. Sleep is the body's way of cleaning house; to "knit up the raveled sleeve of care." The practice stirs up the muck at the bottom of the pool; sleep washes it away. The sleep nourishes everything. That's one thing. Also, you remember Cynthia talking about Rest and Digest? The importance of resting after clearing trauma? This is built in.

And there is more.

In a typical Dancemeditation class, there are multiple shifts between following the teacher or a partner and then closing the eyes and doing your own dance. The pace varies, often super-slow motion, sometimes moderate or fast, always integrating the breath. This is how Dunya teaches, and it is how she was taught. Dunya describes her experience:

"The primary practice was slow movement and breathing; embedded in that would be very tiny movement, micromovement. The energy of the Path was conveyed from teacher to practitioner; 'transmission' is the word that's generally used. That was primarily how we were drawn into deep states, through following this type of movement from the teacher, and then closing our eyes and continuing on our own."

Figure 30 Focus on the inside...

The teacher goes into deep states so the class can also experience them. Thus, the teacher's eyes are often closed. The success of the group is the degree to which the teacher is able to enter into herself—deeply enough to enable the students do the same. This is partly about mirror neurons, through which we experience what we see. And it is internal all the way. As you can imagine, this is quite different from your average belly dance class of counting, drilling, and exactness.

After a period of following, the teacher invites the students to "close your eyes and do your own dance." Dunya describes this in her own learning: "Sometimes one would continue with that type of movement, slow movement and breath, and minute movement, and sometimes with whatever came up or whatever the music suggested, because there was music and the music was primarily Middle Eastern music, which certainly invokes certain kinds of movement. Not small and slow all the time."

It is through movement that the teacher transmits the map for accessing the deeper self; the student then follows the path, exploring this new realm inside of herself. Dunya explains that, "Following is an intentional process. You follow the teacher, *then* you close your eyes and follow your body. This is salient to the cultivation of the All-Important Receptive Movement. It is encapsulated in the phrase, 'to be moved.' To be moved by God. To surrender, surrendering the ego, surrendering to God."

Wait, what? Surrender? God?
Dunya explains that we surrender what Sufism calls *willfulness*. "In modern terminology, willfulness means the ego, which is full of inner scripts, things like, 'You should do this. You should do that,' things that have been cultivated into us that are destructive for us. That's essentially what the ego is; it's wagging its finger at you all the time, whereas God is not full of that. By listening, and following, and letting go of the ego and the willfulness, you have some possibility of *relaxing into kindness* that is much bigger than anything you know how to do on your own."

We are all much bigger on the inside than we are on the outside—as is the dance.

And our dance stands apart.

As mentioned in the previous chapters, there are many benefits to improvisation in and of itself. Of course, one can improvise in many genres, but there is something special about Oriental dance, its movement vocabulary *and* its music, that makes it different from other dances. We feel it, but it's hard to name or even understand. Dunya explains: "I have a lot of reverence for the dance, for the Middle Eastern dance vocabulary, because it allowed me to have experiences on this planet that I had longed for and had never been able to reach."

For many folks, this dance is just another movement vocabulary. They have learned a lot of different dances, and this is one more. You learn the vocabulary and you can do the dance. Like a language, you learn it and then you speak it. But there is more to learning a language than learning words, or syntax (the order of words in a sentence), or even the accent. There is the way meaning is made within that language's culture. There is conversation. There is idiomatic expression (for example, raining cats and dogs). There are jokes. There is poetry. And there is magic.

Belly dance is not just a dance

It's not *just* a vocabulary. It's also a system of invocation, a magical doorway to divine connection. In particular, especially when done to improvised live Eastern music, it is physical poetry, expressed in the moment, addressed to the Beloved. It doesn't come from memorizing a sequence of stylized movements. It comes from integrating movement, music, and breath, letting the body move as it wishes, and entering into the moment—connecting body, mind, soul with the music and the people. This is Sufi Dervish dance, and it embodies the heart and soul of Oriental dance. It is a gift we give—and the gift gives back.

Through this process of going inside, focusing on the breath, and letting the body move as it wishes, we follow the body's intuitive response to the music. We let the body lead.

This is how we learn to be in the moment and how to go there reliably.

The letting go of *I*, the ego, comes from being in the moment, at one with the music, enmeshed in something big, deep, and powerful. The joy of this state is unparalleled. This dance, coupled with the breath, has brought me to places of which I only dreamed. It has opened doorways to my soul. This dance and its music are my go-to. And I am not alone in this observation.

Dunya notes that, "I have not been able to reach mystical states through other vocabularies. I've tried to close my eyes and do more balletic movements, and I can do them slowly and enter into deep states to a certain extent, but I realized that Western dance vocabulary (ballet and modern dance), and Western music come from a different place in the human being. They activate deep imagination, the limbic self and the emotional self. They are not made for meditative entrainment, for inner journeying, or for dissolution of the ego." The imagination makes sense, as ballet tends to be about telling stories to the audience (Western art, remember? It expects meaning. Eastern art is abstract).

Dunya continues, "None of us know where Middle Eastern dance movements came from. It is deep in the mists of time. It feels extraordinarily atavistic, and for me much closer to a primordial self, to a part of me that is pure Central Nervous System, the part that transcends all human control, or in fact all animal control, all life control. It's like the movement that animals do, and clouds do, and trees do. The tree is one of my great teachers, the tree teaching me how to shimmy properly."

"I was practicing in the woods by myself and then fell asleep. When I woke up, I saw this big tree standing in front of me. I stood up without even thinking and started to follow it. I suddenly realized the tree was doing all this beautiful vibration. It was doing the most perfect, natural, relaxed shimmy because the wind was moving through it. That right there was one of those pivot points in my existence. I realized that whole Rumi thing of, 'The wind moves through the reed to make the music.'"

"All this letting go, surrender, because the tree was being moved by the wind but it was dancing. It wasn't dancing, it was *being danced*. I felt the wind through the tree's movement. My shimmy changed after that. It got relaxed, the way that vibration moves through the body in this organic, flowing way. That's what the tree did. It changed me. I think everybody could change that way. I do."

"These movements lead you to this essential piece of energy that is the Universe moving. Not the limbic and frontal cortex, the central nervous system. It's the animal, the physics nature, the cosmic nature—and it's also this difficult journey for humans to drop the ego and be moved by the forces. That's such a high-level thing to say about this dance."

"This dance comes from that and it goes to that—connecting with the movement of the Universe. That can be both cosmic, the way stars form and turn and whirl, and physics, vibrations, movements can also be incarnated things on the planet like little animals, the trees moving—organic life. My experience with the tree was the epitome of natural movement and surrender and receptivity. I was doing it before I knew that I was doing it. I just stood up and did it. Then it dawned on me what I was up to."

The notion that belly dance has a deep connection to our animal core is not so farfetched. Morocco, one of our venerable teachers and researchers in Oriental dance, *casbahdance.org*, points out that this dance uses the muscles of the body in the directions of their natural striations—the way they are designed to be used. Her excellent, thorough warmup leverages this further by moving from the smaller, inner muscles to the larger, outer muscles.

In addition, there is weird semi-correlation between belly dance movement and fetal development. In the Feldenkrais Journal #28, Seth Dellinger describes his training with Sheryl Field, director of The Field Center for Children's Integrated Development in NYC, *thefieldcenter.org*. Field describes a side-to-side wriggling fetuses do in the womb. This movement appears by the seventh week of gestation—and if it *doesn't* appear, the fetus does not survive.

The brain is little more than neurons at this point. Field suggests that "movement builds the brain," that, in fact, these early movements may organize the nervous system. By the twelfth week, the fetus has added folding forward, arching, and a twist, and people recovering from paralysis make these same four movements (Dellinger 2015 with thanks to Nancy-Laurel for the connection.

Wriggling, arching, twists, even forward folds, are integral parts of belly dance. My own observation that belly dance movement coincides with trauma release practices (which are certainly related to a primal past), fits in with all of this.

This dance has so many deep elements. It exists on a level far removed from the average folk dance. Dunya explains, "The thing that makes you live and stop living is a mystery. This is where the dance goes for me; that's what it reaches down into, deep into those fibers. The movements penetrate beneath the cognitive and the limbic to our pure energetic core. It is the fundamental layer of life. How that emerged as a form is a miracle."

"I would say the majority of what I see in performance is very cultivated and *not* that. But you can see it beneath the artificiality; it's there. You can see inside of it; it's there. Inside of all that tiny vibration, inside of the undulation and the wave movements, inside the floating arms is that profundity."

I agree—most of what I see in performance is steps lined up to music, with little to no entrance to any kind of state, either for the dancer or the guests. Yet it is there. And I submit that we have been shortchanged in our learning, as this potential for grace remains unexplored and unmentioned while we focus on technical stylization.

Yes, I hear you: *But we need technique! How do we get better if we don't practice technique?* Let's get that out of the way right now.

Many kinds of technique

In learning this dance, most of us have practiced what's called procedural knowledge—primarily memorization, replication, and stylization of moves and movement sequences. Perhaps we have also practiced our stagecraft. Smiling at the audience. Even making our own combinations and dances. In general, however, we have focused on the outside, the visual—what it looks like and how to do it. And while this has its benefits, it also has some drawbacks.

For example, we forget that the feeling is the most important thing. We forget to enjoy the dance, *and to share our joy with our guests.* We forget to embrace our guests with the gift of our love. We forget that our guests desperately need gracious love and care. And we often forget how to be good guests ourselves, as we squint and judge when we should be good *sammi'ah* (educated listeners), cheering up the dancer with our welcoming, smiling faces.

All of these require skill—technique—that we can practice. With the inner gaze inherent in Dancemeditation practices, we can explore deeper facets of our technique and a more intuitive response to the music. We do this by following our body's feeling—how the movement feels in the body, what the body enjoys, how it wants to respond, and by taking the time to enjoy the physical sensation of the movement and the music.

In the Body chapter, a prime element of trauma healing is opting for the most pleasurable. Enjoying the feeling of the movement for the sake of enjoyment, taking joy in the moving body and the music, these are essential elements of the dance—and of healing ourselves from those "slings and arrows of outrageous fortune." It's a win all around.

We are *not* talking trance. Trance is a separate activity. Both trance and embodiment are valuable states, but they are quite different.

Dancers embodied in the moment—especially in performance—are like meditators. They maintain a detached but keen awareness of everything that is going on around them, factoring it in to their responses and actions—from dodging the waiter with the tray, to including the guests, to turning a slip and fall into a gracious part of the show. They notice and respond in the moment.

People in trance are preferably protected by outside caretakers, for they are in altered state. They may not see the waiter, and may not notice they have fallen. A trancer rolls with the surf. The embodied dancer is present in the moment, riding the wave of the music through intuition and awareness. And this has benefits.

In "real life," much of our time is spent worrying about what happened before or what is going to happen next, and the calamities that await if we don't do X, Y, and Z *right now!* We spend remarkably little time enjoying, or even noticing, the present moment. We are always checking, keeping ourselves in go-mode, living in the past or anticipating the future.

When we step outside of this raging swirl of activity, when we let go of the *I* that controls every moment, these pressing issues don't press so hard. We gain the time, space, and equanimity to see them from a broader perspective, from outside our frantic immersion in the daily rat race, those willful ego scripts of *should* and *must*. We open inward. We trust our intuitive core, not to lose ourselves in the music, but to find ourselves. This is a big difference. Our practice gives us the space to step away from daily strife and control. We can relax, enjoy ourselves, and release our cares.

We can heal: ourselves, and the world.

Healing ourselves and the world

Healing

One of the practices most suited to healing, including increased physical intuition, flexibility, elegance, softening chronic pain, and releasing stress and trauma, is Slow Movement. Dunya explains that in her Sufi training, a primary practice was slow movement and breathing; "embedded in that would be very tiny movement, micromovement. Slow belly dance." Let's take a close look at Slow Movement.

Slow Movement means moving with what Dunya calls "glacial slowness." It's not merely slow; it is incredibly slow, yet a continuous flow. With Slow Movement, we let our bodies discover and feel. Slow is a funny word. Whereas fast has dozens of great words, when I looked for synonyms that might better convey the slow-motion quality we are going for, I found only negative words like listless, torpor, etc. Unhurried, gradual, and languid help, but to see this in real life, to get a sense of just how slow it is, visit bellydancesoul.com/resources.

Slow Movement allows us the time and space for lyrical, refined elegance. When we explore a movement slowly, we have plenty of time to receive and express the beauty of the moment. We find it through softness, attention, and loving grace. We love our body and the movement in every moment, we pay attention to the quality and alignment, the elegance of the line, and we do it with a gentle intensity. Our movements become fluid, rich, filled with subtle glory. Rather than pushing or forcing ourselves, we take the time to effortlessly waft.

But what about technique? This is both healing *and* technique. This honeyed, sleek, effortless quality builds a lot of strength. It takes more muscles, and smaller, subtler muscles, to sustain elegant, languorous movement than it does to drive through a fixed pattern at speed. Holding the intention of evolution, having the patience and engagement in the moment to allow the movement to shift and evolve, gently builds strength and concentration, while developing those languid, effortless lines.

When we explore a movement without the pressure of time, we can feel it far more deeply, allow the body the space to find its way, to be in perfect balance at every moment, making each moment more gracious. There is no suffering of technique—it is enhanced. Top-level musicians practice difficult passages in slow motion—why shouldn't we? And there is still more.

Through this state of relaxed focus, we are able to approach and release pain and even dissolve the residue of trauma. This has been covered at length in the chapter on Body. In Slow Movement, we approach activation sites patiently, as if gaining the trust of wild woodland creatures. We approach slowly, ease back, exhale and soften, so the body feels safe, knowing that it is free to escape.

In this process, we gentle away our frozen places. Over time, we warm them with our breath, allowing them to soften, liquefy, and complete their protective mission. Thus, we free ourselves from the compulsion to project old survival responses onto every interaction that triggers our fear. It is precisely the somatic titration and pendulation.

This dance has the power to melt everyday stress, soften grief, and generally cleanse the body's house of pain and suffering. The first time I spoke of these properties was in 2012 at Yasmina Ramzy's International Bellydance Conference of Canada. After the talk, a woman approached me. She told me of her brother's death, how she held his hand as he died, and how grief-stricken she felt.

On her way home from the hospital, on a whim that seemed odd to her even at the time, she stopped in to take a belly dance class. By the end of the class, she no longer felt that terrible sense of abandonment. She still missed her brother, but she felt at peace with his passing. She had previously thought that it was "just the class," but, upon hearing the lecture, she realized that the dance itself had healed her—through dancing, she had released her pain.

All of us have had the experience of stomping into class in a foul temper and coming out feeling good. It's not the moving per se. It's the dance. This dance. Our dance.

This is the healing soul of our dance.

There is more to the dance, even beyond this.

But first, let's connect some dots...

Connection to the Divine

As humans, we desire to be part of something greater than ourselves. Most cultures conceptualize some framework of a sacred nature, a Sky Father or Earth Mother, a Great Spirit or Creator, sacred sites to whole pantheons of deities, from kind to wrathful and beyond. Many of us who do this dance feel a sacred nature.

The traditional dance has many social ritual functions—celebrations, weddings, and festivities of all sorts. Their explicit connection to something older and deeper has been misted by time, yet still we feel a connection. We know the dance is bigger than a few hip drops and undulations. We've invented many things, but we've had no clear line to which we could point.

Here is a clear line.

As previously noted, Sufi mysticism is ancient. It connects to our dance. Mysticism is not religion. You can be a Christian, Jewish, or Muslim. You can be Buddhist or anything else. Though Sufism has been under the aegis of Islam since Islam's inception, and some folks' Sufi training has been religious, Dunya's was pure mysticism. As she defines it, "Mysticism is the intimate, personal communion with the Divine."

That which is numinous has a mysterious, holy, or spiritual quality. It is a numinous radiance that we feel in the dance—or at least that's what I feel, as do many of the folks with whom I have discussed this. When we improvise, the *I* disappears. We feel closer to God, the Universe, the Divine, or however we characterize it. It is deeply personal, and deeply felt. Belly dancers, including famous dancers of the culture, routinely say, this dance is my heart, it is my soul; it is the best part of me.

Common sense (and Resistance), tells us we have not the time, money, or aptitude to dance; yet our felt connection to something powerful, important, and profound persists. Why do we feel such attraction to this simple dance?

Dunya found that, "I came out of my grayness and my sense of spiritual despair. That's what I definitely left behind, I no longer had spiritual despair." A lot of us feel that sense of spiritual impoverishment. We come to the dance because we sense its power, yet find no inkling of it in the way that we're taught. But it's there.

Belly dance can open our hearts and souls; it can return us to a sense of belonging and depth that our modern world seems hell-bent on smothering under an avalanche of plastic widgets and pre-formed whatsits. Maybe this approach is not for everyone. There are no guarantees. But it is for many.

This dance connects us to the Divine.

We know it. We feel it. It's real.

Do we all start calling ourselves Sufi Mystic belly dancers? No, certainly not. Sufism is a deep pool of wisdom. Classic training takes 1001 days (that's every day, all day, for almost three years). Until we have undertaken such training from qualified masters, let's back off the snazzy names.

Can we incorporate these principles within our dance to open ourselves to this numinous connection? Yes. That we can do right now. Dunya points out that, "Middle Eastern dance, and Eastern traditions in general, are made to entrain meditative opening, the meditative state. This is their purpose—to dissolve the ego. It is a specific intention." This dance is part of that intention.

"Middle Eastern art is all about meditative entrainment. Look at the ornamental work—it's all about infinity, it's all about entrainment. This is always noted about the ornamental art, those gardens of paradise, the infinity of God, the eternal now, all of that. Every Middle Eastern art historian or analyst says this." The music is, too—what is tarab, after all, but dissolution of ego into shared musical ecstasy? If all these Eastern art forms do that, why wouldn't the dance?

Of course, it does. We even make infinity shapes with our bodies.

Entraining into the meditative state and dissolving the ego is the high level of this art form. *The dance is meant for this high purpose.*

Yes.

Mind-body practice

There is a sense among researchers that dance began as sacred activity. Certainly, we also dance for pleasure, for social and sexual connection—even for exercise. It's funny that dance has somehow come to be divested, particularly in the West, of any spirit overtones. There are many sacred dances in other cultures and continents, India, Tibet, Africa, the Americas, Asia. But in much of Europe and North America (except for our First Nations), dance has largely been removed from our sacred rituals. Even in the East, female dancers (and in some cases, any dancers) have recently been pushed out of the historic venues of their social rituals—weddings, moulids, and celebrations of every kind. In the West, even our sacred rituals have largely been abandoned. It is no wonder that so many of us thirst to nurture our spirit.

Religious conservatives have always frowned upon dance—it is too much fun and brings attention to the body. Most spiritual teachings disdain the body, regarding it as a filthy, sin-soaked receptacle for the somehow-pristine soul. Even most meditation practices insist that the body be quieted in order to quiet the mind.

The meditator sits and notices his breath. There may be chants, mantras, or breathing practices. These often focus on the exhale, which calms the body and biologically signals to it that it is safe; thus, the wary, hyper-vigilant lizard brain can calm down and relax for a while.

And we do sometimes despair of our bodies, always eating, shitting, farting, and generally driving us with their insatiable demands. However, without our bodies, we would not exist.

Our bodies are precious.

Our bodies are brilliant organisms deserving of care and feeding, love and respect. The body contains wisdom and understanding that the reasoning, naming mind does not. More and more, science finds that the body runs the show—sending chemical signals to the brain to bump this up, damp that down, or pull out all the stops for fight or flight. The connections between body and mind are too numerous and vital to ignore. Moreover, our bodies are not cars, easily replaced at the first sign of rust or failure. So, instead of hating on the body in traumatic rage, what if we love it? Cherish it? Integrate it? What if we allow the body, with all its wisdom, to heal us? Connect us to the Divine?

In the 1990s, the mind-body fitness committee of the International Dance-Exercise Association (IDEA) defined mind-body exercise as "physical exercise executed with a profoundly inwardly-directed focus." The committee identified five characteristics of mind-body exercise. To determine if these principles still stand, I ran them by Dr. Teresa Hawkes, a neurophysiologist who studies the molecular basis of exercise's effects on cognition, *researchgate.net/profile/Teresa_Hawkes*. She confirmed their ongoing relevance. They are:

1. Inner mental focus;
2. Concentration on muscular movements;
3. Synchronization of movements with breathing patterns;
4. Attention to form and alignment; and
5. A belief in the "life energy," such as *prana* or *chi*, that is part of ancient Eastern disciplines (Dr. Hawkes couldn't vouch for the *existence* of prana, chi, connection etc., as scientists have not found a way to measure it, but we have both *experienced* it, as have millions of other folks)

A mind-body practice typically has *one or more* of these qualities. Belly dance, with this Sufi interoception, has *all* of them. We don't have the prana/chi thing as such, but we do that connection to the Divine, which is certainly in the ballpark.

But belly dance doesn't stop there. It is not an ascetic discipline that seeks to tame the body in order to quiet the mind. Belly dance celebrates the body and its relationship to the world around it, to music, pleasure, and human connection, with playfulness and joy.

Belly dance is a glorious marriage of the sacred and the profane—beautiful, sensual, healing, and redemptive. It aligns the body and mind, washes away stress and trauma, releases us from fear and anxiety, and connects us to the Divine. What other practice has all that? Plenty of practices do some of it—tai-chi, yoga, Zen archery, even sitting meditation. But none include those beautiful, sensual, entertaining, profane qualities. There is no interaction, playfulness, or music. No earthiness. No spangles. No fun. No joy.

Belly dance has it all—with bells on.

This brings me to my final point.

Belly dance is seen as a relatively innocuous occupation with little meaning outside of itself. To those of us who practice it, it is special, and we seek to bring it wider attention; but only as itself, a dance. Many of us have a mission to "elevate the dance," which often means to make it more Western—put it on bigger stages, with bigger audiences—more spectacle, more choreography, more pomp, etc., with ever younger, more flexible, and more athletic dancers. This approach overlooks much of the cultural identity and traditional priorities that are the heart's blood of our dance.

What if we could elevate the dance in a way that valued its cultural context? Without that, this dance is dead. It is an empty movement vocabulary. It becomes like Cheez Wiz or Kool-Aid—an artificial, processed, non-food masquerading as real food.

We don't need more plastic crap in our lives. We don't need harder steps or more of them. We need real things that connect us to our true selves. We need avenues to our souls, ways to accept and nurture ourselves, be kind to ourselves, love ourselves, all of us human beings. We have plenty of work, responsibility, *should* and *must*. We have plenty of *not good enough*. Where is the fun? Let's have more fun, love, pleasure, and joy. Let's have more playtime. This is the numinous soul of our dance.

We have come to our crossroads.
Which way do we go with this new understanding of the dance?

So here we are at the crossroads...

14

MIDNIGHT AT THE CROSSROADS

THE CROSSROADS: BLUES AND BELLY DANCE.

Thanks to Toya R. Smith for clarifying the blues crossroads.

Remember that eerie image in the mythology of the blues —that of the musician who sells his soul to the Devil in exchange for technical brilliance? Back in chapter 1, we learned that it is an amalgam of Western old-world legends superimposed upon an African religious practice.

So why does it keep coming up?

Robert Johnson, for example, a musician who came from nowhere, suddenly exploded into brilliance. While his earlier performances had been nothing special, Johnson became an overnight sensation for his jaw-dropping artistry (and this was back in the 1930s, a time of word-of-mouth promotion). The whispers said he had gone to the crossroads at midnight and sold his soul to the Devil (in Rosedale, Mississippi, according to legendary blues artist Son House—right where Highways 1 and 8 intersect).

Johnson did nothing to quell these rumors—in fact he encouraged them. They added to his dangerous mystique, bringing in audiences and accolades. He wrote several songs highlighting his Devil-given skills (*Me and the Devil, Crossroad Blues, Going up to Rosedale,* etc.).

Tommy Johnson, a virtuoso blues artist whose renown predated Robert Johnson, was also said to have sold his soul. He let it be known that he regularly met a man at midnight, at a crossroad, who taught him any song he wanted to know.

These artists live on, thanks to the miracle of recorded music, and their genius endures. Plenty of today's musicians insist that Robert Johnson (who died in agony at age 27, allegedly poisoned by a jealous husband) must have been recorded at too high a speed, since they cannot recreate his blazing riffs. Artists like Sister Rosetta Tharpe, the godmother of rock and roll, along with the Johnsons, Son House and others (all of whom recorded back in the 1920s and 30s), continue to inspire an endless stream of musicians.

From the blues came jazz, rhythm and blues, rock and roll, soul, funk, and hip hop—a staggering, brilliant artistic legacy. For many of us, this list includes our favorite music. But where did the blues come from? What's up with this Devil stuff? And how does it all connect to belly dance?

Camouflage and Conflation
The blues arose from Africans forced into American slavery. Africa is a huge continent with myriad nations, ethnic groups, languages and religions. Scholars estimate that upwards of twenty million Africans from many nations were forcibly abducted (or killed in slaving raids). Bundled helter-skelter onto ships of death, they were sold into foreign bondage, expected to work or die, or both. There was, by necessity, a lot of fusion and adaptation.

The Africans disguised many of their own old-country traditions beneath a veneer of Christianity to keep them hidden from white owners—a deep part of the power of the black church. Such elements hark back to important African religions, belief systems extant long before their followers were sold into shackles. The bluesman's so-called "Devil," the Keeper of the Crossroads, is a respected, beneficent deity in several African traditions.

The Keeper of the Crossroads intercedes with the gods on the behalf of humans. It is He who opens the way, who helps, who teaches, who is welcomed first into every ceremony. Like the Greek god Hermes, He is emissary, messenger, patron of roads, travelers, and boundaries; a clever bringer of luck, a guardian, and a guide. The Keeper of the Crossroads is a benefactor. He is good. The Devil is not.

But slaves can't be invoking their old gods. They must conform to the culture around them or risk death—or worse. So the Keeper of Crossroads became the Devil. That's the camouflage. And those old-country crossroads myths were right there to confirm it. Conflation happens when people believe the cover story.

Drums were forbidden to the slaves since some African nations used them to communicate at long distances. Deprived of their instruments, the Africans adapted the new country's instruments to fit the music they carried in their hearts.

There was one little problem...

The guitar and banjo (itself of African origin) have predetermined notes due to the frets on their necks. They are locked into Western scales, with specific whole and half steps, like a piano. But the music of the Africans wasn't built on those scales. The blues began with a search for the elusive "blue" note, a microtone, which doesn't exist in Western music. This was not a single note, but an entirely different way of framing notes—one that adapted to the musician's feeling in the moment.

Sound familiar? There's more.

Sylviane Diouf, an award-winning historian, author and a researcher at New York's Schomburg Center for Research in Black Culture, *silvianediouf.com*, finds that as much as 30% of Africans enslaved in the USA came from Muslim cultures. They spoke *and wrote* Arabic. Their musical sensibilities and traditions valued feeling, microtones, and improvisation. It still does (for an overview, see *Muslim Roots, U.S. Blues* by Jonathan Curiel, at *bellydancesoul.com/resources*.

I know—this directly contradicts the myth of Africa as the "dark continent," full of savages. Such lies. Many African nations had highly developed civilizations. Timbuktu, in Mali, for example, has been a center of art, literary scholarship, and tolerance for *a thousand years*. The same for Zanzibar. And the connection between Arabic music and the blues goes well beyond microtones...

- Blues songs explore the pleasure and pain of life and love—and the singer often tempers a song's sorrow with the joy of immediate connection (try the brilliant singer and composer Sam Cooke).
- Simple song structures are venues for instrumental solos. Like Eastern folkloric music, the songs are relatively simple—verse, chorus, verse—but between those elements, each musician gets to strut his or her stuff in solo improvisations. As this is retained in jazz, funk, soul, rock and roll, etc., you can see it is a central element.
- Both cultures lean towards deeper women's voices and higher men's voices, along with *melisma* and "quivery" vocal strategies.

- Blues artists play what they feel—and they pride themselves on never playing a song the same way twice.

Remember the film *The Blues Brothers*? Its greatest accomplishment was rounding up a lot of fabulous musicians of the culture and giving them extended cameos where they could strut their stuff—among them such luminaries as Aretha Franklin, James Brown, Cab Calloway, Ray Charles, and iconic Mississippi blues master John Lee Hooker.

These artists' performances were overdubbed with studio recordings for sound quality. This is standard in films. The artist sings along with their own music, doing it the same way in the filmed scene as they did in the studio. All but two. James Brown was recorded live, though his entire choir lip-synched. But Brown was indoors with a microphone, where there was some degree of control. Not so for the other one.

John Lee Hooker never made a song the same way twice. No matter how many takes they did, he made it new every time. Hooker's appearance (as "Sidewalk Slim," playing an outdoor block party with assorted blues royalty) was recorded live. You can see and hear the difference between Hooker's song and every other song in the movie—in how much time they show him playing and in the texture of the sound of his performance. The infectious, genuine joy and raw power of his voice blows me away. That's the blues.

And here is my final comparison: The blues is a venue for joy. Singing makes suffering more bearable, lifting the heart of everyone involved. When you add in dancing, moving, shaking off the trauma and pain of daily life, we get even more connected. This is a classic example of holding the pain of life in balance with the joy of the present moment.

How does this relate to belly dance?

The blues and belly dance come from the same roots. Try belly dancing to some rich, slow blues and you will feel it (*bellydancesoul.com/resources*). Many songs are about love and pain—as are so many Arabic songs. Are they the same? No. I do *not* suggest that African American music is beholden to Arabic music. Myriad African cultures created this brilliant legacy.

But there is a relationship. And here's a good question:

If the blues is related to Arabic music, why didn't the dance come over with the music? There is a clear connection between African-American dance and the dances of sub-Saharan Africa (just watch video of both and you can see it in the body line and movement quality).

But what about belly dance?

I have a thought about this. It is conjecture, but has potential for exploration. Maybe the dance did come here, and it changed, mashed up with the dances of other African cultures. Or maybe the dance did *not* come because the African-Muslim music was, like other Arabic classical music, tarab music—meant for listening rather than dancing.

Perhaps turning the music from devotional listening music (gospel) into secular dance music (the blues) was a contributing factor in the sinfulness that those who adopted the Christian worldview associated with the blues. We may never know. But the musical connection is clear. And the Oriental dance community can learn much from the blues.

Belly dance is not Islamic dance any more than the blues is Islamic music. Both the music and dance sidestep Islam, but have roots in the same region and encounter misperceptions as to their "low-class" origins. Both have been heavily appropriated (and appreciated) by Western artists and audiences. However, only one has gained respect in the global arts world—by staying true to its roots, true to its traditions, true to its soul (Hint: Not belly dance).

In the Western version of the story, the Devil only got one's soul after death—but we dancers haven't made such a good bargain. In selling out to political expediency, Western cultural values, xenophobia, racism, Orientalism, and an uneducated marketplace, we have too often let go of the Eastern qualities of the dance: Improvisation. Feeling. Joy. In a word, Soul.

What do we get in exchange?

Spectacle. Difficult, showy movement. Densely packed combinations. Drilling rather than dancing. Stylization. Novelty. Empty music, rhythmic counting, choreographed everything. Group precision. Big stages. Rote movement. Shallow presentation. The fixed grin.

No catharsis. No feeling. No joy.

So here we are at the crossroads...

The blues tradition began with the search for a microtonal note that did not exist in Western scales—that "blue" note that hearkened back to African and Eastern music. The blues begat jazz (12-bar blues is the basis of early jazz) and rock and roll. All three of these genres enjoy worldwide acclaim. If Westerners can value microtones, feeling, and improvisational expression in music, why not in belly dance? Maybe we have under-estimated our students —and our guests.

I would submit that one of the reasons this dance caught on in the 70s had a lot to do with experimentation, improvisation, and expression in the art and music scenes—much of which came from the blues into jazz and jam-band rock music. Maybe dancers in the West have more in common with Eastern dance than we think. Maybe it is nurture rather than nature. Maybe we have been selling ourselves, our students, and our guests short, as well as the dance.

James Baldwin said, "Not everything that is faced can be changed, but nothing can be changed that is not faced." And yes, as I invoke Baldwin and the African American experience, there are more essential things to face than belly dance.

Let's face the *othering* and disdain that patriarchy has ingrained within all of us, our little places of superiority, taking comfort in being *better than*: misogyny, racism, homophobia, strippers, immigrants, and so forth. Hierarchical thinking perpetuates bitterness, shame, and misery. We are all in this together.

Let's face the unflattering history and ongoing devastation of Western colonialism and slavery, that we may understand its effects and ameliorate the violent oppression heaped upon folk of color through centuries of state-supported racism.

In light of the above, let's face the hurtfulness of using terms like *dark* and *black* in ways that mean bad, depressing, grim, or the like. White and black are as ill-suited to characterizing good and evil as yang and yin would be. The devil on the cover is white, but is he good? No.

Oops…

Let's face all of this so we can begin the process of change that will bring us closer to the heart and soul of our dance and to our True Self.

We change the world, one undulation at a time.

What can we do?

- Embrace and model the Eastern cultural values of the dance, their importance, and their myriad benefits.
- Support Eastern cultural assets. Go there. Immerse yourself. Learn from artists of the culture. Sponsor them. Promote them.
- Elevate the core principles of the dance—feeling, improvisation, joy.
- Promote quality improvised live Eastern music and dance.
- Downplay stylized drilling and choreography. Yes, choreography is a great tool, it's fun to make dances, and students feel safer. But when students are fed only upon choreography, their own creativity plummets. Fast. They become anxious, serious, and stylized.
  Instead, let's empower students with the agency native to Oriental dance (see *aliathabit.com/groups*).

And, of course, there is more.

Belly dance has the power to heal.

We have been valuing the external, how things look—pretty girls in pretty costumes doing what they're told. This reinforces patriarchal power structures and the pressure on women to be defined by male desire, to be at all times attractive to and available to men.

This focus devalues women's agency, power, and beauty. It discredits, denies, and discards women past a certain age, without a certain look, or a certain weight. It reinforces cultural stereotypes (both Eastern and Western), and co-opts the power and beauty of dancers and of this dance.

We have valued stylization, athleticism, and perfectionism. This has decimated dancers' ability to love and honor themselves, their individuality, and their feeling for the music in the moment.

This has reinforced the shame-based, traumatic message that we are never, ever, good enough. We have been judged and found wanting. We have been pushed to judge ourselves, hate ourselves, and denigrate everything we do. This is the opposite of the messages inherent in our dance—self-love, acceptance, unity, and joy.

What if we change our focus?

- What if we allow this dance into our hearts and souls—not as an outward facing display, but as an inward, personal practice?
- What if we value interoception, personal growth, soul healing, and spiritual connection?
- What if we practice self-compassion? Through forgiving ourselves, we heal our relationship to the world.
- What if we grow our ability to appreciate, honor, and accept each other—even as we all seek to deepen our relationship with our art, our bodies, and the Divine?

What if we celebrate the dance's cultural identity and values?

Not the "dancers are whores" part—patriarchal misogyny is everywhere. Instead, let's value the transmission of joy, the personal agency and expression, the luxuriance of movement and endless variety of micromovement, dance for the sake of pleasure—the human, interactive, communal joy that comes from this dance and dancing together with friends and family. I'm talking about stress-healing, self-love, compassion, and the pleasure of moving in a beautiful, loving, self-accepting way.

And that means a couple of changes.

What if we stop pushing performance?

I sometimes hear dismay about "hobby dancers." You know, the folks who take classes, fill workshops, and pay the bills? The ones with relatively normal lives who want to dance and have fun? Because we all should be Serious Dancers Who Work Hard. Well, surprise! Maybe the hobbyists have the right idea.

I'm all for performance. I am a performer. I love it. Many of us do. I love teaching. I'm good at it. I get that. Keep doing what you love! People feel called to open studios, develop professional companies, dance at birthday parties, and I say YES to all of it. But this dance is also a folk dance, done by folks, in their homes. Those folks would never perform except to take their turn at the center of a circle of family and friends. FUN is a legitimate, honorable relationship to the dance.

What if we stop beating ourselves up for "not going anywhere" with our dance?

Those little voices keep ragging on us to quit and be done with it because our dance will "never amount to anything." We should all quit if we can't be World-Class Famous Dancers awash with money and fame. Why are fame and fortune the benchmark of success in our dance? Few of us dance solely for adulation or money. It's awesome that dance can give us these things, but the dance is deeper than this. It's the connection to the music we crave—the sense of oneness that we value. Yet all the emphasis is the pretty girl on stage in costume.

Think of all the people who do yoga, meditation, or tai chi. They don't look to be performers. Few even want to be teachers. Most go to weekly classes, maybe a workshop or retreat. The activity is part of their life. It gives them physical and emotional benefit, maybe a community. And they enjoy it.

The same with this dance.

The physical interaction with the music is pleasurable in and of itself. And the more in sync we get, the better and more beautiful and delicious it feels. Think how lovely a twenty-minute dance practice would be if we focused on sensual enjoyment of the moves and their relationship to the music. This is a reason for pursuing mastery—for the pleasure of the activity, all by itself.

The pleasure of the activity

Mastery as transmission of joy

That sounds radical, doesn't it? Most of us don't practice for the enjoyment of it. We practice to get better. We work. What if we danced instead?

No one thinks their yoga practice ought to have an audience, their sitting meditation—or their evening boogie at the local disco. But belly dance in the West is viewed as a performance activity, even though it is social activity for millions of people in the East—who have always danced, but rarely have performance careers except out of desperation. And while many non-performers are great dancers, they dance for fun, with friends and family, for the joy of it.

Joy is here for all of us. Social activities are lovely. Let's have more. For regular folks to play music together, dance together—these used to be common activities, but now, alas, they are virtually extinct. We play recordings and everything has to be fancy-fancy. But social fun is beneficial all by itself. Studies have shown that an hour a week with friends uplifts better than antidepressants.

Social dance—and social connection—heals and uplifts. Why, then, is every hafla stuffed with performances, with no time left for open-floor social dancing? There's a chicken-egg conundrum of everyone wants to perform—but maybe it's because they have been told they have to since day one, because the highest regard is given to performers.

I LOVE that belly dance as a performance art is open to everyone. I LOVE troupes of middle-aged ladies up on stage in their spangles and glory, beaming with joy. Belly dance welcomes all bodies, all genders, all ages. It is a gentle, loving dance that anyone can do. In its cultures of origin, groups dancing together make circles. Each dancer basks in the center as their friends and family cheer them on. Everyone gets to shine.

Yes, performers also have a place. Professional dancers fulfill valuable social rituals, bringing everyone together, starting the party, and giving the guests permission to have a good time. And yes, we have artists going far beyond this in theatrical and brilliant ways. But we need that social time, too. After the dancer performs, everyone wants to get up and dance. Let's make room for that—a lot of room.

What if we cast our performances as healing benediction for our guests?

Instead of self-glorification and accolades, let us extend the gift of love to our guests. Through our own joy in the moment, we bring joy to others. We may present differently onstage than in a home practice, but presenting something true and glorious onstage, sharing that with our guests, is profoundly moving for everyone involved. What if our shows were cathartic, pleasurable, loving journeys for the guests, experiences that leave them changed, soothed, at peace inside?

They can be.

What if men and women danced together? What if we let go of our patriarchal conditioning, the trauma of our past, and join together as equals through dance? Couple dancing in Oriental dance does not involve touching. It does not involve mirroring. Each party dances their own expression of the music—together, relating to each other, incorporating each other, enjoying and playing with each other. We can do even this. It seems hard, but it is so easy. All it takes is the tenderness, the incredible risk, of joy in the present moment…

We can do this.

We can do all of these things.

Do we dare?

Dare we accord the courage, time, space, and conviction to love and heal ourselves, our dance, and our world?

Dare we not?

It's clear by now that belly dance is much more than a shiny little toy. It's more than a sexy treat for the male gaze, a movement vocabulary, a fun way of getting exercise, or a dress-up opportunity. It is more than entertainment, more than art. We can use it this way, and it is wonderful, but it is like playing marbles with pearls. Another world is possible.

This is a wild, free dance. It has resisted oppression, fundamentalism, naming, and shaming. It lives, it evolves, it survives. It is our gateway to healing, spirit, and joy. It is our strength, our heart, our soul. We who dance this dance know it is sacred. Why tame it, water it down, or make it live by Western rules? Rather, let's celebrate—for ourselves, our students, and the world—the power and wonder of this dance.

Belly dance is more than an ethnic genre. It is a healing, joyous miracle. The dance frees us from pain and tragedy. It gives us confidence and power. It connects us to the Divine. Through accepting, affirming, and loving our bodies and ourselves, we find the courage and the kindness to love others. Little by little, this love radiates outward, touching others, healing as it goes. It extends out, all over the world, finally returning back to us, energizing us along with everyone it meets.

Am I suggesting that belly dance has the potential for world peace?
　Yes. Yes, I am.
　The dance is meant for this high purpose.

Through this dance, we spread love, healing, kindness, and joy. We connect our guests and ourselves to the Divine. We heal the world, one undulation at a time.

The door is open.
　Will you step through?

Through the wardrobe..

PART IV
HOW-TO

"Where a dancer stands, that spot is holy ground." —Martha Graham

15

PRACTICE: THE DOOR TO HEALING, SOUL, AND JOY

THERE IS A KIND OF GRUB THAT ANTS LOVE. NOT TO EAT—THEY love its scent. They love its scent so much that they take the grub into their nests. They feed and nurture the grub, lavishing care upon it. Yet all the while, the grub is eating the ants' eggs, as fast as it can gobble. The ants, fanatically careful of their eggs, are so enamored of the grub that they don't even notice.

Like that grub, traumatic stresses suck up all our attention. We are so busy with these vortices that we have no space to relax, enjoy, or open ourselves to the moment. Another world is possible.

As improvisers, we learn to let go. We decouple from the scurrying, thinking, anxious mind, and revel in the moment. We free ourselves to express our intuitive response to the music, engage with guests, and bring joy into our lives and into the world. Even a moment of relief can turn off the alarm bells that hound us. This opens the door to engagement, discovery, and confidence. That's a pretty great thing to do.

Trauma expert Bessel van der Kolk defines trauma as an inability to live in the here and now. As we roil in the pain of *there and then*, we don't see what is *here and now*. And all the while, our present, our potential, the seeds of our bright future, are gobbled up by anger, fear, and despair. The strategies in this book help us release ourselves from *there and then* and return to *here and now*.

The basis of this practice is a 20-minute period of free improvisation.

This is neither long nor short, but it is effective. Twenty minutes is the time it takes for the neurotransmitter bath in the brain to shift—for actual change to happen in the brain. From my own experience, and that of hundreds of dancers, I believe this because I have seen that shift take place, day, after day, after day. Ideally, practice every day. Changes happen quickly when you do. But even if you dance only a few days a week, you will feel the difference.

If you have not yet begun to improvise, this practice can jumpstart your journey. Though it may be challenging at first, it can be infinitely rewarding. If you already improvise, these practices can help you go further and teach others. Learning to engage with and trust the body flows from dance to life, even into the lives of those around us. As we step back from our established patterns, we grow into our strength and confidence. As we grow into our confidence, we make space for others to do so. Our growth gives others permission to grow.

In this section, we will look at **Preparation, Practice, and Process** for how to do that. This is all optional. You can start with nothing. But sometimes it's nice to feel prepared and safe. Your call.

1. Preparation

Safe space, music, and props and equipment. Let's take these one at a time.

Safe Space encompasses inner space and outer space.

Outer Space is your physical environment. You want a place that is private, sufficient, and comfortable. Ideally, it is also easy on the eyes.

Private can mean whatever you want. In this practice, you might roll around and let it all hang out. You want a space in which that's okay. It might be that you use thumbtacks and fabric to curtain off a personal space. It might be you close the drapes, or go out into the woods, or retire to your bedroom. As long as you feel safe in your space, it's fine.

Many of us don't have a room of our own, or we are responsible for others much of our day. We might have to be creative; we might have to create our safe space out of thin air. It's okay to experiment. Don't get wacked about the perfect space (there isn't one). Don't bother with mirrors. Do keep away from anyone who might snipe at what you are doing. Do make it as easy on yourself as possible.

Sufficient means that there is enough space to do what you want. A yoga mat or two (or a bed) is usually enough space. If you like to travel and roll around a lot, you might want more, but it doesn't take a lot to have enough.

Comfort is personal, too. You want to feel safe, to avoid sharp edges, splinters, or other ouchies. You want enough matting to feel protected. You might want a window, or a nice light. You want to be warm enough, cool enough, whatever you like.

"Easy on the eyes" gets bonus points. Because trauma resolution includes grounding in the visual and the present moment, it's nice when that visual has a soothing, loving affect. If you feel triggered and scratchy everywhere you look, you might want to make some changes—even curtains can help. I went through a long period where I only moved with my eyes closed, for my personal space at the time was so chaotic it threw me out of my zone. Outer Space definitely can influence Inner Space...

Inner Space is your internal environment. In preparing your inner space, you want, oddly enough, to develop an external orientation, so that you cultivate enough Stabilizing Blue. When one feels triggered, it helps to open the eyes and ground in the present moment, which is why we want a safe space. The more things you see that soothe and nourish you, that your eyes enjoy, the easier it is to ground, to breathe, and to remember that you are safe.

All of the elements of this practice, focusing on the body's feelings, the breath, the connection to the music, the connection to the here and now—all support a grounded, resilient inner space.

Teachers: Make your class space as warm and welcoming as possible. Of course, we are often at the whim of the studios we rent, but do what you can to build a safe container. Build safety with your presence as well. Developing the inner space is not only for you, but also your students. Focus on building rapport. Help the students feel safe with you and each other. Avoid overwhelm —watch for those who seem to be sinking into pain or getting too high. Change the music to change the mood (gently), or even fade out what you are doing and change the activity.

Students: In choosing a class, look for a teacher who creates a safe container for the group. Look for someone with whom you feel rapport, one who treats you and everyone else respectfully and with genuine warmth. Look also for a space that feels safe and inviting, that soothes your eyes and heart.

Important Note: For those of us who may be in the grip of traumatic dysregulation, or who may want to work with such folks, it's vital to work with a qualified trauma therapist. While you can do this work at home, it is safer and far more productive to have a professional at your back. And if you teach, in particular, take the time to learn the process through your own growth. Reading this (or any) book is not enough. You want experience and practical application. There is a list of Somatic Experiencing® providers and training at *traumahealing.org*.

Music

There is a lot of music that works well for this practice (and a lot that doesn't). Generally, you want music that is deep and made for entrainment. Dunya explains that *entrainment* means to draw us down into a state; it helps to choose music from cultures with a dance underbelly to carry us down.

Nothing too cerebral, no Western classical. Persian and Arab classical music emerges from that place, but for Westerners, it may not always be the thing. Skip songs that have negative associations, affect you with negative emotions, or make you think.

Avoid English lyrics (or those in whatever language you normally speak). They can make you think or get too emotional; they can take you out of the now. You want things that are a little more neutral, plain rhythm and structure, such as Klaus Weisz's *El Hadra*. There are links to *El Hadra* and other suitable music at *bellydancesoul.com/resources*

It helps a lot to have a playlist or collection of music that you want to use for your practice at the ready. Skipping through your CDs or device menus is distracting and pulls you out of your zone. You can have a big selection of assorted songs or build each day, whatever suits you, but you want it to be easy for the next song to come on, and easy if you want to change the mood to do so.

Props and Equipment

There are a few things you may like to have in your practice space. The more you can leave them there, the easier it is to practice: a mat, any props, practice clothing, and a sound system or earphones, etc.

A mat or a bed (something soft) makes a big difference. We often work in Low Space (on the floor), and we lie down to rest after our practice. A yoga mat is inexpensive and one is enough, though you are welcome to build a nice cozy nest with multiple mats, pillows, blankets, etc.—whatever feels right to you.

Other props go along with this cozy space. I always have a silk veil nearby, for covering up when I sleep, and for dance, often with slow movement. I also use the veil like a yoga strap for stretching. I keep a notebook and pen, to I can write down any ideas or thoughts, or for journaling after my practice. I might have some water, in case I get thirsty. A pillow or a cushion for seated work is also nice. Whatever you like for your practice, have at the handy. You won't know it all at first, so relax. Over time, you will learn what you want to have around.

Practice clothing is another nice thing. There is a transformative process of changing clothes, as there is when changing into a costume. It helps set the intention and helps us shift into the practice mindset of interoceptive exploration and discovery. Comfortable clothes in which you feel good are best. Keeping them in the space makes life easier.

Use a timer. You can't be climbing out of your zone every five minutes to check the clock. Set a timer for twenty minutes and let go of one more niggling anxiety.

Arrange for sound. While you may, of course, practice in silence, having the option of music is much nicer. You can use anything from a huge stereo to your phone and some earbuds. It's helpful to have good quality sound; feel free to indulge yourself on decent earbuds or speakers. Stash this all in your space so it's there when you need it. You want your workflow to be as streamlined as possible. Even the simplest equipment will do a fine a job.

Take breaks

2. Practice

Once we get our space and music set up, there is nothing to be done but to go dance. However, the idea of going out and just improvising, boom, can be scary. The moment of transition from one plane to another includes a certain amount of what Dunya calls "crust." You have to go through the crust to get to the richness inside.

Even in our daily practice there is a quality of crust that separates our everyday self from our dance self. It can help to have a transition ritual. I'm not a big ritual person; mine are bone-simple. You can make yours as simple or as ceremonial as you like, but the longer or more complicated you make it, the less time you have to dance.

Transition into Practice

One way of transitioning is to change into practice clothes. Like changing into a costume, this can help set the mood and provide a sense of shift all by itself. It helps to have your practice clothes ready to wear, maybe even waiting in your space. You want things in which you feel beautiful. As you are dancing for yourself, anything loving and comfortable is fine. You may be rolling around on the floor, so choose things that you can do anything in and feel good. Now, how to get moving?

Sometimes I put on upbeat music and get revved up with Rhythmic Breath. I don't care what I do; my only intention is to expend energy and get warmed up. I often use old rock and roll for this. Some days this is my entire practice. I need to do it, and this does it.

Another go-to transition is Slow Movement. It is low stakes and hard to mess up. My music choice depends on how tired, crappy, or resistant I feel. I might choose upbeat music to get some energy or slow music to coddle myself. I use Rhythmic Breath to get in sync with the music, but I don't move fast or do anything notable—I ooze around for a while without any attention to what I'm doing. I attend only to my breath and the slowness with which I move.

I also find Dunya's Opening Sequence to be luscious transition. Opening Sequence (OS) is a series of slow, elegant, dynamic stretches that flow seamlessly from one to the other. It has the benefit of something that you follow rather than invent; this means there is no pressure to come up with anything. As we move through the shifts and stretches, we focus on the feeling in the body, the feeling of air moving through the lungs, and the languorous sensation of slow movement.

OS uses a gentle, movement-based breath, inhaling and exhaling with the expansion and contraction of the movement—the long exhales sooth and calm the body. It feels grounding, soothing, and present. It gently warms the muscles and oxygenates the blood, readying the body for practice. Its movement quality can then be continued into the practice period. Best of all, it can be extended into the entire practice time if need be.

You can find a demo video and an offer for Dunya's tiny instructional video at *aliathabit.com/dos*. Opening Sequence also brings us effortlessly into the mind space we need for our practice—grounding in the present moment.

Ground in the Present Moment

Grounding in the present moment is grounding in the here and now—but what does the word "grounding" mean? It means settling in. It means connecting, being present. It means experiencing the Now (remember Be Here Now? That's what it means). "Here" is the physical space you currently inhabit—not the future or the past. Not the plans you have for the afternoon, the worry about that meeting, or last night's text, or whatever. Right now, right here. Only this. Think of it as Orientation (like Oriental dance). When you are Oriented, you know where you are. You have the security of confidence.

Any time you feel triggered, anxious, distracted by thoughts or emotions, or focused on some other place or time, re-Orient. Open the eyes, come back to the breath, and ground in the present. Check in with your senses. Feel the sensations in your body. It is an interoceptive sensory experience—sight, sound, smell, touch, and taste—all five senses. What do you see, smell, taste, hear, feel, right now? Look around. Listen. Breathe. What do you find?

Scan your body. What sensations do you feel? Where are you tight, relaxed, stiff, warm, cold, heavy, numb, crimped, tingling, loose? Breathe into these areas; consciously exhale the stress and let them melt and drain away, out of the body. What do you feel as they do? Whatever arises, memories, images, sensory impressions? Breathe. Let them float out. Build your Stabilizing Blue.

Let your eyes rest upon whatever they enjoy, what gives you feelings of safety, beauty, and comfort. If there are none in your space, of if you find an element of your practice area that is scratchy, what could you add or remove to make it more soothing? Even a piece of pretty fabric thumbtacked over a distracting visual can make a big difference. It's worth the effort.

Continue to breathe and move. Close the eyes again and notice the sensations of the body, the muscles as they slide over one another, the bones as they shift, the breath as it moves in and out of the body. Let your body move in response to the music. Change the music if it is part of the distraction. It's challenging at first, but over time, you get better at it. Much, much better.

Modulation

Modulation is the shifts and changes of tempo and energy, and the arc of these changes. Like a novel, you build over time towards a climax, and then relax into the denouement, the wrapping up. Of course, dance practice is more flexible than a novel, because you can change it up any time. Some days you may want to start fast and others slowly. However you begin, bring some energetic shifts into your session, and close with a relaxation period.

Those shifts can come from the music or your approach to the music. You can bring Slow Movement to fast music, using Rhythmic Breath to stay grounded in the song. You can even let go of Rhythmic Breath and let the movement create your breath for a different effect. There are myriad options to music and motion: Rhythmic Breath with upbeat music, Slow Movement with taqsim, Movement Breath, Low Space, etc. For more on breath, check out aliathabit.com/road-to-joy.

Any time you feel too high or too low, change it up. Remember, back in the Music section above, about being able to change the mood. Have some playlists available to upshift or downshift. You are not married to any song that comes on. While it is an interesting challenge to play Song Roulette and dance to whatever, don't be a hero in your practice, at least, not right now. The goal here is to learn how to easily enter an improvisational zone, to relax the body, and to allow it to move. Stick with that.

Rest

Plan to rest afterwards for ten minutes or so. This is the most important part. This is when the body gets to reorganize itself, when change gets to happen. The more we rush out of practice and go on to the next thing, the *less* benefit we get. In every yoga class, there is shavasana at the end, where you get to lie there and breathe. In Open Heart belly dance, we also build in this rest period. Turn down the music. Make it dreamy or turn it off. Lie down on your mat. Snuggle with your veil. Some lie stretched out like shavasana. Some lie on the back with the knees up and feet on the floor. Some lie on their side. Whatever is comfortable to you is fine. Scan the body, relax what is tight, and focus on long exhales. Let yourself go. Rest.

Thinking about the next task (or anything else) is *not* rest. Critiquing your practice is *not* rest.

What is rest?

> To rest is to give up on the already exhausted will as the prime motivator of endeavor, with its endless outward need to reward itself through established goals. To rest is to give up on worrying and fretting and the sense that there is something wrong with the world unless we are there to put it right; to rest is to fall back literally or figuratively from outer targets and shift the goal not to an inner static bull's eye, an imagined state of perfect stillness, but to an inner state of natural exchange. The template of natural exchange is the breath, the autonomic giving and receiving which is the basis and the measure of life itself. ... When we give and take in this easy foundational way we are closest to the authentic self, and closest to that self when we are most rested. To rest is not self-indulgent, to rest is to prepare to give the best of ourselves, and perhaps, most importantly, arrive at a place where we are able to understand what we have already been given.
>
> — DAVID WHYTE

Reflect

It's helpful to keep a journal in your practice space. After resting, write. Another ten minutes if you have the time, or make some notes on what you noticed and how you feel. Writing is an important source of expression. Freewriting (writing quickly for a set period of time without thinking or planning) is another form of improvisation. All the ways we practice improvisation reinforce each other.

3. Process

It helps to let our practice run over into our daily life. All the things that help us to become effortless improvisers help us navigate the everyday as well. We all benefit from learning to build our resilience, sidestep triggers, and live in the here and now. To do this we rest, write, develop our practice habit, and invest in self-compassion.

Rest/Relax/Decouple

The practices and benefits of our 20 minutes can be brought into our everyday lives. Throughout the day, take breaths—long, slow exhales, twice as long as your inhale, bring calmness in a moment or two. Allow yourself to step back from worry and anxious or angry thoughts. The world will not end, and your mind will be sharper for the rest. Orient yourself. Ground in the present moment. Much of our perceived danger is in our heads and bodies. In this case it is safe to step back. (If the present moment involves immediate danger, exhaling will help moderate freeze and return you to agency. Running like hell is good, too. Or an Aikido class).

Write

Making even ten minutes a day to freewrite can have a wondrous effect. Better yet is the 30-minute Morning Pages of Julia Cameron's *The Artist's Way*. This can be part of your practice, as above, but it can also be done any time of the day or night. It is another example of Diffuse Thinking, in which the working brain gets to rest and the subconscious is free to ping around making random connections.

Studies have shown that for women especially, journaling about traumatic moments can help to free us from their grip. Remember to breathe, or even get up and move to release any building tension. Remember also to be kind to yourself. There was a time when you did not get the love and comfort that you needed to process the danger that you survived. Now you can reach back and give yourself that love and caring.

Develop your practice habit

Putting dance and joy first is a pretty simple thing, but it is devilishly hard in real life. Because real life is full of other things, each one screaming for attention, the things we do for ourselves somehow get lost. There are some highly developed methods for developing and anchoring new habits, and they will help you to make real space in your life for this (or any) practice. Check out, for example, Stanford researcher BJ Fogg's *tinyhabits.com*; Charles Duhigg's, *The Power of Habit*; or Nadira Jamal's course on developing a practice habit *bellydancegeek.com/practice-habit/*

Find your anchor

Invest in Self-Compassion

Many of us, especially women, are alarmingly hard on ourselves. We hold ourselves to rigid standards of perfection and berate ourselves when we fail to meet the self-imposed mark. I believe that for most of us, this self-cruelty, this self-loathing, is a symptom of unresolved trauma. I know it was for me. We have been made to feel responsible for every evil that has ever befallen us (what were you wearing?). In response, we have taken to judging ourselves before anyone else gets the chance, stirring our own flies in the ointment, never letting ourselves rejoice, relax, or savor the good. It's time for this to change.

I always thought the vicious little voices in my head were telling the truth—that I was as much of a loser as I thought I was. As I traveled upon my road to health (primarily via acupuncture and Chinese medicine), I discovered that those voices were symptoms of imbalance. When I was well, they largely disappeared or had no power. When I was ill, they had all the power. I took herbal medicine and changed the way I ate, and it helped. But trauma resolution helped the most, and has been the most permanent and relatively effortless shift. That is what has prompted much of this book, understanding that our dance has this potential for healing.

When I was ill (most of my life), I sneered at my own pain. I had no idea how lost I was. Now, I like myself. A conscious adoption of the principles of self-compassion helps to crack the brittle shell of self-loathing. Self-compassion allows in the warmth and sunlight of health and love. Trust me, this is where we want to be. Trauma healing helps us get there.

Not sure if this is you?

Kristin Neff, a researcher who studies compassion, has put together some excellent resources to help with this process. Check out Dr. Neff's Self-Compassion quiz here: *self-compassion.org/test-how-self-compassionate-you-are*; then see how you might be able to bring some of your native goodwill and kindness to yourself.

Trauma healing is about recognizing and celebrating the gifts and strengths that got us through—the resilience that helped us survive—and we did survive!

If you are reading these words, you survived.

Begin to see your bounty, your goodness.

Begin to find your True Self.

Open Heart: Numinous Belly Dance

I have a mission statement on my website. I made it a long time ago, and it has remained constant over the years. Here it is:

- Awaken people to their own beauty and power
- Enable them to express their unique individuality through art
- Bring honor and appreciation to Oriental dance
- Enjoy a life of creativity, adventure, mystery, abundance, and ease
- Cultivate a radiant oasis of warmth and delight

This book is part of my mission.

I have a vision, too.

I envision more people dancing for fun, more people enjoying the music—live, improvised, quality music. I envision men and women, children and old folks, dancing together for joy, playfully enjoying themselves and each other. I envision us all dancing, alone, together, as couples, as small groups, in circles—having fun, releasing our cares, and finding joy in the moment.

It's not about pushing the dance backward. It's about inviting dancers forward, out of their fears and into their joy. This dance has a long, long history. A silver thread connects us to every past dancer, to all the joy of ages past. Let's find and feel the thread of love that connects us to each other and to every dancer before us and after us.

Open Heart.

This is my vision. As I have experimented with the ideas in this book (and much more), I have integrated them with other practices such as gaze direction, weight shifts and movement initiation that help to create a more grounded relationship with the dance as well as facilitate trauma healing and soul connection. This I have come to call Open Heart. Open Heart began as a free web series in 2015, and it has been expanded and developed since then. It is this material that we will explore in depth in the next 90 Day Dance Challenge.

The 90 Days

A personal improvisation practice helps build skill in intuitive movement, soften and release stress and trauma, and find a soul-connection to the dance. All this can be accomplished with this simple 20-minute practice of free improvisation.

Developing such a practice is challenging on your own, but it can be done. I started my own daily dancing in 2011, committing to dance 20 minutes a day for forty-five days. I danced every day, but I found that the habit of daily dance did not stick. In 2012, I upped the ante to ninety days and invited dancers worldwide to practice with me. Over four hundred dancers took up the challenge. The 90-Day Dance Party Challenge was born.

Every other year we run the Challenge. I write and email daily Love Notes to the dancers. We have a Facebook group for camaraderie and accountability. Many dancers participate regularly, and many have found friends through the process. They testify to growth and changes they have made. The flexible structure accommodates everyone's various needs. For more information, if you prefer a structured approach, or for the pleasure of a group of like-minded seekers, please check out Alia's 90-Day Dance Challenge (*aliathabit.com/90days*).

Thank you

Thank you for reading this book. Thank you for thinking about these things. Thank you for tending the dance's roots that the living tree may flourish and bloom, nourishing all with grace and beauty.

If these ideas have resonated for you, we have a Facebook group for readers of this book that you might like to join. Here, like-minded dancers can share ideas, strategies, accountability, and friendship. For an invitation, please see *bellydancesoul.com/unite*

Like-minded friends

Please write to me how it goes for you. I will write back.
My address is *midnight@aliathabit.com*.
All my love,
Alia

THE END?

No.
The Beginning...

Acknowledgments

Before this was a book, it was a talk at the 2012 International Bellydance Conference of Canada. Thank you, Yasmina Ramzy, *arabesquecanada.com*, for giving me the opportunity to put these thoughts together! That talk became the outline for this book. Lynette Harris of Gilded Serpent, *gildedserpent.com*, pushed me to write down that talk. Much of the first chapters here were an article in GS's first Belly Dance Reader. Thank you, Lynette!

Much of that article was originally written for the Bonus Pack of Joy subscribers of the first 90Day Dance Party, *aliathabit.com/90days*. The wonderful dancers who embarked upon that journey gave me the confidence to write this book. Thank you!

Thanks to business mentors Nathalie Molino, *nathaliemolina.biz*; and Julie Anne Eason, *julieanneeason.com*. Thanks to Paul Wolfe, *howtoplaybass.com*, for the challenge that became this book. Special thanks to Sean D'Souza and Renuka Menon, *psychotactics.com*, for wisdom, encouragement, accountability, and cartooning!

Thanks to Lisa for space to write. Thanks to William (and nanowrimo) for showing me I could write a full-length work.

Profound thanks to the fearless Kickstarter backers who maintained their faith in this book over the years it took to complete it. Special thanks to Lisa Mancuso, Katherine Sandberg, Joanna Shellenberger, Stewart Hoyt and Shakti Smith, Frances Goldin, Jennifer Bowen, Tamalyn Dallal, Janet Morgan, Deborah Rubin, Sally Pelkey, Rachel Bond, Catherine Barros, and Kathy Brinkerhoff. Extra-special thanks to Amity Alize and the ladies of Raq-On Dance, Lisa Talmadge, and Erika Zeitz. There is a list of backers on the website and in the ebook. Thank you!

I am deeply indebted to the beta readers, each of whom gave valuable insights, corrections, and clarifications along the way: NYTimes bestselling author Karleen Koen *karleenkoen.com*; world-famous belly dance pioneer Tamalyn Dallal, *tamalyndallal.net*; Leila Farid, *leilainegypt.com*, a top professional dancer in Egypt and worldwide for over a decade (and producer of a great series of music CDs); all the dancers in the Secret Center (you know who you are); Corina Carlson; Lisa Talmadge; Amity Alize of *raq-on.net*; our sensitivity reader, the brilliant Palestinian artist Roula Said, *roulasaid.com*; Toya R. Smith for clarifying the blues crossroads material; and finally, wisdom-woman and dance icon Morocco Carolina Varga Dinicu, *casbahdance.org*. Thank you all. This would be a far lesser book without your guidance.

Thanks to our wise, forthright editor, Lizabet Nix of Wordcredible!, and to Benjamin Carlson for design help. Thanks to Rachel Bond, *inspirebellydance.com.au*, for eleventh-hour copyediting. You all made this book special.

The Arabic music and music theory information comes from the world-class teachers at Simon Shaheen's yearly Arabic Music Retreat, *arabicmusicretreat.org*, an immense gift in my life (thanks Ranya Renee, for the push). I am especially grateful to Dr. Jihad Racy for his lectures on Arabic music history, his nay instruction and his music.

Dr. George Sawa, *georgedimitrisawa.com*, is a generous (and hilarious) musical scholar and beloved friend with an astounding understanding of and love for our music and dance. He kindly vetted the music chapters, offering a wealth of information and clarification. Thank you! All the glory goes to Drs. Racy and Sawa. Any errors are my own.

Thank you, Cynthia Merchant for guiding me through the trauma section. Cynthia's knowledge and wisdom far outshine this small taste. An incredibly busy person, she made time to talk with me and to comment upon portions of the work. All glory goes to Cynthia. Any mistakes are my own.

Dunya McPherson of *dancemeditation.org*, friend and teacher, for the generous support you have given to me, to the world, and to this book, Thank you. I can never thank you enough.

ALL you wonderful dancers over these decades, all my friends, students, teachers and mentors, everyone who talked with me, laughed with me, and let me sleep on your sofas. Without you, there would be no book. Thank you.

ALL you wonderful musicians who gave me the joy of dance, I thank you every day of my life. Without the wonder of live music, I would never have understood this dance as I do now. Thank you. The world thanks you.

Jeanne Thompson, my first teacher and dear friend for forty-five years. Look what you've done! Thank you.

Bobby Farrah, you taught me how to *dance*. Thank you.

Elena Lentini, *elenalentini.com*, teacher, mentor, artist, friend, I love you. From you I learned drama, artistry, and intention, and the joy of the flow state. I will be grateful until the day I die, and a few lifetimes down the road. Thank you.

Deep gratitude to all my family for loving and believing in me. My mom, Frances Thargay, introduced me to the music of the Middle East. She is living evidence that you don't need Eastern blood to feel the music. My daddy, Walter Thabit, advocate city planner, supported my dancing from day one without reservation. If I were not Arabic, I never would have gone into this dance that has given me such undiluted joy. My brothers, Darius, Nick, and Paavo, my children, Corina and Ben, you are precious to me. Thank you all.

And finally, dear reader, for reading and supporting this work, thank you.

ABOUT THE AUTHOR

Alia Thabit, a Levantine-American dance artist, writer, and teacher, celebrates belly dance's cultural ideals of feeling, playfulness, and joy.

An international and online instructor with forty-five years of experience, she specializes in improvisation, composition, and performance skills.

Alia enjoys travel, coffee shops, reading, cartooning, and conversation. She believes that each of us is filled with our own unique beauty and magic, treasure waiting to be found. Come find your treasure at bellydancesoul.com

ALSO BY ALIA THABIT

Improvisation is scary

Where do you start?
> **Effortless Improv: A 6-Week *Online* Crash Course**
aliathabit.com/effortless

∾

Cringe at video of your dance?

Want to stop?
> **Focus on the Feeling: How to Get and Give Great Critique**
aliathabit.com/focus

∾

Want to level up your art?

How to Create Dance Art
> An *Online* Composition Intensive, for Improvisation and Choreography
createdanceart.com

∾

Want help getting through this book and developing your practice?

Check out our 30 Midnights Challenge!
bellydancesoul.com/challenge

∾

What bugs you?

Have a question? Something needs to be clarified or revised?
   Found a typo or other annoyance?
   Tell me (and get a prezzie!):
   alia@aliathabit.com.

Thanks for making this better. Remember, no issue is too big—or too small ;).